AF348543

CASEY DANCER

CASEY DANCER

A Memoir About Dating, Stripping, and a Little Hot Yoga

By Kristin Casey

RARE BIRD
LOS ANGELES, CALIF.

RARE BIRD

THIS IS A GENUINE RARE BIRD BOOK

Rare Bird Books
6044 North Figueroa Street
Los Angeles, California 90042
rarebirdbooks.com

FIRST HARDCOVER EDITION

For more information, address:
Rare Bird Books Subsidiary Rights Department
6044 North Figueroa Street
Los Angeles, California 90042

Set in Dante
Printed in the United States

10 9 8 7 6 5 4 3 2 1

Library of Congress Cataloging-in-Publication Data
Names: Casey, Kristin, author.
Title: Casey dancer : a memoir about dating, stripping, and a little hot yoga / Kristin Casey.
Description: Los Angeles, Calif. : Rare Bird Books, [2025]
Identifiers: LCCN 2024056572 | ISBN 9781644284469 (hardback)
Subjects: LCSH: Casey, Kristin. | Stripteaser—United States—Biography. | Women authors, American—Biography.
Classification: LCC HQ127.S77 C37 2025 | DDC 792.802/8092
[B]—dc23/eng/20250129
LC record available at https://lccn.loc.gov/2024056572

To Bob Schneider

Ian Moore

Charles Rieser

George Reiff

Alejandro Escovedo

Craig Marshall

Tucker Livingston

James Speer

Charlie Richards

Jon Napier

The Scabs

Soulhat

Mingo Fishtrap

Endochine

The Grooveline Horns

Boombox

Indagroove

Jerkuleez

Gnappy

Wayne's Donkey

Oliver Future

Papa Mali

Del Castillo

La Tribu

The Resentments

…and all my favorite mid-aughts Austin bands & musicians

PROLOGUE

In the summer of 2006, I took a walk through Austin's Zilker Park and stumbled upon a large, outdoor memorial service. It was for Kim McLagan, former model and wife of Faces keyboardist, Ian McLagan. I hadn't known her, but since I'd once met her husband and was friends with some of her friends, I took a seat in the back row and listened to them speak about what a special person she was. During Ian's speech I surprised myself by tearing up. Their life together sounded like a movie script, much like my former life with my own rock star partner had been, albeit without all our fighting, cheating, and out of control addictions.

I'd been sober for almost a decade by then, but still had a lot of healing to do around men and relationships. I cried through the rest of that memorial service, wondering if I would ever release the resentment I harbored toward all the men who'd abandoned me. All the men I hadn't been able to depend on, particularly my dad. My dad, who'd delighted in me and cherished me. Who made me feel smart, interesting, and funny, but who, when push came to shove, had forever deferred to my hypercritical, emotionally abusive mother. In my teens, Dad pulled away from me more and more as my relationship with her deteriorated to the point of barely existing. He'd always chosen her over me. And when I'd been all alone and dying of alcoholism in Las Vegas, he'd shut me out entirely.

Three months after that memorial service, I returned to my previous career as a stripper. I'd been selling real estate for seven years by then, but after a six-month dry spell I felt backed into a financial corner and grudgingly took on a second job at a strip club north of Austin. I'd expected to hate it (at my relatively advanced age, having just turned thirty-nine) but was delighted to find I didn't. Quite the opposite, in fact.

The most satisfying aspect of stripping—something I had ten years' experience of by then, in my younger years—had always been that every lap dance I did was like winning my father's attention away from the original other woman: Mom. All night long, my inner child and oldest core wound could be soothed and treated with the imagined "win" of securing the attentions of men who didn't belong to me but were choosing me over their wives, their girlfriends, and my fellow strippers aplenty. Looking back on my decade of dating in sobriety up to that point, I'd have to say that the appeal of having sex with married or otherwise unavailable men was not at all dissimilar.

Part 1
LOVERS

(vulnerability)

CHAPTER 1

January 2007

I WAS THE FIRST DANCER up that day, waiting till a smattering of lunchtime customers arrived before the DJ put me on the main stage for three songs. Early in my third song, as I slowly spun topless around the pole to Tom Petty's "Saving Grace," I saw him. He'd just entered and was sauntering across the main floor toward me. His eyes were locked on my face, a neutral look—or at least one I couldn't gauge—on his.

He was hot as fuck and the walk was part of it. Plus, I quite liked brown skinned men. He was Latino, late thirties, five nine or five ten and stocky, wearing faded jeans, a long sleeve Penn State T-shirt, and a dark brown leather, flat-brimmed cowboy hat. I slinked over to him, preparing to do my standard edge-of-stage dance—grinding my hips and gently bouncing my crotch to the beat, at his exact eye level—but he was having none of it. His eyes remained on my face as he waved me down, placing a ten-dollar bill at my feet. I rested on my knees.

"Hi, there." I smiled at him.

"What're you doing today?" he asked in a velvety smooth, casually confident voice.

I cocked my head. He'd just seen me dancing nearly naked on a strip club stage—what the hell did he think I was doing? But all I said was, "Working. Why?"

"Wanna do some drinking?"

I laughed. "No thanks. I'm way more fun sober."

He looked doubtful at that, but shrugged, like either I might be worth it to find out or the conversation was already boring him. I couldn't tell which and felt my heart rate shoot up for fear of losing his interest already. "All right," he shrugged. "Well…meet me in the VIP room if you want." Then he strolled off.

I couldn't get there fast enough. The moment my stage set ended I grabbed my red plaid, mini schoolgirl skirt and matching lace bra and raced to the VIP room. I found him in my favorite corner—the darkest one—on a sagging loveseat next to the faux fireplace (a feature made all the more ridiculous every time the manager came over to hike up the air conditioning on a nearby thermostat). Hot guy was alone, and I couldn't believe my luck. Usually by one in the afternoon, enough girls had drifted out of the dressing room to pounce on anyone with a wallet, much less a youngish handsome one headed straight for VIP.

Hot guy's name was Lalo. He was a thirty-eight-year-old married man and father of one, with soft brown eyes, full perfect lips, and a sharp, dry sense of humor. When he took off his hat, I melted—a shaved head did that to me sometimes. We opened up to each other right away and were almost immediately cuddling in a way I rarely did so quickly. Minutes later we'd fully debriefed each other; me about my past addictions and current boundaries. Him on his miserable marriage, day drinking habit, and recently abandoned coke business.

Twenty minutes later he "debriefed" me in a whole other way, as I lap danced for him, standing on the loveseat straddling his face. I was bouncing my crotch softly back and forth again—this time closer to mouth level than eye level—when I let him tug my thong to the side and slide his tongue around what he found there. He gave me two orgasms in the span of one song, the second rudely interrupted by a waitress friend of Lalo's, who came up behind me and started jokingly yelling at him in Spanish. How he heard her with my thighs clamped over his ears I don't know, but her intrusiveness cheated me out of the last twenty percent of my orgasm. I sighed, dismounted Lalo's face, and redonned my bra, to make small talk for a few minutes before politely running her off from our private VIP corner. (It was weeks before I'd understand that Lalo had a lot of "friends" at Perfect 10, partly because he was super cool and good looking, and partly—perhaps mostly—because he'd been supplying a bunch of them with cocaine on a weekly basis.) Before Lalo left the club that day he gave me a third orgasm, this time as I sat on his lap with his fingers tucked inside my thong. When I came, for some inexplicable reason, I looked at him and we gazed into each other's eyes until I was done.

It's safe to say we'd sparked. I'd crossed more of my personal boundaries in that single hour than I had in the entire three months I'd been back in the stripping business. I would've done it again (and again) in a heartbeat. Right then I asked for his number, thinking Lalo would make the perfect fuck buddy. Mainly because the odds of me falling in love with a married man with a young daughter, and apparent substance abuse problem, were slim to none.

I was three months away from getting my ten-year AA chip. Selling real estate six days a week and writing two books and multiple short stories on the side. Lalo was staying in a horrible marriage with an emotionally unstable, physically violent woman, in order to be close to his daughter. He was working a landscaping business that until recently had been a front for his drug dealing income. Our lifestyles couldn't have been more different, but we certainly identified with each other. For one, while his lifestyle probably looked like pleasure-seeking to most people, I knew different. I knew pain management when I saw it, and while I was (mostly) long past that kind of thing—with substances anyway—I'd just overcome a long habit of using sexual connection in a similar way, as a salve for the pain of my lingering clinical depression. We were both incredibly lonely. I managed by staying busy. He managed through drinking, drugging, and cheating on his wife (who was likewise cheating on him). At least Lalo was honest about not being ready to change anytime soon. I actually thought it was a good thing he wasn't clean and sober—I might like him too much if he were.

Between my two jobs and multiple writing projects, I hardly had time for a restroom stall quickie anymore, much less a regular fuck buddy or genuine relationship. With Lalo I thought if I were really lucky, I'd get a once-a-week hookup for a month. When I called him at work the next day, he sounded surprised. I knew he'd felt our chemistry as strongly as I had, but Lalo knew the stripper mindset as well as anyone and had written me off as a fun lunchtime distraction he may or may not see at the club again. As I was relaying my home address to him, I got the feeling he was looking over his shoulder to see if one of his buddies was pranking him. It was a risk for me too. A strip club spark doesn't always translate into the cold light of day. Regardless, we made plans, and I met an entirely different side of him than the suave confidence of three days earlier.

He arrived at my apartment in a beat-up work truck that I tried to hop in, to guide him to guest parking, only to find a child's car seat and loads of junk on the floorboards in my way. Lalo nervously cleared a space, having no idea his embarrassed, tongue-tied state was charming the pants off me—literally. The only thing hotter to me than a confident man was a confident man being vulnerable. Which he was, since, as he told me later, he wasn't used to hooking up sober, much less with sunshine slipping through the blinds and an aging, arthritic cat curled up on the pillow next to us.

The parking lot awkwardness followed us into the bedroom. Some things flowed and others didn't—namely, enough blood to his penis. I didn't care (much) though because I understood what was happening. Performance anxiety can be crippling. We switched gears to cuddling and talked for an hour. Then we tried again the next day, and the exact same thing happened—or failed to, as it were. Still,

I didn't care. I knew this guy was special and that everything would soon fall into place. Which it did on our third hookup and first real "date." Suddenly all bets were off and this charming, awkward, suave, embarrassed, sexy-as-fuck strip club customer, former drug dealer, current playboy, miserable husband, and loving father, became my best fuck ever…with potential for more.

❧

I'D ORIGINALLY QUIT STRIPPING at age twenty-three, in 1991. After five years in the business I left Austin to move in with the love of my life—guitar legend and rock star Joe Walsh—at a house he'd bought for us in Studio City, Los Angeles. Four years later we'd broken up for good and I returned to stripping—this time in Las Vegas—for another five-year stint. I spent half that time trying to drink myself to death before finally getting sober in 1997. The following year I moved back to Austin and got a "respectable" job as a Realtor. I was done with stripping for good…or so I'd thought.

Since then, I'd been selling homes, for seven years, with plenty of ups and downs, dry spells, and windfalls, but the last year had been a rough one. I'd recently broken sales records at my new hill country broker, leading me to believe that might be the year I finally earned a six-figure income. Six months later I hadn't made a single new sale. Business sucked and I refused to beg for clients with annoying email campaigns and useless open houses, showing a bunch of looky-loos the same generously sized closets I'd spent the day fantasizing about hanging myself in once they were gone. The writing was on the wall. If I wanted to pay next month's rent I'd have to dust off the old Lucite heels and wrap up my thirties by unwrapping my body for a living again.

Things had changed since I'd been gone. Thongs were remarkably smaller, for one, and I found myself having to tell customers that despite the postage stamp size, no, they could not, in fact, lick them or peel them off (before Lalo, anyway). For the most part, Texans were less entitled and pushy than Vegas customers had been. And managers no longer complained about dancers working in multiple clubs, so my schedule was finally completely my own. I could show up late and leave early any day or night I chose, though I almost never did. I'd selected dayshift at Perfect 10 as my home base because it was in Round Rock, just north of Austin, near the Dell Computer campus and plenty of North Austin businesses. The white-collar lunch crowd adored me, and—as far as their financial generosity went—the feeling was close to mutual.

Initially I'd dreaded the idea of returning to the sex industry, having left Vegas in my twenties so incredibly burned out. Also, one of my biggest fears when I got sober was discovering that my only real value in the world was what I could do for men sexually. Finding a different line of work seemed a vital step in disproving that theory. Working as a Realtor not only taught me qualities of reliability, accountability, and tenacity, but I'd come to excel at certain aspects of it: negotiating investment properties and winning bidding wars for fixers and flips. I also loved advocating for first-time home buyers, but working for free so much of the time defied my belief system and chipped away at my self-worth. My first day back stripping a lightbulb went off as I was reminded how wonderful it felt to be compensated for my labor. Above all I couldn't help feeling like *I'm home!* The music, lighting, fog machine, skimpy outfits, sexual energy, constant praise, free back scratches and body caresses, and even the weird dressing room odors (far as I could tell, a mixture of hairspray, body spray, cigarette smoke, spilled booze, and mold) all brought me back to the one place in life I'd ever felt supreme confidence. Right or wrong, stripping was something I'd always loved and excelled at in the extreme.

At thirty-nine—despite severe insomnia and increasingly long bouts of lumbar, hip, and sciatic pain—I at least *looked* in better shape than at any other time in my life. One of the fittest dancers I worked with asked how often I went to the gym.

"Once a week," I replied.

"Damn, you look like you go every day!" she exclaimed.

My tits were as full and perky as ever. My legs garnered just as many compliments, and my dancing was frequently called "best in club," including by DJs and management. The best part was that since returning to stripping, my occasional suicidal ideation— something I'd dealt with since the day I'd gotten sober—had completely disappeared.

At the end of that first day though, I felt every minute of the past four decades when my knees gave out halfway through my final stage set. A few minutes in, the ache I'd felt all day suddenly escalated to mind-numbing agony, so I slid my back down the pole and crawled like a cat to center stage where I finished with nothing but floorwork. It would be two weeks before I got through an eight-hour shift pain free. But after one month I was earning fifty percent more money stripping part-time than I earned working full-time as a Realtor. I was able to pay off a six-thousand-dollar IRS bill two months later.

Still, I continued working both jobs, often negotiating real estate contracts and home repairs in the dressing room restroom (until my coworkers' toilet flushing became distracting and my manager offered to let me use the locked VIP restroom, saying, "Anyone trying to better themselves gets all my support."). I worried early on about running into colleagues at the club, but it turned out residential agents didn't frequent strip clubs—probably for lack of time and money. We got lots of farm and ranch guys (who were the best tippers), brokers (who always tried to hire me away from my current broker without asking anything about my sales record), and developers (who never even found out I was in real estate because they only ever talked about themselves). When customers at the club found out I was a Realtor they'd say one of two things. First, "How's the market?" I was asked this so often I finally decided to start charging ten dollars apiece for the answer.

(They never paid, but the line was always good for a laugh.) The second was that they were considering buying a new home and could they have my number? Not only would they not get it, but I'd say they now owed me five dollars for insulting my intelligence with their little ploy to get my number. (Again, they never paid, but always laughed at themselves for asking.)

The bigger issue was keeping real estate clients from discovering I was stripping on the side. Or, rather, keeping their constant demands for my time—carting them all over Austin and the hill country, unpaid, in the hopes of earning *something* for it someday—from interfering with my far more fun and lucrative stripping schedule. One client in particular, a pharmaceutical CEO from Dallas, had been taking up weekend after weekend, viewing dozens of homes and developments, in my first ever seven figure price range. Six weeks later, I was already out two thousand dollars due to missing four days of stripper income and filling my tank twice to haul him and his wife around. In that time, they'd narrowed down seventy-five homes and twenty-seven subdivisions to twelve homes and six subdivisions, but as agreeable as the husband was, the wife tended to nix anything he liked and was becoming more nitpicky by the day.

I needed them to buy and soon. After paying next month's rent I would have forty-five dollars in my bank account. Meanwhile, I had dental and medical bills piling up, not to mention a stream of veterinary bills for my aging, beloved cat. Anyway, I liked Big Client (less so his elitist wife, who'd made quite the point one day of disparaging anyone who hadn't graduated college—shortly after discovering I hadn't graduated college). I just hated doing so much work for them for free. It ate at me constantly, but walking away from a potential twenty-five-thousand-dollar commission wasn't in me. Meanwhile, I enjoyed work at Perfect 10 so much I braved black ice on I-35 to get there on time one day. I felt almost proud to state that I was a dancer again, yet it was becoming more uncomfortable than ever to admit that I was a Realtor.

❦

I WAS ALSO A PUBLISHED WRITER, or poet, at least. My work had appeared in print and online six times by then, including one photograph and a joke in *Reader's Digest*, which I was counting as a publishing credit until I got one of my short stories into print (besides, *RD* was the only magazine of the six that had paid anything). I did occasional poetry open mic nights and workshopped my short stories on Zoetrope.com, reaping high praise that boosted my confidence that I'd get one published someday. I'd finished a rough draft of a novel about a punk rock, teenage, meth addict that I was considering revising into the memoir it should've been in the first place. I was also collaborating with an old friend on a how-to book for strippers.

I never lacked for inspiration. I felt like I needed to write every day for the rest of my life to get all the stories and ideas out of my head, where they'd sometimes pound on the backs of my eyeballs and eardrums begging to be released. One month before meeting Lalo, I started a stripper blog on LiveJournal: *My Dancer Diary, a sexy/smart sober stripper blog,* which was growing in readership daily and that my memoirist idol, Jerry Stahl, had commented on twice. My stripper name was Casey and my profile moniker was CaseyDancer. My collection of blog avatars were sexy shots I'd taken with my digital camera—bought for real estate purposes— and a handful of even sexier shots taken by one of Austin's best photographers, Todd Wolfson. Todd's girlfriend, Mickey, was a friendly acquaintance from the downtown music scene. She'd read my blog and passed it on to Todd, who'd loved it so much he insisted on shooting me for free. I'd sent the new blog link to my ex-fiancé, Joe Walsh, who promised to give it a read.

The last time I'd seen Joe was a mere four months earlier. He'd been in San Antonio for a corporate gig with his band, the Eagles, and had invited me to spend the weekend with him. It was the second time in recent years we'd done this, the first being three years earlier, in Dallas in 2003, when the Eagles had a gig there. Like then, he got me my own hotel room down the hall from his. On the elevator I ran into Timothy B. Schmit, Eagles' bassist. I knew Timothy from Ringo's second All-Starr Band, in 1992, and he'd been nothing but friendly to me on that tour. But in San Antonio he seemed baffled to see me, suspicious even. I assumed it was because almost no one knew yet that Joe was getting divorced. Timothy must've thought I was either showing up uninvited or having an affair with Joe. I wanted to snap at him that Joe had asked me to come, but instead shrugged it off and went to meet Joe in the hotel's business office.

I wore my favorite spaghetti strapped crop top; faded, low-rise jeans; caramel colored Candie platform mules (Joe's favorite style of women's shoe); and hair in a loose upsweep (his favorite hairdo on me). As I checked email with my back to the door, he came in behind me. I pretended not to know he was there until he greeted me with a surprise kiss on my neck. I jumped up and gave him a long, tight hug.

"You haven't aged a day!" he said, stepping back to take me in.

"Aw, thanks," I replied, choosing not to mention my recent surgical eye lift.

He looked great too. Tan and healthy, with a tiny belly yet still as handsome and boyish as ever. The next twenty-four hours were as good as I could've hoped and everything I'd wanted and needed for so long. Which I daresay Joe did as well. We went to lunch and talked at length about aging and energy, at one point comparing our daily vitamin regimens. Joe said life had become a lot about acceptance, though he didn't accept having to slow down. His marriage had been difficult he said, and he'd "lost himself" during their years together.

"The problem is, I'm not good at taking care of myself. I need someone to do it for me," he laughed. "But dating is confusing."

I agreed wholeheartedly and shared a few of my recent failures in that vein as well. We talked a lot about sobriety and Joe's foray into Buddhism and meditation. I showed him how MySpace worked and directed him to multiple Joe Walsh fan accounts, which fascinated him.

"How do I read my messages?" he asked.

I laughed, "Contact the profile owner, I guess."

That night, he came to my room after wrapping up the Eagles (private, corporate) gig. We watched TV on the bed, and he did this thing he used to do, which was to maneuver me like a ragdoll into a position he liked to do some kissing. That's as far as it went though, for a lot of reasons I suspect. Our history was so complex, especially in regard to our sex life. It was such a strange place to be with him—potentially on the verge of something new, but ancient too. Unknown but familiar, comfortable but confusing. Joe had matured, mellowed, and gained wisdom. He was my dear friend and soulmate, but our history had a distinct flavor. In our former six-year relationship, the number of times we'd had uninhibited, lustful sex—the kind I most liked—I could probably count on two hands. Perhaps it was the memory of his many sexual rejections, or his propensity for bondage, dominance, and submission, that kept my libido from kicking in right then. So, the next day, when he suggested we pursue dating again by taking it very, *very* slowly, I was relieved. Also, unsure.

Not that it mattered. In the four months since, I'd barely heard from him.

I SPENT MOST OF the past ten years exploring my sexual and romantic needs, and by exploring, I mean attempting to indulge them, yet just as often being suffocated by them. I tried to approach people— friends and suitors alike—with an open heart. To make genuine friends and explore attraction and chemistry as a fun way to share something of myself while getting to know some seemingly great men. The problem was that authenticity required vulnerability— the capacity to see and be seen, and to allow for occasional disappointment and rejection. That part didn't come easily. It didn't help that the men I always fell for—while "good" in most of the important ways—were rarely emotionally or logistically available. Therefore, they weren't always good for *me*—long term anyway, which was very much what I craved.

Before meeting Lalo, the most recent object of my lust was the dayshift manager at Perfect 10. I called him "The Suit." And despite the fact that I had just sworn off married men completely, in my heart I didn't mean a lick of it, so I flirted with The Suit shamelessly. To his credit, he flirted back just as much but in a hands-off kind of way.

Before The Suit, I'd spent five straight years immersing myself in the downtown music scene, dancing three or four nights a week to the best, funkiest bands around. In the process I'd met all kinds of fabulous lovers, casual flings, flirtations, and short-term romantic partners. But by late 2006, attending the same old gigs and venues as always, I was starting to see—or rather having to avoid—my favorite men and former lovers, who, I supposed, like me were finally maturing. My favorite two partners from this time were recently sober themselves, and like many of the rest, were suddenly showing up at gigs with wives and girlfriends in tow. It stiffened me, emotionally and physically. Suddenly every night out dancing brought an ache to my heart and my left hip. I decided to end my schedule of dancing and trolling for men five nights a week. My loneliness was still crippling and the sexual salve I'd been using had officially dried up. But sex wasn't the only thing missing in my life. The truth is I'd have killed for a great guy to go hiking with or simply spoon with while watching TV all night. But I rarely tended to date those kinds of men.

I had issues. Intimacy issues, trust issues…whatever, it was complicated. Thank goodness therapy was one of the many benefits covered by my Comprehensive and Affordable Stripper Group Insurance Policy as well as my Platinum Realtor Group Medical Plan! *Pfft—not*, though I was in therapy and had been for five years. What my therapist helped me see was that I'd learned at a very young age that reaching out for attention, affection, approval, or support resulted in rejection and shame. My mother was depressed and overwhelmed. My father worked long hours and could only do so much with five needy kids when he was home. So I spent years convincing myself I didn't need any of it and that's exactly what I manifested—a life shockingly free of any real intimacy.

Believing at a core level that I was going to be disappointed and hurt meant that I frequently put myself in a position to be disappointed and hurt. I'd been working on it slowly since getting sober, trying to build trust, lower my walls, and resist the overwhelming urge to sabotage. Once I got all that down I supposed I'd have to hit the local happy hours, since Austin was on multiple top ten lists for the "Best City for Dating" (and while I'm not sure what that even meant, it was probably that we had more bars and college students than most cities and therefore a record-breaking number of drunken hookups on any given night). Meanwhile, swearing off married men effectively cut my options in half. Of the remaining prospects half were recovered alcoholics like me, which meant they were just as messed up in their own ways, so we'd invariably end up trying to scale each other's walls at the same time pouring hot tar on each other's head to avoid the dreaded intimacy. The rest were either budding addicts, compulsive gamblers, or worse, normal, in which case they'd bore me to tears.

Loath as I was to admit that I gravitated toward the familiar. I was drawn to men who were like me—damaged. Three of my ex-boyfriends were Vietnam vets, one was severely emotionally abused, and almost all had lost a parent (usually a mother) at a young age. I wasn't sure what that said about me but doubted it was that I was reigning queen of Well-adjusted Land. What I did know was that I wanted a special man in my life before I passed my sexual peak, *that* was how *my* biological clock was ticking. Enter Lalo.

Goodies, Goodies, Goodies!

January 30, 2007

Current Location: Devil's Playground
Current Mood: aware

My behavior with Lalo yesterday—specifically sitting on his face within twenty minutes of meeting—was way out of character for me, and I've been thinking about it since.

A psychic told me recently that I would find much happiness *in my fifties*. I wanted to kick him. Sorry, dude, but I'm not waiting around that long. Listen, I like my dignified life and I'm damned lucky to have it. But, as a recovered addict, I've spent too long worrying that to (literally) stay alive I had to avoid certain indulgences. Because while I do have to avoid some, there's no way I'm sidestepping all of them.

My friend Rob told me once that, for men, masturbation was as commonplace as looking at their watch. Like, you look down and think "Oh, it's noon. May as well break for lunch," or, "Oh, it's six, may as well have a beer." Rob said whenever he looked down and noticed his dick hanging there, he'd think, "Oh, my dick. May as well jerk off." Not that I'm striving to emulate the male population, but I gotta admit, they're kinda onto something here.

I guess the question is, do men jerk off at work? Because I'm certainly all for orgasms off the clock, I just am not in the habit of letting customers give me one (or three) *inside the club*. I'm laser focused on making money there because I have to be. I have goals to reach and no time to waste. Neither do I regret what happened yesterday one bit. Point is, I'm starting to come to terms with my urges and activities, and what would seem to be my rather flexible boundaries.

It's all coming together for me right now—this thing about being in recovery making me hesitant to indulge in pleasure because of where it might lead or what it might mean I'm giving up. Because in the distant past, when I partook in certain pleasures—drugs and alcohol mostly—I set no boundaries. I had them (boundaries) of course, instilled in me as a child, but I denied their existence so that when I crossed them, I could pretend I really WASN'T filling up with shame and guilt.

See, all this time I thought my lack of boundaries had totally screwed up my psyche, but I think maybe my screwed-up psyche is what made for my near total lack of boundaries. Anyway, now I have this dignified life. That I live all alone. With no adventure, little excitement, and no real thrill. *I need thrill.* I need to maintain my dignity in the throes of passion; keep my self-respect while giving in to the heat of the moment; share something of myself without necessarily giving it away; indulge in some hedonism while staying accountable for my actions.

I hear the Devil whispering to me and he wants to know—he's waiting to see—if I can express my inner hellhound without actually selling my soul.

Oh yeah, no sweat, sugar. The name's Casey and I think we'll get along just fine.

CHAPTER 2

February 2007

I DIDN'T GO ON a lot of traditional dates. I usually met men at live music venues. On rare occasions I'd meet a hot fellow Realtor (twice) or client (thrice). I'd sparked with a few guys at the gym and men I met through friends. I met one man on a dating site. I'd met three lovers in AA, then two more through an AA sponsee, during her court case when her legal counsel and character witness both turned out to be hot as fuck. (I dated them simultaneously for four months while she did a yearlong stint in jail for taking Valium and nodding off behind the wheel with her kids in the car.) But far and away, most of the men I hooked up with were local musicians I got to know by dancing every week to their music, then letting them chat me up afterward when the lights went on. They weren't really the "dinner and movie" type but more the "let's flirt like crazy for a few weeks until we can't take it anymore then start up a monthlong, wildly intense fling until we burn out and / or I go back to the ex-girlfriend I'm still pining for" types.

Before Lalo, most lasted between three weeks and three months. Two had lasted three years, but only because they were both married and thus only available once or twice a month, so the burnout took longer to come around. I wasn't complaining about any of it. While I would've loved to have something longer, deeper, and more out in the open with some of them, I prized the thrill of my adventures highly. Higher than any traditional dating scenario I might've otherwise forged. I'd had a hell of a lot of fun. And almost as often I learned something about myself that made me a better person and potential partner for the right man in the future.

In the last year, I'd had two "traditional" dates, one with Bruce, my longest crush ever, which was precisely why it never led anywhere. Digging a guy that much while simultaneously having zero confidence in myself as a quality partner for him in return, turned our date into an exercise in crippling self-consciousness for me. We'd gone to see Joe Rogan at the Capitol City Comedy Club and laughed our way through the evening, but walking back to my car I became too nervous to let him kiss me goodnight. So instead, he sweetly suggested going on a second date sometime, making my heart soar just before my brain suddenly cowered in fear. Next, in what was probably a subconscious attempt to sabotage something I didn't feel worthy of, I emailed him about my packed schedule and overly stressful life, effectively throwing up an emotional wall and pushing him away. Soon afterward he fell in love with a lovely young woman who seemed perfect for him, and we went back to being flirty friends. It was the only type of relationship I could have with him where I didn't feel exposed, raw, vulnerable, and on the edge of rejection. Meaning the only one that, to me, felt safe.

The other traditional date I'd had was with Brad, my high school boyfriend, with whom I'd reconnected years earlier. I wasn't nervous with Brad because there was nothing at stake. We weren't in love anymore and I didn't expect we ever would be. He was easy and fun, and we had occasional sex for a few months, until he eventually faded from my life, as rare-to-occasional lovers are wont to do.

The same week I met Lalo, I had a date planned with the sexiest guy in my AA home group—Danny. We'd flirted off and on for years, then finally decided we'd be crazy not to give it a shot. Danny had solid, long-term sobriety. He was rugged and sophisticated all at once. I loved his tall, muscular body, deep tan, faded jeans, spectacle glasses, and thick southern drawl. From the day I'd met him, I thought, any girl would be lucky to date a guy like that. But after two dates with Lalo, erectile dysfunction notwithstanding, I knew I had to follow my heart and cancel my date with Danny. I debated it for two days, worried about being more drawn to an unavailable man like Lalo, with a lifestyle I rejected a decade ago, than to a sober prince of a man like Danny. Was I putting too much stock in chemistry? Or was I following the needs of my soul?

See, I saw sexual chemistry as a physical sign of a spiritual connection. I was such a highly sexual person that I figured my soul—or higher power, if you will—had decided to speak to me through my sex drive. It was certainly the best way to get me to listen. So, when I didn't feel that erotic "charge" with Joe six months earlier in San Antonio, I resolved it as a sign from God that we were incompatible, or at least that the timing was off. I suspected the same applied to Danny. The boy could not have been hotter. Intellectually I marveled at how perfect he was for me and how much I *should* want to rip his clothes off. But I didn't, and it wouldn't have been fair of me to string him along until I invariably dumped him.

When it came to men, my intuition spoke loudly. Whether someone was perfect for me on paper didn't matter. The heart wants what it wants, and in my case, a body part eighteen inches lower knew better than any other part of me—including my brain. And when it led me astray, well, I often had to experience the wrong thing for me in order to know what the right thing was. Sometimes it was the only way to learn that I deserved to be with someone better and to *be* someone better myself. Although I didn't always think it through in those terms, I grasped the concept, then in practice simply paid attention to how badly I craved someone sexually, romantically, or both. If I craved someone, I pursued it. If I didn't, I didn't. With Lalo, I craved closeness on multiple levels.

❧

Our third hookup was our first real "date." We decided to see a movie and quickly agreed to the most morbid thing in theaters—a documentary about suicide called *The Bridge*. We didn't choose it because it was morbid. We were drawn to it because we'd both spent an inordinate amount of time pondering and contemplating—and in my case, actively pursuing—a similar way out. Most people wonder what goes through a person's mind in those final moments, like the documentary subjects pacing restlessly next to the railing they were about to hurdle. But I knew. They were weighing the difference between the courage needed to jump and the courage needed to stay and fight to make themselves a better life. The difference was that, while it takes courage either way, they rarely had enough self-worth to balance out the weight of inner peace they perceived on the other side of that railing.

I had been suicidal for two years after the breakup with Joe. In getting sober, I'd found the courage to stay and find a purpose to my life, and while I knew I'd done the right thing it had taken nearly ten years to feel at peace with my decision. My writing was going well, and I knew that's where I was meant to be. Between my former addictions, current sobriety, and slightly unconventional perspective on sex and sexuality, I believed I had something to say that could make the world a better place. What's more, stepping back into stripping had meant stepping out of the mold my friends, family, and peers had shaped for me. Acknowledging my work in the sex industry as valid and, frankly, important, was one of the most empowering moves I'd made. No one understood it yet, but through stories, articles, and books I intended to change that.

I didn't yet know what made Lalo fantasize about suicide as well. I just sensed that, like me, he was deeply lonely, underappreciated, and overworked. In the same way that many of my validating connections had been severed with the loss of my music scene fuck buddies, Lalo's friends were slowly disappearing one by one as his party favors dried up. He'd recently quit dealing cocaine, he said, because one of his runners had gotten popped crossing state lines with multiple kilos. The guy hadn't squealed, but he was sentenced to two years in jail, which put the fear of God into Lalo. Since then, he'd turned his fake landscaping business into an actual job, doing long hours of manual labor while trying to quit his coke and occasional crack habit.

Knowing I was clean and sober kept him abstinent at my place. He started coming over every day after dropping off his daughter at school, before heading to work. I'd unlock the door and wait for him in bed, then watch him peel off multiple winter layers before crawling into the warm sheets to spend the next hour having some of the most amazing sex of my life with me. Having his arm around me felt like breaking a twelve-year diet. Exiting a movie theater holding hands was like wearing a gorgeous, red-carpet gown I wanted everyone to see me in. Having someone to kiss every day was like finally getting my driver's license—so exciting I hardly knew where to go with it. He gazed at me during sex and moaned my name when he came. He made me look at him when I felt shy and call him out when he was being cocky. He was the first guy to help me change the sheets ever, my whole life. The cuddling, private jokes, surprise gifts, and sweet voicemails were all so rare for me it was basically Christmas in February. But I knew better than to expect it to last, since there were too many forces against us and only a couple in our favor. We decided to keep it casual and have low expectations of each other.

I thought I could do that easily—I'd practiced my entire life, after all. Then twelve days after we met, I saw him at the club getting a lap dance from another stripper and my whole world came crashing down. The look on Lalo's face as he drank in her twenty-year-old beauty—plus what looked like half a dozen tequila shots—as they cozied up together in a corner of the VIP room stopped me in my tracks. My stomach turned, then I did too, marching into the dressing room to catch my breath and regroup.

I'd told myself, *and him*, I wasn't the jealous type. Certainly not over the dalliances of a man I barely knew! We were a fling, for God's sake. It was absurd and I felt ridiculous. It wasn't his fault that my workspace happened to be his playground. I pushed it out of my mind and went back to work.

Besides, I had other shit to worry about. Big Client was trying to renegotiate our buyers agreement to cut eighty percent from my commission if he decided to build instead of buy. Should that happen I'd barely recoup the stripper income losses I'd incurred, plus losses from other real estate business I'd turned down to drive him around every weekend. Between my two jobs, I was working every single day that month except one—the day of my movie date with Lalo. Eight hours per shift at the club, plus another two to four hours daily at my desk, managing real estate shit—largely for Big Client, who was suddenly refusing to consider a home with the wrong shade of kitchen cabinets. (Honestly, anyone who believed the sex industry was exploitative never considered what life as a Realtor was like.)

On top of that was the situation with my aging cat, Tippy, who'd been throwing up and peeing on the floor for some unknown reason. I administered pain meds for her arthritis two to three times a day, but lately the reprieve seemed to last only a few hours. And I was pretty sure she was mad at me for being away from home so much. That morning she wouldn't stop crying, which was so unlike her it made me cry too. She was alone and hurting, and I was all she had, yet I was being pulled in every other direction. I simply could not keep working so much, and yet I had to keep up with bills *and* not blow the opportunity to close my biggest deal ever.

An hour later I met Lalo at the VIP room bar, the twenty-year-old from earlier nowhere in sight.

"There you are," he said, throwing his arms out wide. I sank into them without a word. "You okay?" he asked, holding me tight.

"I'm fine."

"Come sit with me then."

"I have to work."

"I got money, girl. I got your back!"

I smiled at that. It felt a little strange taking his money this time, even though that was the nature of my business. So, I tried to find a balance between our personal connection and my professional routine of hustling lap dances out of a guy. After he left I missed him for the rest of the day. That night my "Juicy Days" started—the three-to five-day stretch of my hormonal cycle during which I ovulated and became hornier than an entire college football team. A time when every molecule in my body, every atom of tissue, became focused on the ancient, primal, unwavering urge to procreate (except for my fallopian tubes, which I'd had soldered years before). All systems were *go*. The floodgates opened. I'd be as wet as Austin's Shoal Creek during the rains, as there was basically a flash flood in my pants for four straight days out of every twenty-eight.

My most recent block of Juicy Days had been two weeks before meeting Lalo, when I felt in such dire need of sex that I'd screamed at a wall (I don't even know what I said; it was completely unintelligible) then burst into sobs for thirty minutes. No lie. My body craved sex so badly I was sobbing. It didn't have a clue what else to do. This happened every month and it was painful enough not having sex those days, but when I couldn't channel the sexual energy into banking at the club it was all the more frustrating. All the next day I showed lake homes to Big Client for eight hours, in jeans with no panties and a wet spot the size of an egg in my crotch. The following day I showed him homes for another five hours in the same condition, then worked at my desk all evening. Lalo snuck away from home long enough to see me for the briefest visit, then we made plans to celebrate Valentine's Day at my place, two days later, on the thirteenth.

I got him a card with a little silver charm in the shape of a tequila bottle glued to the front, with my wishes for his future health and happiness written inside. I tied it together with a homemade gift using ringlets of red ribbon. The gift was a CD with a custom cover—a photo of me on my hands and knees, nude, long red hair spilling everywhere. The interior insert was another nude of me, reclining on plush pillows with a dreamy look on my face. The CD recording was an AA lecture about the latest research on addiction and brain chemistry. It was an excellent speech for someone receptive to hearing it. If not, a good gag gift, I supposed.

When I found out Lalo was standing me up for Valentine's Day, I told him he could pick up his gift bag on my doorstep and that I was unavailable to see him again for at least a week, unless he came to the club, which wasn't my preference. He'd called eight times that afternoon with eight excuses. I stopped answering after the fourth and spent the night curled up with Tippy, who was doing much better after five hundred dollars in medications and yet another veterinary house call. The cost was a hit, but whatever… Tippy was all I had. I'd break my back to keep her alive until she was truly ready to go. And even though she was twenty years old, Dr. Burnside said she still had some good quality of life left in her.

The next day Big Client called to tell me his father-in-law was deathly ill and his home buying plans in Austin were on hold. Weeks later, he called one last time to say his father-in-law had died. His wife had a lot on her hands, being the executor of his will, with a lot of sibling infighting over his assets. They'd probably stay in Dallas after all, he told me, but thanks for all the hard work. I never saw him again.

I was out five grand in missed work thanks to him, but at least I now had my weekends free. As I basked in the rare luxury of choosing between the gym, errands, and working on a writing project, Lalo showed up to apologize for standing me up on Valentine's Day. I had shopping to do, and he agreed to come along, dutifully pushing a Costco cart as we discussed our feelings and what might be best for us moving forward.

"I've got to get a divorce soon, and all that entails…find a lawyer and a new place to live, that whole drill. And with working nonstop, it's just a lot going on."

"It's a lot to deal with, I know," I replied. "I'm just as busy with stripping, real estate, and my writing. We were probably crazy to think we could fit into each other's life for very long."

"At least let me keep paying for your biweekly massages," he insisted. "I know how much your hip and back bother you and I really want to help."

"If you must," I said with a shrug. He'd bought me three massages already and they really did help some.

No one since Joe had concerned themselves with my lifelong back pain or bought me massages to help. I never had anyone help push one of those huge Costco carts. No one to pump my gas or stroke my hair while I cried about Tippy's health issues, but Lalo did all that and more, while agreeing with me, sadly, that with everything going on in our lives we were better off as friends. Then, when we were done talking, we went back to my place and had "friendship sex" for the rest of the day.

Two days later he returned, and we had sex again. He'd been in San Antonio for his daughter's game and passed up an opportunity to spend the night with a hot soccer mom because he couldn't stop thinking about me.

"That's weird, right?" he asked.

"I understand completely," I replied. "I feel the same way, Lalo. I don't want anyone else but you."

"Really?"

"Really."

"Then maybe that's what we should do."

We promised to tell each other if our feelings changed. When he left, he said, "I adore you."

I said, "Me too."

Two days later, in bed again, he said *I love you* in the middle of sex.

I said I did too. I didn't understand it really and didn't equate it with the love I'd had for Joe in my twenties or even Brad in high school, but it did feel like love. It was love with walls around it. Love for a man with substance abuse issues, a young, vulnerable daughter who needed to be his priority, and an upcoming messy divorce with a crazy person I'd do well to stay away from. A careful, limited kind of love. But a lot more than anything I'd had in a long, long time.

Give Me an "S"...!

March 18, 2007

Current Location: Rah, Rah, Raw
Current Mood: horny

"Do you know that my clitoris has 8,000 nerve endings?" I ask him. "That's twice as many as the head of your penis, you know."

"I know," he says.

"Really? Did you count them? Is THAT what you're always doing down there?"

"I'll never tell..." he whispers, sliding his hand under the sheet and slowly up my thigh.

"That's fine. Whatever you *are* doing it's working for me." I see him slide his other hand under the sheet and come to rest near the top of his own thigh. "Do you know there's a theory," I continue, "that the G-spot is nothing more than the back end of the clitoris?"

"I like it when you talk like that," he says, speeding up the motion of his hand stroking my inner thigh. His eyes are getting dreamy.

I think for a moment, then say, "Vulva."

He jumps me.

Yes, it's another fabulous sex-filled Sunday at Casey and Lalo's cozy South/Central ATX love nest. And I haven't even donned the cheerleading outfit yet.

CHAPTER 3

1998–2001

ALLOW ME TO DESCRIBE the ten years of my life leading up to when I first met Lalo.

When I left Vegas, in 1998, I was making one thousand dollars a night or more, stripping at the Crazy Horse Too. Some of the "more" came from moonlighting—hooking up with occasional horny strip club customers I'd rejoin after work, at their hotel, for an hour of sex. None of them ever lasted an hour, which meant I typically earned one thousand dollars at the club over eight hours, then another five hundred for fifteen minutes in a hotel room with some nice enough guy who was invariably delighted, complimentary, quick, and generous. Sometimes they gave me money to gamble with and we'd hit the blackjack tables together. I also made sure they gave me an orgasm, every time, though that was less about my personal enjoyment than a practice I undertook to ensure I continued to be able to come easily and quickly with new partners. (I looked at it a little like public speaking, meaning the best way to combat the mental block of self-consciousness was to undertake the practice regularly.)

The problem was that to make that initial thousand at the club I had to let customers cross all manner of personal boundaries. I did it because I was newly sober, and, to me, cash still better quantified my value as a human being than any set of personal morals or principles could. Making that extra five hundred was simple enough but entailed giving someone access to my body I wouldn't have otherwise. The result was that I paid off twenty thousand dollars in credit card debt ridiculously quickly, while developing a handful of quirks hinting at a certain emotional instability. Meditation helped, as did daily AA meetings, but for the most part the habits I displayed in early sobriety were just as compulsive, if not as ruinous, as the drugs and alcohol I'd just quit.

After every paid date I took rigorous, abrasive, almost Silkwood-style showers followed by curling up in the fetal position on my sofa all night with my back to the TV. I hoarded money, obsessively clipping coupons while shoving almost every dollar I made into a Palace Station lockbox, watching stacks of hundreds grow week by week, month by month, in tandem with my twisted perception of self-worth. I'd see a couple on the street holding hands and have the urge to vomit over the fakeness of their absurd display of devotion, because I didn't think there was any such thing between men and women. I'd want to claw out the eyes of some guy at the airport who gave my body a polite once-over followed by a relatively innocent nod of approval. All of that is why I left Vegas, in fact. The knowledge that it was me, not them, who was fucked up in the head. And that every dollar I'd stuffed in that lockbox would be spent on therapy for life if I didn't get out of the sex business.

Also because I was gaining weight. I'd quit smoking six months after quitting drinking, then immediately started eating everything in sight. Within a month I had a full-blown binge eating disorder and put on enough weight that I didn't feel comfortable stripping at a top Vegas club anymore. In 1997, none of the good clubs employed heavyset girls. No one I worked with was bigger than a size six and I was slowly exceeding that. I moved to Austin and took a year off work. I started running daily, hitting the gym, and seeing two (nonsexual) sugar daddies to keep a little money coming in. I already had a major caffeine addiction, on top of which I added daily ephedrine in the form of "workout supplements." Eventually I flipped from hoarding money to spending my savings as fast as

I could, mostly on beauty and body treatments, travel, and bad stock investments—subconsciously purging myself of the financial security I didn't feel worthy of having.

My first job outside the sex industry was credit card processing sales. I cried the first time I had to buy business attire, as I'd not worn anything as straightlaced as a collared, button-up blouse since Catholic high school. When I discovered the owner of the company—one of my strip club customers from Vegas—was screwing over our clients, I quit the job. I tried to return to stripping for lack of anything as profitable to do, but quickly realized it still wasn't a healthy place for me. I wanted to be better at boundaries but didn't know how. When the men I'd danced for in Vegas hadn't set them *for me* I'd grown resentful—as if it were their job all along. I sniped at my new coworkers and seethed at customers who didn't spend as much as I thought they should. I was redirecting my financial fears and resentments toward myself, onto my (mostly) innocent customers, so I quit again, after a mere three weeks dancing back at Sugar's in Austin.

What I really wanted to do was write a book, but I abandoned the idea as soon as I excitedly told my parents about it over dinner and was met with silent, disapproving looks. I was still too tied up in what they expected me to be and too guilty over wasting my twenties to trust my own instincts. My father had always been in real estate, so I signed up for classes and got my license, then promptly became a raging workaholic. I was also a work*out*-aholic, spending hours in the gym every evening, after running miles of streets every morning, often boxing and swimming laps in between. All the weight I'd gained in 1998 melted off in 1999, through fasting, crash diets, stimulants, and excessive cardio. I was in a hurry to look my best again. My sex drive—which had disappeared the day I got sober and stayed gone for almost two years—was back *with a vengeance.*

In early sobriety I'd only had personal sex (versus professional sex) with two men. The first was Beeper, a former fighter pilot and fuck buddy from my drinking days, but since he was still drinking, I lost interest almost immediately and promptly brushed him off, to his wounded chagrin. The other was with a waiter in Reno, where I stripped for a month while my Vegas club was being renovated. He was a young, long-haired hippie who worked at a vegetarian deli I frequented. One day I called and asked him to deliver my lunch to the club, hoping the sight of me in a sparkly, red, thong bikini would turn him on, which it did, though it also made him slightly uncomfortable, never having been in a strip club before. That night at his place, during our first kiss, I realized—having recently quit smoking—that kissing a smoker was, in fact, as much like licking an ashtray as nonsmokers always claimed. From there I rushed us into sex, hoping to lose myself in it the way I used to when I was drinking. Instead, our connection was awkward and boring, and as soon as it was over, I got dressed and left. The look on his face as I did was just like Beeper's—wounded and confused. It was my first clue that sex and dating might work differently in sobriety, and I was going to have to learn what that meant and how to navigate it.

A year later, I moved back to Austin and joined an AA home group in Cedar Park, northwest of Austin proper. At the end of my first meeting, a shy, serious young man approached me to chat. Knowing I was newly back in town he offered to hang out, suggesting we hike Enchanted Rock together. I needed to make new sober friends, so I agreed. A week later I heard through his sponsor's wife that he thought he was dating me.

"What?" I yelped.

"Didn't you go hiking with him?" she asked.

"Yes, as *friends*."

"Well, did you tell him that?"

"I didn't think I had to. I thought he was just trying to make the new girl feel welcome."

"But he's a guy."

"That's insane," I retorted. "This isn't 1950. I have loads of male friends who don't think we're dating when we hang out together."

The situation felt so bizarre I never returned to that Cedar Park group. Then a similar thing happened when I was hanging out with my sister and her friends. We were at UT's student union with one of their friends, a quiet young man calling himself DJ Mel. There was a movie starting that I wanted to see, but my sister and her friends had to leave, so DJ Mel and I watched it together. When it was over, he asked where I wanted to go next, my place or his.

"Actually, I need to get home," I said, turning to go.

"What the hell," he fumed. "I thought you liked me. I thought we were on a date."

I had no answer for that. I didn't know what he was talking about and ducked out of there fast. Were men outside of strip clubs just as clueless as men inside strip clubs? Was socializing in sobriety always this presumptive and weird?

I switched my AA home group to one in the Cat Mountain area, where I met my new sponsor and a bunch of other lovely sober people who'd go on to become my friends for many years. One was Marty, a handsome thirty-five-year-old, new to AA, with a slight build, honey blond mustache and goatee, and the silkiest, sun-bleached locks around. There was a surfer look to him, with his long shorts, sandals, and Baja poncho, that combined with his raspy southern drawl to make him the sexiest man I'd met in two years of daily meetings. His eyes were hypnotic and penetrating. An old-timer there once referred to him as "blond Jesus" and everyone in the room knew who he meant. I didn't expect him to look twice at me—I hadn't lost all my extra weight yet—but damned if we didn't catch each other in a sideways glance. A few weeks later, chatting after a meeting, I said something about being grateful for how well he seemed to get me. I might have made it sound flirty. He definitely responded in kind.

　　　　　　　　　　　　　　　　　　Kristin Casey

We hooked up a handful of times. My sex drive had recently escalated from barely there to beyond voracious. Still, the first time he came over I broke out in a nervous sweat. Sex in early sobriety, without the usual crutches, was a whole new, terrifying experience, like having sex for the first time ever. I mean, I'd had lots of paid sex and a few short boring fucks in those two years, but Marty was the first guy I'd been genuinely and severely hot for—the first to trigger real sexual arousal in me for twenty-four straight months. And despite that I'd been one of the best paid escorts in Vegas, waiting for Marty to arrive that day, I started to wonder if I'd remember how to do it.

As it was, we did just fine. Marty was breezy, good-natured, and playful, and knew how to make a woman feel desired and special—at least for the time he was with her, which in my case was extremely sporadic. Still, sex with him opened the floodgates, triggering an ocean of suppressed feelings I hadn't been able to access in sobriety yet—from tenderness to connection to sorrow. I didn't know how it worked, but I was grateful for it. Sometimes, in the middle of things, I'd even be flooded with waves of rage and resentment, like a purge of stuck emotions his thrusting had forced to the surface—having little to do with Marty himself. Strange as it sounds, it was incredibly cathartic. Isn't anger the other side of the passion coin? I had both in spades, and they needed to come out however my body would let them. For two years in sobriety, I'd been drowning in depression and anhedonia—the inability to feel pleasure, not uncommon in early sobriety. To open any floodgate was a blessing. It made me feel whole and connected and human again. The problem was I needed it more than he did—or I needed it with him more than he needed it with me (because for all I knew, Marty was getting it from multiple other women).

I tried hard to play it cool, to be the tough chick. Answering every call in my breeziest voice, never letting him know that I thought of him every day, in between our too rare hookups. Sex with him was the only time I felt connected at all to anyone. But, for reasons unknown to me, he eventually moved on and that was probably a blessing too. The spontaneity had been delicious. It added to the intensity of the sex, but after a few months it was no longer worth the pain of uncertainty to me...the constant wondering *when can I have him again?* Later that year, long after we'd ended things, he left a voicemail praising my wit, spirituality, and intelligence. Another time he let me know that he'd cared for me as much as I would let him. He wasn't wrong about that, I had to admit. I was capable of having sex again, but of true emotional intimacy? Nowhere close to it.

I tried to fill the gap at an AA conference in Colorado, coming on strong to the leader of the Alateen group—a good Christian college boy who took my sexual advances as a sign I wanted to date him and become a committed couple, something he seemed shockingly eager to do after knowing me a mere week. I backpeddled like mad, telling him it was just a sex thing for me.

"I'm sorry, I didn't mean to lead you on," I said. We were standing in my bedroom in Austin, where he'd come to see me the weekend after the conference ended.

"How can you do this to me? I really liked you," he whined, on the verge of tears it seemed.

Getting that muscular, weeping jock out of my condo and back into his car, bound for Dallas, was the most awkward moment of my sobriety thus far. I changed my number afterward to avoid having to hear his mournful voicemails.

Soon after, I met someone new at the gym. We were on stationary bikes, one seat away from each other. Rob was reading *Conversations with God*, a book I'd recently finished. Without thinking I leaned over and asked how he liked it. He had an exceptionally muscular body, short dark hair, and a classically chiseled jawline. I'd already noticed his reading glasses, which had long been a turn on for me, but not how good-looking he was, so when he first glanced over I practically gasped. He didn't notice. Turns out he was almost as shy as me right then, if his stammer was any indication. When he started talking, the sweet vulnerability of it sliced me right in half.

"I-it's good. I mean, it's interesting s-so far. Pretty d-different s-stuff, right?"

"I suppose," I replied, finally finding my voice. "But infinitely better than the God that I grew up with."

He laughed at that, and we continued chatting. He was a project manager at a software company and amateur MMA fighter. He asked what time of day I usually worked out and said maybe he'd see me again tomorrow night. The next night I was so tired I crawled into bed, then sighed and got up and dressed again. I went to the gym and sat on a bike. He promptly sat down next to me. We talked some more, then traded phone numbers.

Our first date was at the park and then to lunch at Central Market where I told him about being clean and sober. He was as sweet and gentlemanly as could be. I was nervous the whole time, wondering if I was boring him. Freaking myself out by how much I liked him. Our next date, watching TV, I was so nervous again I must've adjusted the thermostat ten times. I was thirty-two years old for Christ's sake. When would I get past this cringey dating anxiety? When he left, he kissed me on the forehead and gave me a hug. I locked the door, rested my head against it, and touched my fingers to it. I couldn't stop smiling. I hadn't felt like that in so long.

On date number three we made out. On date number four sex happened. That's when I discovered Rob practically had a PhD in sexual technique. It wasn't wild and uninhibited but perfectly choreographed and deeply satisfying. We continued to see each other, going to dinner with my sister and her boyfriend and watching football at my sponsor's house. I was falling for him hard, and he seemed to be on the same page. He called multiple times every day, even from work.

Then his ex-girlfriend showed back up in his life, bringing all kinds of drama with her. Turns out they had quite the back-and-forth relationship. I could see he had unresolved feelings for her, though he still called me regularly. I couldn't believe this normal, gorgeous, successful man was into me, and I tried hard to accept the limbo state we were suddenly in. I again fell back on the tough chick ethic, pretending nothing phased me. That there wasn't a cloying, needy little girl screaming inside me. Rob said he needed to step back a bit while he "settled things" with her. One night he and his ex—if indeed she could be called that—had a fight and he ended up in my bed. Things were getting sticky. She accosted me at the gym, proclaiming Rob's devotion to her. I turned my back and continued lifting weights in silence. She got friends who worked there to bully me. They ignored me at the counter, told me they were out of towels when they weren't, rolled their eyes when I grew impatient, and mocked me when I raised my voice at them. It felt like high school all over again.

I was falling in love with Rob, but he asked for another few days to sort out his feelings. I saw the writing on the wall. He started pulling away. He said it wasn't about me, but I blamed myself for revealing too much too soon. The sobriety thing, the bulimia. I suspected I'd also become too sexually aggressive and that Rob preferred a more traditionally feminine partner. I was no good at casually dating someone like him, it was too much pressure to be perfect. And no matter how much he was in my life, it wasn't enough. If I hadn't heard from him that day, I'd wish we were emailing. If we were emailing, I'd wish we were talking. If we were talking, I wanted to be with him. When we were together, I wanted to have sex with him. Every time we had sex, I wanted to be his girlfriend.

He still called occasionally, but I started playing games, not returning calls for days, then suddenly being extra friendly at the gym. Other times, on the phone or in emails he'd glimpse my clinginess and mood swings and try to soothe them. Sometimes we hung out, sometimes he canceled plans on me. I'd bought two tickets to see Kid Rock and ended up going alone.

The first time I'd attended a concert in sobriety was to see Chicago at the Aladdin, with no ability to enjoy or feel the music. I'd been sober six months and my anhedonia was deeply entrenched. Sitting among an entire auditorium of people standing and waving their Bic lighters, I cried quietly in my seat, terrified of feeling nothing but numbness and depression for the next fifty years. But two years later, dancing my ass off to Kid Rock playing the best songs off his fourth album, everything was different. He had strippers on the stage—*my people!*—and just enough Joe Walsh in him to endear me completely. For the first time in sobriety, I felt truly alive, like my old self in all the best ways, full of passion and joy, dancing without self-consciousness or inhibition. Completely present, completely in my body. It was a good sign to feel like that again. I had missed that part of myself far more than I'd realized. And I hadn't needed Rob at my side to access it, though, lonely as I was, I continued to obsess over him.

WHEN MY SEX DRIVE RETURNED, two years into my sobriety, I'd felt like a teenage boy at parochial school. My needs were so strong and unmet they were painful, and the handful of sporadic trysts I'd had with Marty were hardly enough to get by. Months later, my monthlong fling with Rob felt much the same, leaving me forever hungry, albeit with him in my heart as much as my body. So, I threw myself at my kickboxing instructor, to no avail beyond two flirty phone calls in return—one of which he'd left me on hold for an hour, *while I let him*. I was beginning to question my affinity for choosing severely unavailable men.

Around that time, I interviewed with real estate brokers and had my pick of where to hang my license. I went with a broker named Hank at a North Austin office, and within a few weeks had developed a major crush on him. Chatting in his office we discovered we were both runners. He usually did three miles on his lunch hour. I told him I averaged six a day.

"Really, what's your long run?"

"Twelve miles, most Sundays," I bragged.

"That's amazing! You should run a marathon."

I smiled and shrugged it off. I'd never considered it, but three months later, partly to impress Hank, I did.

He was another former fighter pilot, and who doesn't love a flyboy? He was also handsome with bronze skin, a gorgeous smile, tidy hair, and a lean, compact body that I couldn't stop fantasizing about. He had a confidence about him, business-wise especially, that attracted me to no end. He was supremely professional yet extraordinarily caring. I'd never worked in an office setting before, thus had no way to know if the way he took care of his agents was the norm, but I suspected it wasn't. One day I was struggling to learn some new paperwork and he could tell. Without saying anything to me, he suddenly made a little speech to the new agents about how hard things can be in the beginning, with a couple funny anecdotes about his own early mistakes.

I enjoyed our rapport and respected him tremendously—despite how many times per day I imagined him in compromising positions with me all over the office. After all, he was everything I was not—successful, sophisticated, casually confident. Likewise, I represented something missing in his life—a certain wildness and adventure perhaps, for a grounded flyboy stuck behind a desk. He made me feel good about myself and I made him laugh. We developed a friendship and mutual attraction that was impossible to repress.

Three months after I started working there, Hank invited me to a charity event at the Four Seasons. I spent an entire day shopping for the right dress, a formfitting lavender, beaded evening gown with a leg slit up to my hip. When I climbed into his truck as he held open the door, the slit showed my entire leg—the one I'd run a marathon on one week before. I thought his eyes were going to pop out of his head and we had a good giggle about it as we drove off.

He was attentive and jocular. I was nervous but greatly enjoying myself. At one point we stepped out to the courtyard for air and ended up in an exquisitely tender kiss. The moment couldn't have been more perfect. At the same time, I sensed we weren't compatible. I was far too wrapped up in myself and my many emotional issues to be a full-fledged partner to anyone just yet. I wanted to use him for sex. But he was a more traditional guy and I sensed he wanted more from me than that. Having the power to hurt him terrified me. It was the only thing big enough to override my yearning to ravage his body. Hank was the first truly available man I'd been attracted to in sobriety, yet because of that he was vulnerable to my indecisiveness, mood swings, and trifling tendencies. He was also the best boss I could've asked for and heading down that course with him all but ensured an iceberg ahead. A few days later, at the office, I told him we should probably cool it.

"The flirting and sexual jokes, you mean?"

"All of it," I replied. "Look, this whole thing makes me nervous. I feel like I'm slipping into some bad habits."

He seemed confused, and why wouldn't he be? He barely knew me and had no idea the kind of wreckage I'd created in the past by being sexually self-serving. Which was one thing in a strip club or out in the world, and another thing entirely at the office of my first mainstream job.

"I've hurt people...men, I mean, and I'm trying so hard to change. To be more considerate and stop indulging my desires at the expense of other people's feelings."

I meant every word of it. I'd quit the sex industry and gone mainstream. I desperately wanted to be a respectable member of society. Yet here I was, three months into my first civilian job, dating the boss and flirting like crazy whenever the other agents weren't looking. We'd even kissed in the copy room. I felt like such a cliché. Hank had no idea about my checkered stripper past or why I might need to separate my sexual self from my workspace. I couldn't feel legitimized in my new life otherwise. Even Kurt, the owner of the credit card processing company I'd worked for the previous summer, had not only been a strip club customer but an escort customer as well. I'd helped him produce his first porn movie with actors sourced from the Crazy Horse Too. (He'd stiffed me on that deal entirely, much like he'd screwed over our credit card processing clients the following year.)

I'd never been so honest about why I was ending things as I was with Hank that day. He was clearly disappointed but said he understood. We thought we could still hang out as friends, but the first time we went out, to shoot pool, watching him smoke a cigar and sip on martinis, I couldn't stop fantasizing about fucking him. Worse, he started talking about how good we might be together long term. He'd invited me to Hawaii, and I'd crazily said yes, but suddenly I put the kibosh on all of it. The look on his face was crushing and the whole thing left me sad. Sad that I'd hurt him, and sad for myself that I couldn't take him to bed without hurting him more. Had I been more mature I could've made our connection a win-win, for sure. I could have given him the closeness he needed while instilling a few boundaries to create space for my continued freedom. But with a mere three years' sobriety and even fewer successful dates under my belt I didn't have the skills or experience to move forward in a way that would honor either of our slightly skewed desires.

❧

Dating in sobriety was unbelievably confusing, but I continued to try and fumble through it. Later that year I finally agreed to go out with a fellow Realtor named Lance. I'd put him off for months because a) he was a Realtor and there's nothing sexy about that, and b) gorgeous as he was, we had nothing in common and I expected to be bored stiff.

That's not what happened. After trying unsuccessfully to align our schedules for two weeks, I agreed to swing by his place one evening after work on short notice. Unfortunately, it turned out to be the same day his parents made a surprise visit, so by the time I got there we had to be super quiet in order to not wake them in the next room. After whispering in the living room for a while, a spark appeared. We moved into his bedroom and proceeded to peel each other's clothes off.

Three and a half long years I'd been waiting for someone to tap into and match my passion like Lance did that night. Since before Hank, Rob, Marty, Beeper, and that Reno waiter. Since the day I'd gotten sober and wondered if I would ever feel wholly sexually free again.

Lance and I clicked in bed better than I had with anyone in sobriety and plenty of the men (and women) in my bed before it. And just when I thought things couldn't get any better, he flipped me onto my stomach and nudged his way into a different orifice altogether.

A whimper of pleasure escaped me, for which he urgently shushed me. "My parents, remember?" he whispered, pressing my face into the mattress, nudging himself farther and farther inside me.

It wasn't my first time having anal sex, just my first time in several years. And perhaps because I had no expectations of him or "us" as a couple, I could fully and immediately relax and open up. Muffled as I was, I could make all the noise I wanted directly into his bedding and mattress. The pleasure was indescribable—deep, pulsating waves of arousal through my entire ass, pelvis, clitoral structure, and more. He fucked me like that until I came as hard as I ever had, exactly at the moment he did. It was one of the most satisfying sexual experiences of my life.

Not much opens the emotional floodgates like truly amazing anal sex. The thing about allowing a man into that forbidden zone, without the pain that tensing up can cause, is that it demands an immediate release of walls, barriers, and ego. Letting go of the mindset I lived in all the time—that of doing, directing, accomplishing, repenting, and forging a new life in sobriety. Anal sex done right was about yielding, which took me out of my head and put me in my body, where I needed to be to have great sex. Anal sex was also a deeply intimate experience of trust, in which one must relax and surrender to receive—to embrace receptivity, the hallmark of feminine energy. My life, since the day I'd gotten sober, had been all about harnessing masculine energy to make the changes in life I needed to make. Three years into sobriety I was firmly cemented in my yang, but in that one moment, when Lance flipped me onto my stomach and took charge of my body, I reopened to the yin within me, a space I'd denied existed for longer than I should have.

I never saw him again. The next week he emailed that he was getting back with his ex. Whatever. Our one night together had been worth it. I was coming closer than ever to feeling whole again.

Months later, I got a call from a woman who wanted to buy her college-aged son a condo. Shawn was thirteen years younger than me and as pretty and buff a young man as I'd ever seen. He was Persian, in my opinion the most beautiful group of men on the planet. And he was sweet. Also, playful in the way hot twenty-year olds can be. I remained professional, having no presumptions about whether he'd want to play with me. But after three or four property

　　　　　　　　　　　　　　　　　　　　　Kristin Casey

tours we established a friendliness that led to him coming over to my place where we ended up in bed. I initiated it—which was rare for me—indicating I'd finally leveled up my confidence in that area.

It wasn't love or anything close to it. It couldn't have been a more casual, one-time thing, and as we lay there afterward, I decided to pick his brain.

"What do guys *really* think about women who have casual sex?"

He didn't miss a beat. "We like 'em!"

I laughed. That was the end of my questions for him.

NOT LONG AFTERWARD, I was fixed up by an old friend. I'd complained to him about not meeting enough available men and he'd told me about his actor friend Christian. Then he told Christian about me, and the next thing I knew Christian called and asked to meet.

He was selling his old record albums in the parking lot of Whole Foods downtown. I went there to say hello and chat, not expecting anything at all to come of it. While I trusted the friend who'd fixed us up, I based all my decisions about who to date and fuck on chemistry, something too unpredictable and complex for anyone—myself included—to arrange or predict. So no one was more surprised than me to feel sparks fly the second I got close enough to lock eyes with Christian. He was tall and lean, at least six foot four, with a shaved head and a mind for poetry and philosophy, though on that day our conversation was short and tame. Still, we never took our eyes off each other. The intensity of our chemistry was insane.

It lasted three weeks. Three weeks of hours-long phone calls, lunch and dinner dates, and make out sessions that went on all night. But we never had sex, because, as Christian put it, "There's something incredibly special between us and I don't want to rush into anything that might ruin it."

Bizarrely, I agreed. The chemistry was so strong I had no reason not to trust his assumption. I thought it might be nice and appropriate, for once, to not rush into sex. So, we made out on my bed like young teens, petting, and grinding endlessly, never getting naked or even going down on each other. Then he went on a weekend retreat with his men's group and sent me the strangest text I'd ever received—something about him having a (psychedelic induced, presumably) epiphany that women were man-eating insects who mate, then kill, and that he had no choice but to save himself immediately by breaking up with me.

I was a little crushed and a lot pissed off and called the friend who'd fixed us up. I told him Christian was acting crazy.

"Oh, Christian is batshit crazy, for sure," he replied.

"Then why the hell would you fix me up with him?!"

"Because when it comes to dating you're batshit crazy too."

I couldn't help but laugh through my tears.

❦

Rob, the muscular project manager with the endearing stammer I'd met at the gym two years earlier, had been in my life ever since. We'd become close friends. I'd been in love with him the whole time but kept those feelings to myself, determined to play it cool, the tough chick with her feelings in reserve. Meanwhile, he'd dated other women but had repeatedly gone back to his ex. I recognized the unhealthy pattern of addiction he was in (if not the one that I was in with him). Finally, he'd moved to California and broken up with her for good. Now he was returning to Austin and calling me a lot, suggesting we spend time together and making countless sexual innuendoes in the process. I, of course, developed outsized expectations that he wanted to escalate our relationship to something not just sexual but romantic. In the interim, he met someone else. When I found out, I had a full-on meltdown, sobbing and clutching his legs like the unstable, brokenhearted child I was.

He forgave me for making a scene, calling me honey and sweetie, and soothing my embarrassment and hurt feelings.

I sent him home, then took two days off work (unheard of for me), got a tattoo on my wrist of a starfish, bought some MDMA, and went to see the Toadies play, dancing like a woman possessed. And while I knew the use of MDMA was considered a relapse by most people in sobriety, I didn't. I used it solely in a last-ditch attempt to medicate the crippling depression I'd lived with for my entire sobriety. Fearing antidepressants (having heard horror stories about withdrawal symptoms and sexual side effects), I believed in my heart that were it legal any therapist worth a damn would prescribe MDMA exactly how I used it—in miniscule doses, a tiny nibble every other day for a month to simply feel normal again. To get a break from the misery of suicidal ideation and experience a brief spell of proper mental functioning for a change. When I ran out of the four tablets I'd bought, I never used MDMA again. Instead, I finally got on antidepressants, realizing it was probably the best option for me just then.

Once my mood swings leveled out, Rob and I went back to being good friends. Friends who on rare occasions still had amazing sex. Friends who loved each other, just not in the same way as the other.

CHAPTER 4

2002–2006

During those first five years of my sobriety, none of the men in my life stuck around longer than for a few weeks or a very sporadic few months. Over the next five years, I had slightly better luck.

In December 2001, my AA sponsee Nicole went to court for reckless child endangerment. Before getting sober, one day on Valium, she got in the car with her kids and fell asleep behind the wheel. No one had been hurt, but Williamson County courts were some of the toughest in the nation. Her character witnesses were me and her sober friend Paul from Los Angeles. My first sighting of Paul was down a long courthouse hallway. He had his back to me so all I saw was a lean man in a dark suit with a shaved head, but I had an instant premonition that I was meant to have an intimate connection with that man. When Nicole introduced us, I looked in Paul's eyes and knew I'd been right, but Nicole's case was our main concern, and we kept our eyes on that ball all day.

She was convicted and sentenced to one year in prison. The judge gave her two weeks to get her affairs in order, so Paul and I stayed with her after her sentencing, on suicide watch, as Nicole was the most emotionally delicate person I knew. He and I ignored our chemistry all that day. Weeks later I went to visit him in LA. He picked me up at the airport, then took me to an AA meeting. Afterward we went to Trader Joe's to pick up tuna steak and fudge pie for dinner. The heat between us was overwhelming but, aside from our arms touching at the AA meeting, the entire time we played it cool, discussing AA philosophy, Nicole's case, life in general, my writing, his industrial rock band, and his prolific session work as a bassist. To meet a man who was so talented and established in his creative career, considering how far from that place I was, was part of the attraction. Paul was like a humble, spiritual, edgy rock star, with long-term sobriety, leather garb, studs, tats…the whole bit. I got wet just sitting across the table from him.

Once the dishes were put away, he approached me with the softest imaginable kisses on my neck. I'd hoped for something a little more intense, but also figured I could die happily with just more of this. He cupped my breasts softly, then harder, then suddenly yanked my blouse down as roughly as I'd first hoped. Then he pinned me to the wall by my wrists, and I thought, *finally someone to dominate me.* Much like being pinned to the bed by Lance with his dick in my ass, I desperately needed one place in my world where someone else—someone I trusted—was in charge.

Using his belt, a blindfold, his extra-large dick, and a firm tongue, Paul ordered me around, telling me what to do and how to do it. It went on until five thirty in the morning. One month later I was back in LA, wearing my black suede, knee-high, Jimmy Choo boots in bed, doing it all over again. We went to the Knitting Factory, a live music venue where he worked, and fucked in the restroom over the sink, watching ourselves in the mirror. Then we ran into a bunch of old friends from my Joe Walsh years: Terry Reid, Jack Tempchin, Rick the Bass Player, Waddy Wachtel, and some roadies I used to know. We hung out backstage at Rick and Waddy's show where Paul knew as many musicians and crew as I did.

I missed my rock and roll life. Being with Paul brought all that back for me—brought up buried parts of me. It was a thrill to be with him. He called me beautiful, sensual, and erotic, and loved how in touch I was with my sexuality. But I sensed it wouldn't last. Paul was too intense to maintain a long-distance relationship and neither of us had money for airplane tickets. I put up walls to protect myself from the pain of its end—playing the tough chick again; I couldn't get away from it. On the other hand, perhaps it was a good thing I was finally learning not to give my power away, become too attached, have too many expectations. Three months in, he told me he was manic, which I took to mean bipolar. I saw his comment for what it was—a warning not to rely on him—and I told him not to worry, that I wouldn't get clingy. He wanted phone sex, but now that he was pulling away I couldn't access my arousal that way. Knowing he had one foot out the door killed my ability to open up sexually. I'd had too much rejection in recent years, starting with Joe but also from Marty, Rob, and Christian—all of whom abandoned me when I most craved them, much like my father had done. Which was probably why I'd subconsciously chosen them.

I emailed Paul sexy pics, but as I predicted he started calling me less. At the four-month mark he ghosted me, then eight months later called to make amends. By then I was over the pain of it. We went on to become close friends and occasional lovers, whenever I was in LA, or he was in Austin.

It hurt to be ghosted but, ultimately, I was fine, partly because I was dating two other men. One was Nicole's legal counsel. Larry had been one of her escort clients who happened to be a former lawyer. He was giving her free legal advice in prison. I was their conduit, since she was only allowed to be in contact with a limited number of people, and Larry hadn't been her trial lawyer.

Larry was a venture capitalist from the Bay Area, in Austin every month working a deal with Michael Dell of Dell Computers. Neither of us expected our chemistry to appear the way it did. Shortly after Nicole was locked up, Larry came to Austin and called to discuss his needs appealing her case. He cared about Nicole and wanted to help her. He asked about Sugar's gentlemen's club because that's where Nicole had been working after she'd gotten busted, in an attempt to keep food on the table for her kids. The DA had had a field day with that tidbit in court, insisting no one could stay sober while stripping, until I'd gotten on the stand and testified about my own excellent track record and that of dozens of sober Vegas strippers I'd worked with. (It hadn't helped, and if anything pissed off the DA more and made her more aggressive about prosecuting Nicole *and* disparaging her for being a stripper.)

"Do you know anything about this club she worked at?" Larry asked me over the phone.

"Of course," I said. "I worked there for five years myself."

Larry paused, then slowly repeated what I'd said. "You worked there for five years."

I tried not to giggle. Larry was as sexy a man as I'd met, with long hair, pouty lips, and a certain tousled elegance. But he was also a neurotic Jew who seemed a little fartoost about things like stripping and sex and what have you. Regardless, we decided to meet at the club so Larry could see it for himself. There we covered as much of Nicole's case as Larry felt necessary, then spent three hours chatting about ourselves until it dawned on us that we were on a date. Larry asked a hundred questions about me. He watched one of my stripper friends give me a lap dance, and when the subject turned to stripper shoes—which Larry liked very much—I casually mentioned still having mine at home. Next thing I knew I was giving Larry a lap dance at my place. He tried to kiss me but was too drunk to do it well, so I suggested calling it a night and driving him back to his hotel. Instead, he jumped in my bed naked, so I followed suit. We traded back scratches before falling asleep in each other's arms. Two days later he invited me to spend the weekend in Vegas with him.

Saying no to sex had rarely worked out so well for me. But it turned on Larry to be rejected by a sober former stripper who'd thought he'd had too much to drink. The more I got to know him the more I suspected Larry identified as much with sex workers as he did with lawyers or venture capitalists. One time, when I asked about his parents, he told me his father was the worst person on the planet and that his mother was a whore.

"Larry! Why would you say that about your mother?"

He looked at me flatly. "Because she was a whore. An actual prostitute."

"Oh," I replied sheepishly. "How did you know?"

"I had a different uncle every night," he said with a shrug.

We started seeing each other one weekend per month, mostly in Austin. Larry was beyond successful, and it was exciting to be with him. He'd grown up dirt poor, without food in the cupboards or a kitchen table on which to eat it. Now he owned more homes all over the world than I showed buyers on an average property tour. We had the same yoga mat, books, and bathrobes—his bought at a five-star hotel, mine swiped from one. The first time he got in my car I played an Allman Brothers CD that turned out to be his favorite ever rock record. Driving around, I wondered suddenly if he'd like to play video games, something I hadn't done in decades. When I asked, he lit up. "That's wild," he said. "I was just thinking I'd love to play video games right now but was afraid you'd think it silly!"

One morning he told me he'd been sleeping better than ever.

"Why's that," I asked.

"From being happy."

"Why are you happy?"

He looked away, bashful. "You know…when you're with someone you like, you're just happy."

I felt a surge of excitement and simultaneously a moment of dread. I had trust issues. As soon as things started working out with a man, I'd wonder when he was going to change his mind or get bored of me and bail. But it was so easy to be with Larry that my anxiety never got too bad, until he told me one afternoon that he thought I might be oversexed. I was so taken aback I had to talk to my therapist about it. Dr. Tina told me to stop worrying. She'd grown up in the same area of New York as Larry, within blocks of him, in fact. "It's different for Jewish men," she said. "It's a good thing. It means he doesn't just want you for sex."

On one hand that sounded grand. On the other, too hard to live up to. With sex, I had it in the bag. But if he liked me just for me, I had to wonder how long it would be before I screwed that up somehow. I loved being with him, including his charming as hell awkwardness in bed. I wasn't in love yet felt like I could happily spend the rest of my life with him, in a strange kind of romantic friendship. Alas it was not to be, as right at the four-month mark, he pulled a Paul and temporarily ghosted me. We had plans with Michael Dell to see the Eagles open their new tour in Reno, but Larry never followed up about it, and once his working relationship with Michael was over—and Nicole's appeal hit a dead end—he stopped coming to Austin altogether. Again, the ghosting hurt, especially coming within weeks of Paul doing it. However, I was prepared for it. I toughened up, played it cool, and pretended to be unaffected by it. I may've also sent him one or two chastising emails that served mostly to embarrass me after hitting send then rereading them. If they had any effect on Larry it was minimal. In time, like with Paul, we reconnected and remained friends, occasionally, over the years, meeting up in Vegas for fun and friendship sex.

There are men out there—respectable, sophisticated, successful men (lawyers frequently)—who identified with or understood the sex worker side of me as well as or better than I did. Larry was one of them, and that's probably why I felt so comfortable and content in his company. Without trying or meaning to, he made me feel good about myself, that I was good enough just being me. When he left, I questioned all of it, but in the end decided it was real and that it would behoove me to continue believing I was worth something. That I was good company, interesting, sexy, fun, and the type of woman who could and would attract more high value men.

THE THIRD MAN I was dating at that time was Zed. I met him at Momo's in downtown Austin, in early 2002, within weeks of meeting Paul and Larry. Unlike with them, I immediately felt like I'd known Zed my entire life. Like a super-hot twin brother that just might be the male version of my sexual self. And long before it was over—more than three years later—he'd breathe life back into the part of me that had been battered, deflated, and sexually wounded after breaking up with Joe.

A Realtor friend had insisted on taking me to see some live music. He said I seemed stressed out a lot and like I could use some fun nights out. He wasn't wrong about that. Austin was the live music capital of the world, after all, and aside from a handful of nights out with my sister, I hadn't taken advantage of that fact in the three and a half years I'd been back.

Zed's band was one of the first my friend took me to see. He brought two other friends along and the four of us hit the dance floor till closing time. I caught Zed staring at me from the stage multiple times and noticed how hot he was and how much his playing style and my dancing aligned. I approached him as the band packed up. "Great show," I said.

He looked at me for a long time, not saying anything. Long enough for me to feel embarrassed. I was just about to walk away when he finally opened his mouth. "Goddamn, girl. You are the sexiest dancer I have ever seen!"

I blushed, not sure what to say.

"You really kept me going tonight. What's your name?"

We chatted for a while, then I rejoined my friends, but just as we got up to leave Zed appeared and asked if he could walk me to my car.

"My car is at home, but you can walk me outside."

On the sidewalk we broke off from my friends who waited on the corner while I said goodbye to Zed.

"I want to kiss you," he said shyly, "but your friends are watching."

"I don't care," I said dropping my purse on the ground and wrapping my arms around his neck for a long, wet, satisfying kiss.

Zed was my age—thirty-four—married, with no kids, and someone who still drank and partied quite a bit. He was tall and muscular with short hair, a strong jaw, and piercing eyes. A natural musician, he was considered one of the best in Austin at his instrument. High in demand and in more than one band, Zed called the scene "incestuous" in a fun way, not as a slam.

He asked for my number and called one week later to tell me about a gig he had in Pflugerville, just north of Austin. I met him there, and during his twenty-minute set break we escaped to make out in a shadowy outdoor niche of a neighboring commercial business. Over the next four months I saw him play every other week. Almost every time, we had sex somewhere nearby, all over downtown and the surrounding areas—in the grass at Pease Park, standing against a brick wall in an alleyway near Momo's, in the backseat and front seat of my Lexus, parked at the Steamboat, The Saxon Pub, multiple parking garages, and one dark, residential curb in Hyde Park. I'd follow him to Houston for gigs so we could do it in my motel room after the show. Sometimes he'd drive north of downtown, to my condo, so we could use an actual bed.

The sex was intense but also as natural a feeling as dancing or running. There was none of Paul's dominance, Larry's deferring, Rob's withholding, or Christian's hard limits. Zed and I had no limits. With Zed it was all passion, instinctual and free. We were two horny kids full of lust for each other. Our drives and needs matched up perfectly. I didn't get to see him as often as I wanted— which would've been every day, had I had my way—but every time I saw him, he let me know how bad he wanted me, then showed me, making me come multiple times that way. That may've been one of the most therapeutic aspects to our relationship—to feel so wanted and desired, attractive, sexy, and special, by one of Austin's most talented, sexiest men. To be wanted so badly and to feel so much desire for him in return that we had to find a place to fuck as quickly as possible, without rules, boundaries, social etiquettes, or the banality of four walls and a mattress, was the best. It made me feel like a child again. Zed was nothing if not playful with an overriding childlike sense of wonderment. For him, I sensed I fulfilled a deep-seated need for wildness, expression, and adventure that the woman he'd married didn't.

But he did love her and loved being married to her. Ultimately her groundedness was good for him and he knew it. So, one day, exactly four months in yet again, I got a call telling me it was over. The guilt was getting to him. "It gets easier and easier to be with you and it shouldn't be like that," he said. "Also, if someone found out it could ruin my wife's life. Upset my in-law's, too, you know… the whole extended family."

"I understand completely," I said. Because I did. I understood not being able to get everything you needed from one partner, despite desperately wishing to. I told him about loving Joe Walsh, yet having a yearlong, guilt-ridden affair with his road manager, Smokey. But in my heart I knew that had Joe and I stayed together we would have surely agreed to a non-monogamous arrangement at some point. We were simply too complex of creatures to get all our needs met by one life partner.

The truth is, until relatively recently (around ten thousand years ago) and for millions of years, most people—men and women alike—had multiple sexual relationships going at any given time. That most men still want multiple sex partners through their twenties and thirties, is hardly breaking news. Yet most men decide at some point that securing *reliable* regular sex is preferable to putting in the effort to find multiple partners every year for twenty years. Which is why, if you offered 100,000 men the choice between a decade of monogamy in their thirties or a guaranteed decade of reliable, regular, satisfying sex from *multiple* partners, 80,000 of them would choose the latter. Unfortunately, that's a choice usually offered only to celebrities and rock stars. Now, Zed was a local rock star and could get as many side pieces as he desired, but he was also one of those men who truly treasured the partnership his marriage provided. That it didn't provide the sexual adventure he craved was a sticking point, to be sure—and a valid one in my mind—but it wasn't my place to convince him to override his conscience or vow of fidelity to his wife. That was on him to work out—or not—with her, whether now, in the future, or never.

Regardless, I told Zed that I thought he was amazing, and I respected what he was trying to do. And that maybe I was beginning to like him too much anyway. I told him about Paul and Larry, who'd both drifted from my life in recent days. I suppose I was poly before anyone really started to use that word. "I don't want to start craving you too much because you're suddenly the only man giving me what I need."

Zed gave me connection, but more than that he provided space for me to escape the constant stress of trying to make something of myself…the space to delight in something. The space to just be playful.

I told him not to have regrets, just to treasure the good memories. "Don't feel guilty," I said. "Look at it this way. It wasn't your fault…I'm just *that* hard to resist," I joked.

He laughed. "It's true, you're amazing. And the sex, Jesus…"

"I'll miss you," I said. "Call me if you ever change your mind."

He did change his mind, dozens of times over the next three years. And sometimes he called just to talk because during the time of our affair he was battling substance abuse issues, which for obvious reasons I understood and withheld judgment about in ways his friends and family couldn't. As promised, I was always discreet, though on occasion I'd get clingy and pouty when he'd cancel on me last minute or bow out because of guilt. But for the most part it was pure fun and connection. Connection through the most fun activity I knew of. Sex was the easiest way for me to experience intimacy and for him to feel authentic. Because that's what sex was for some of us—a place to feel connected, authentic, and secure. For much of my thirties, sex was the only place I *could* feel that.

As for my partners, nowhere does a man reveal himself the way he does in bed, displaying a level of openness and willingness to *be seen*, that he doesn't—and often can't—experience anywhere else. Sure, sometimes the vulnerability of the moment backfires, making him run the other direction never to return his partner's calls. But for the most part, a man's quest for intimacy and approval, his desire to feel valued and worthwhile, and his urge to express his inner caveman *and* inner child through the act of sex is a gift and beautiful thing. Unfortunately, like in Zed's case, it's one not always made clear to or recognized by the women in their lives.

In the middle of my three-year affair with Zed I fell for someone new. One year since my initial foray downtown, I'd become as much of a fixture there as the bands I went to see. Bob Schneider's two bands were chief among them. Whether with his self-titled band or his beloved, funky, raunchy, party band, The Scabs, there was no one better to dance to all night long, and nowhere better to do it than Antone's Nightclub, where they played regularly. Among The Scabs' incredibly talented band members was Charles Rieser, whose guitar solos were so good they sent me to another realm. I finally got up the nerve to tell him one night.

"Your 'Beatomatic' solo makes me want to pay your mortgage."

"Thanks," he said, blushing and scuttling off.

Turned out, Charles wasn't much for taking advantage of the many horny female fans hanging around after every show, if for no other reason than he hadn't a clue how. The next time I saw him,

I chatted him up during the set break. We talked about our favorite bands and venues, and my work as a Realtor. I came up with an excuse to give him my card. Almost six months later he used it to ask me out. By then I knew him as the shyest member of The Scabs, nine insanely talented musicians and delightful personalities, oozing in charm and sex appeal. Charles was the tallest, but because of his humble posturing, the one who faded into the background the most—until one of his solos that is.

He invited me to La Tazza Fresca, an artsy UT area coffeehouse club, on a stormy Friday the thirteenth, where he was jamming with Wayne Sutton and a third guy on bongos. Zed happened to be there, and I spotted him as soon as I walked in. He waved, happy to see me, and with my eyes still on him I went to hug Charles and promptly smacked foreheads with him. It was an awkward start to the evening.

I watched the guys play, sitting alone, sipping an iced tea all evening. When the band took a break, Charles went outside to smoke in the rain. He hadn't waved me over or invited me to join him, but when I did, he asked what my plans were for later that night. I had none but he didn't pursue the question. As soon as the show was over, he took off with Wayne, saying, "Sorry, he's my ride. Thanks for coming!"

I'd thought we were on a date, but he hadn't even hugged me goodbye. Maybe the forehead slam had embarrassed him. Or he'd simply decided he wasn't interested. I motioned to Zed who followed me to my car, where we promptly had sex, my back on the front center console and head resting on the dash, Zed sandwiched between my thighs in the backseat, fucking me. Afterward, as we sat next to each other pulling on our jeans, I asked, "What's up with Charles, do you think?"

"I don't know why he left like that, but you should give him a chance. He's an awesome guy."

"Yeah?"

Zed nodded. "I highly recommend him."

So, with my favorite lover's endorsement, when Charles called the next day to apologize, I gave him a second chance. Besides, his excuse was ridiculously sweet.

"I got no game," Charles said. He'd rushed out because he hadn't known how to talk to me or advance our date into the evening. His vulnerability touched me deeply.

We made plans for lunch a few days later, but in the interim I worried. In eight months of crushing on him I'd been drawn to his wit, hyper intelligence, and philosophical way of talking. I loved his silky, wavy hair, soul patch, spectacles, and broad shoulders. But I was suddenly privy to his insecurity around women, which gave me the power to hurt him. It was a bit of a turnoff and I decided to proceed cautiously. On the one hand, he seemed so safe and kind that I was eager to spend more time with him. On the other, I'd need to see some strength in him to move forward and was wary of ending up on an uncomfortable second date.

I needn't have worried. From the moment he opened his purple front door, it was like the skies parted. He practically glowed, and when he smiled a sudden warmth spread through me. I'd long thought he was good-looking, but had he always been *this* handsome? A call came in just then about a record he was producing for someone. He stayed on the phone twenty minutes while I wandered around his clean, colorful, little house taking everything in. I couldn't help feeling like something in my life had just changed or was about to.

We went to Guero's for Mexican food and TCBY for frozen yogurt, talking all about our past relationships, favorite music, and life philosophies. Back at his place the talking continued for hours, until at one point he suddenly sat back and said, "I'm finished."

What an adorably odd thing to say, I thought.

We were on a couch in the spare bedroom that he'd converted into a recording studio. I was reclining longways with my toes tucked under his thigh. The silence went on a long time, with enough sexual tension to finally push the slightly-less-shy one of us—me—up to grab his arm and hike myself right onto his lap. We looked into each other's eyes for two seconds before sharing the best kiss of my life. As we started making out, I marveled at how skilled and sensual he was. When he went down on me, I came so hard I slipped into outer space just like during one of his "Beatomatic" solos.

We made plans to get together in two days. On the way home I stopped by Café Mundi to see Bruce Hughes and Matt the Electrician play. I ran into my friend Jud and told him I'd just had the best date of my life.

"It lasted nine hours and felt simultaneously like a full week and the blink of an eye," I said beaming.

"Very cool," Jud replied. "I don't think I've ever seen you this happy, Kristi."

On our second date, Charles and I moved into my raspberry painted bedroom and started having sex. In the middle of everything, he whispered that I still made him a little nervous. I told him he made me nervous too. We stopped for a minute.

"Why?" he asked, lifting his weight off me.

"I'm just not…" I trailed off.

"Go on," he said with sweet concern.

"I'm not used to letting someone in. To getting close to someone."

What I meant but didn't say was that I was terrified my feelings wouldn't be reciprocated. That I wasn't someone who'd learned how to not become emotionally dependent on the men I loved, and therefore not someone who knew how to handle rejection from them when it came.

He said he understood, and maybe he did. He'd had three long term relationships and two of the women had been "psychos"—in his words. He'd only recently gotten out of the last one. We were both fearful of getting hurt and hurting the other person. But we clicked like crazy. He started asking to see me almost every day and nothing could've made me happier. I went to all his gigs to see him in all his bands, multiple times per week. We watched *The Sopranos* and *Law & Order* together, went to the lake and the greenbelt, and had sex every which way all over his house. But every few days we'd confront our feelings and get scared all over again.

"What do you think is going on here?" he asked me casually one day.

"I don't know. All I know is I want to see you every day. I've never been so comfortable with anyone," I said.

"Me too! What is that?!"

I laughed and shrugged.

Later he said, "You confuse me. You're so easy to be with, but it's hard to be with someone in general."

"I get it," I nodded. "I feel that way too. You scare me a little."

"Yeah," he said. "You scare me too."

I didn't want to ruin it by thinking about everything that could go wrong. But I told him my biggest fear: that I would lose myself in him. His was that he'd screw it up the way he always did, by being a self-centered flake. I wondered if he sabotaged relationships. I wondered if I did too. And I couldn't help noticing that our biggest fears could not be more at odds with each other. Also, that both of us had just admitted how hard it was to "be" with someone in general. Either we were being faced with the opportunity to enact a positive psychic change upon each other, or we were headed for a completely predictable romantic disaster.

"We'll take it one day at a time," he said, holding me tight.

One night at my condo I put on Peter Gabriel's *Passion*, lit candles, and turned on strands of colored twinkle lights. I was dozing by the time Charles arrived. He woke me with the most tender, sensual caresses, pulling off my nightie and kissing me everywhere from my neck to my ankles, his silky hair trailing my skin, his soft breath warming it as he kissed and licked my toes. He was magnificently sexy, The Scabs' best kept secret, snaking his way back up my body as I reached out to entwine my fingers with his, hoping to convey how I felt about what he was doing to me, physically and emotionally. He kissed me endlessly. He kissed me more than any man ever had, and it was healing in the extreme. He told me again how easy it was to be with me.

Every day Charles asked if I was free to see him tomorrow. Every day I was grateful he took the initiative when I couldn't. I was so into him, and so intimidated by those feelings, that I couldn't even ask to see him the next day. It had to be *him* asking *me* out, never the other way around, or I feared I'd never know for sure how much he truly wanted me from day to day. Within a week of our first date the power dynamic had shifted over to him completely. And by giving him all the power to direct our time together, I'd reverted to the twenty-year-old girl I'd once been who'd let a rock star dictate everything about their relationship *and* her identity.

One night at a Scabs show, after the lights went on, he found me in the crowd and I jumped into his arms, wanting the world to see us together…to witness us falling in love. That night in bed he asked, "What are we going to do about this?"

"About what, us?"

"Yes."

"I don't know…give me some options," I said, playfully.

"We could get married," he suggested.

I burst out laughing, not because it was funny but because I was so happy to know he was on the same page. I probably should've explained that to him. Instead, he dropped the topic, possibly hurt by my odd reaction. I wanted to explain myself but as often happened with him, I couldn't find the words, or didn't trust that I could make them come out in a way that my true intent would be heard. Anyway, he'd already told me he didn't want to see anyone else and that was enough for me. Later that night, after having three nightmares in a row, I woke him up.

"Charles?" I whispered in the dark. *"Charles?"*

"Hmm?"

"Do you want a girlfriend?"

"I don't know," he finally said.

I appreciated his honesty but coming from a guy who'd just suggested marriage, it also really hurt. I was beginning to better understand his earlier comment about self-centered flakiness, that was for sure.

"That's okay," I said evenly. "It's probably too soon."

After a pause he asked, "Do you want a boyfriend?"

"I don't know." I whispered. Then, "But yeah, I think maybe it would be nice."

He squeezed my hand and we agreed to wait and see.

I wasn't really the marrying kind, but I was falling in love with him. We'd spent almost every day together for a month. He invited me to New York to meet his daughter. I invited him to Crested Butte, Colorado, where I went with my parents every year to an AA/Alanon conference. "That's not a hint or anything," I laughed lightly.

"I quit drinking heavily about a year ago," he replied. "In case you were wondering."

I had been, but I neglected to ask how he defined "heavily." He played a lot of out-of-town gigs and kept crazy musician hours. Hiding a drug or alcohol problem wouldn't have been challenging. And had I been paying attention I would've seen that was precisely what he'd been doing. One morning Charles came over at five unannounced. He'd had a gig in Dallas that night, and instead of crashing when the band dropped him at home in South Austin, he'd gotten in his car and driven fifteen miles north again, just to see me. And if it occurred to me right then that he might be using coke to stay up, I just as quickly dismissed the notion because it didn't fit my image of our storybook romance.

Still, he said he'd love to go to Colorado *and* meet my parents. Also, that he was currently producing someone's record and if he didn't finish in time, it might not be possible.

The record he was producing was for a folk singer. A decent one. A bubbly, corn-fed woman with straight brown bangs and a day job as a social worker. We met accidentally at his house/recording studio when she showed up early to their session one day. Charles introduced us and she said hi, then giggled at everything Charles said for the next five minutes. When she left the room so I could say goodbye to Charles in private, I asked him, "So how long has she been in love with you?"

He seemed surprised by the question, and not nearly as indifferent as I would've liked, but then shrugged it off like I was crazy.

He couldn't join me in Colorado but drove me to the airport and promised to pick me up when I returned. He didn't, claiming to be working late when I called him from baggage claim. A few days later I discovered it was over. He wouldn't say why, which stung as much as the breakup itself. Regardless, I had my suspicions, and the folk singer was one of them.

There had been multiple problems between us. For one, his drinking and drug use were far worse than he'd originally let on. And for us to make it as a couple that would've needed to end for him. Charles knew all along that I would never partner with a man who had a substance abuse problem (and while I didn't know the extent of it yet, I was beginning to suspect it). The folk singer, however, was so in love with him, and so clueless about his issues—in fact she drank with him—being with her was simply easier.

The larger issue, though, was that he and I couldn't take care of each other emotionally. A therapist once told him that his big heart was locked in a box. He quit therapy a week later. I saw a therapist weekly, but at my core I was still quite needy. Years later, Dr. Tina would diagnose me with PTSD from the final two years of my drinking—years when I was actively suicidal and everyone I loved and should've been able to depend on, physically and emotionally, abandoned me, Joe and my father especially. By the time I met Charles, I'd been so closed off for so long that our chemistry felt like a drug. And every time I feared losing that drug, I reacted either by clinging or withdrawing, but rarely by simply taking a breath and explaining how I felt. I'd wanted many times to tell Charles how I felt; Lord knows he asked me often enough, but I was so terrified of being vulnerable I'd usually revert to the cool chick schtick and immediately act blasé. I had a high need for intimacy but a low tolerance for it. So, I oscillated in and out of emotional proximity with men who weren't any more available than myself. Charles was no different than the others that way. When he'd have his own moments of detachment, I'd do a one-eighty and become dependent on him for my emotional security. It wasn't a good recipe for a long-term relationship.

On top of everything, we'd moved too fast. He'd been too huge to me, too magical. He told me later that in the beginning he'd been completely in love with me but had worried about not being enough for me. We'd both been too scared, overwhelmed, and passionate about each other, and not just inside the bedroom. It interfered with his work. It had been distracting and obsessive. When I'd gone to Colorado the spell was broken.

The breakup broke my heart. It was my father all over again—absolute adoration followed by sudden and complete abandonment. I hadn't opened up to Charles fully and we'd only been together for one month, but I'd allowed him into my heart deeper than any man since Joe Walsh. To have him suddenly be so elusive pummeled me. He finally said that he wasn't sure he wanted to be in relationship anymore. He still wanted to "see" me, but the unevenness of that suggestion was galling. I reacted by demanding back my house key. He reacted by leaving everything of mine he had on his doorstep—my makeup, toothbrush, and other personal items. When I saw that I snapped in half. I went into a kind of shock, tearing up as the sound of him and the folk singer playing guitar together drifted outside to me on his porch. I drove downtown and wandered around in a daze.

It was early on a weekday, and no one was out yet. I saw a light on in a gallery near Antone's and walked that way. In the window was a mixed media painting of a nude woman with a blue face and kaleidoscope swirls around and inside her. It was so beautiful it jarred me out of my shock. I went inside and talked to the artist, Ricardo Acevedo.

"She seems so strong," I told him.

"That's what inspires me," he said. "Strong women."

I needed to emulate that image but couldn't quite muster it. A psychic had once told me that I gave up my power around men, that I was a strong woman who'd convinced herself she was weak. Regardless, I was a wreck and spent the next three months scheming to get Charles back. He and the folk singer became a couple in that time. So much for not wanting to be in a relationship! But despite our amazing chemistry and that I "got" him sexually, we were ultimately romantically incompatible. Meanwhile, the folk singer was as normal, stable, and ready for a comfortable kind of love as could be. She was grounded, just like Zed's wife was and I absolutely wasn't. Hell, aside from the enabling, she was probably good for him.

Still, I had him back in my bed within days, and then in his bed, my bed, my car, a neighborhood pool, and various hotel rooms whenever one of his bands played in Dallas or Houston. The back and forth was insane and happened sometimes every few days. I'd promise to be content with something secret and casual. We'd have amazing sex, then he'd disappear on me, and I'd lose my shit, beat him up verbally, and then afterward beat myself up for losing control. He'd always forgive me instantly—Charles was nothing if not forgiving. Then we'd have amazing makeup sex, and the cycle would repeat. It went on for three glorious, exhausting years. I developed an anxious attachment to him; he had an ambivalent one to me. Despite my best efforts, my fears, mood swings, and immaturity rose to the surface on multiple occasions. He said to me once, "Please, *please* do not take this as an insult or some kind of slight. You are a beautiful, sexy, hyperintelligent woman who might want to relax a little emotionally." I knew he was right. But for a long time, I had no idea how to take his advice.

Eventually, however, I found myself mellowing without even trying. A three-year long affair will do that to a girl, if she's paying attention. Especially because, once the extent of Charles's coke addiction became apparent, I was attracted to him less. Also, no matter how many times I yelled at him or admonished him for hurting my feelings, he never shamed me for being dependent and needy. He never failed to praise my good qualities and tell me how much he cared for and desired me. And in sharing his own struggles with self-esteem over the years, he taught me by example how to be vulnerable in an intimate relationship. All my lovers and fuck buddies did. All of them opened up to me over time and almost all stayed in my life as friends. Not one of them ever shamed me for my neediness—not Marty, Rob, Larry, Zed, or anyone else— and as the years went by they all continued to show me affection and validation. If there was one thing I learned in ten years of dating these men, it was that being needy didn't make me a lesser person, and that I didn't need to be so damn needy. That I would be just fine on my own in between my many flings, affairs, and adventurous trysts.

I finally ended my affair with Charles after he and the folk singer married. I fucked him one last time after he put a ring on her finger, so that—whether she knew it or not—she never had a faithful partner in their courtship, engagement, or marriage.

Was I proud of that behavior? No, but I didn't lose any sleep over it either.

I hadn't taken any vows of fidelity, and I didn't believe in long-term monogamy as the default way for couples to be. It hadn't worked for Zed, it didn't work for Charles, and it certainly would never work for me. How was it natural to sacrifice our erotic selves for some puritanical dictate that served no purpose to most mature, childless people?

Most men don't want to be monogamous for life. Why would they and why *should* they? What most men *really* want is for their partner to be monogamous, and the price they're willing to pay for that is to abide the monogamy dictum themselves—as best they can anyway. While I'd concede that a small minority of men probably felt most comfortable in monogamous relationships, a much larger contingent simply saw it, at best, as a welcome break from the rat race of searching for sex and having to constantly prove their masculinity through bedpost notching. Unless a guy was exceptionally handsome, powerful, or famous, that shit became exhausting.

Ultimately, there is nothing inherently natural about a lifetime of monogamy. I believed that most people sensed this on some level, some—like myself—quite consciously. Zed and Charles didn't want to be monogamous. What they wanted was to be "good" men, and modern society says good men are monogamous. So, they bought into the lie and managed their occasional waves of guilt over our trysts as best they could. When the wave passed, they always called me back, and I almost always showed up. I had no guilt or shame over any of it. I thought modern society was full of shit. And that if a guy couldn't get what he needed at home, he was entitled to get it elsewhere, especially if he was discreet about it.

It wasn't just about sex, after all. Sex was rarely, if ever, just about sex. It was also about identity, about being seen. And I saw and understood aspects of Zed and Charles in ways their wives didn't want to and therefore probably never would. I understood their darker sides and sexual selves—which were extensions of their authentic inner selves—because they showed those parts to me. I didn't condemn or judge them. I met them halfway and so they felt safe in doing so with me.

Should they have been open with their wives about their needs? Absolutely. They held back out of fear, which was a chickenshit thing to do. But the fact remains their wives would not have been receptive in any way to that information. I wasn't stealing anyone's husband here. I was simply reciprocating the desires of autonomous individuals who, like me, were still young enough to need the space to work out our childhood shit through multiple intimate connections. I wasn't onboard with the institution of marriage as it typically functioned. Thus, I was no more responsible for declining their husbands than I would be responsible for turning away a North Korean refugee seeking asylum.

All that aside, in my first ten years of sobriety, my long, lovely string of lovers—overlapping and otherwise—taught me invaluable lessons in vulnerability. Mostly they taught me that with every new romantic connection I could accept the possibility of rejection, even when (*especially* when) it was personal. Because when men stopped calling, sometimes it wasn't about me, but sometimes it was. While sometimes a girl just never knows, when men say things like, "It's not you, it's me," sometimes they're straight up lying. But that was okay, because I didn't have to base my self-worth on whether every man I wanted wanted me back as much in return.

Besides, there was always another one around the corner, if not already right on top of me.

Part 2
PARTNER

(authenticity)

Shame My Ass

March 3, 2007

Current Location: falling
Current Mood: shameless

The first time I slept with another girl's boyfriend I was a fifteen-year-old punk rocker. He was a seventeen-year-old high school dropout. His girlfriend was a beautiful, Amazon blond, punk rock chick who cornered me at a party and beat the crap out of me. My scrawny little arms were no match for her, so I (ineffectively) tried to protect my head until she got bored. I wanted to swing one solid punch but couldn't muster the self-protective adrenaline. I could neither fight nor flee. I just froze, outwardly and inwardly.

I guess I figured she had a right to her anger as much as I had a right to her boyfriend. After all, if he'd wanted to reserve his genitals for her alone, he surely would have. It was his dick. He could do what he wanted with it, was how I saw it. My takeaway that day, along with a few bruises, was *discretion is vital*, versus *adultery is not in my best interest*. I don't believe the only choice in life is monogamy. I don't like to limit myself. Clearly neither did he.

Lalo's soon-to-be-ex-wife called me ten times yesterday, leaving three messages. I eventually answered, denied the affair (I have no shame), sympathized with her pain (I'm without shame, not compassion), stated my position ("not so much about the drama"), and hung up. She called back later, armed with Lalo's cell phone records and diminishing control over her rage. By then I was bored with her, so I turned off my phone, put on Lalo's favorite red garter belt, and let him fuck me senseless till I had two of my most intense orgasms of this year.

I've been the other woman at least a dozen times in twenty-five years and don't regret any of it. Every one of those men were stuck in relationships or marriages that weren't fully honoring their needs. But I never tried to break anyone up; I was just in it for the thrill of a temporary fling...a mutually beneficial, intensely passionate connection that tended to run its course before anyone found out or any damage was done. Usually, anyway. Aside from the aforementioned "Amazon incident," three wives or girlfriends suspected an affair, but never from me (in a word, guys: *password protected online cell phone statements—Jesus*).

Discretion is vital, and I do my part to that end because I really don't want to hurt anyone. However, I'm not so powerful that I alone can ruin another woman's marriage. *Her relationship is her problem.* My libido is mine. And if Lalo is unhappy and unloved at home, well then, what we do together becomes OUR business (cell phone records notwithstanding). Anyone who thinks they own another person's sexual energy is acting entitled and crazy. If any of these men had truly wanted to be faithful MORE than they wanted sexual variety, *they would've been*. Should they've have been honest with their partners about their desire for nonmonogamy? Absolutely! But again, *not my problem*.

I don't have a gun to anyone's head here. And I sure as hell never vowed a lifetime of monogamy to anybody.

Thursday night Lalo's and my plan was that I would stay home and write while he hung out with friends. My writing and his social life are both suffering because of working nonstop (sex breaks notwithstanding). It was a good plan, until he invited me to come out with him and I immediately had a fascinating (and extremely unsociable) meltdown. Torn between the discipline that keeps my life running smoothly and the fun nights out I miss so terribly, I actually started crying. Poor Lalo had no idea of the difficult position he'd put me in, nor that my only possible choice (to stay home and write) would haunt me all night, especially after watching him leave looking so incredibly sexy. What hot as hell, soon-to-be-single man leaves a raving lunatic home with her dying cat and laptop and ever comes back?

I eventually stopped crying, wrote the first worthwhile shit I'd written all day, snuggled with Tippy and went to bed, prepared for the possibility I'd never see Lalo again. And that's when I realized where the shame in this is—or might someday be.

It's not in our quickie hookup or the demise of his severely dysfunctional marriage. Not in his drinking, which I've hardly seen since the beginning. Not in our exhaustive overworking, since our lovemaking offsets it. Not in my meltdown and not in the intensity of my feelings, because he definitely feels similarly. The shame would be in acting against the instincts I've come to trust over the years, which are telling me—*screaming at me*—that I can trust these feelings for Lalo. And that right now I belong with him, and he belongs with me... as well as a few of my things.

Like my spare cell phone, a spare drawer, closet space, my cat's side of the bed (with her permission), and my spare house key. In turn he's given me loads of unbelievable sex, a warm (hot) body to spoon at night, countless foot and back rubs, a bonsai tree, a book about bonsai trees (I'm so fucking whipped right now), a necklace inscribed, "Be fearless, Choose love" (I melted), laughter in my sleep (so weird, since I rarely laugh when I'm awake), someone to cook for, affection, a new appreciation for anal porn, and a renewed appreciation for anal sex (heh). I could go on, but I'll stop here.

Except I can't stop. Obviously, I can't stop. Or I don't want to stop, or slow down, or feel shame or regret, or any of that shit.

Sitting next to me right now, rubbing my sore hip and leg, patiently watching me write this awkward, faltering attempt at something cohesive, is the source of it himself—Lalo—who tells me I've been smiling the whole time I've been typing. I had no idea.

Maybe it's all the orgasms. All the Lalo lovin'. Because I think I am, actually...*loving*, I mean. Loving Lalo. I think I'm falling in love with him. Or I'm blinded by the orgasms, but whatever...I'm running with it.

Fuck shame.

CHAPTER 5

Spring 2007

THE NIGHT LALO TOLD ME he loved me, we went to Magnolia Café for dinner, then Bookpeople, where he bought me a stack of books and a silver necklace. A few days later he stopped by the club with two hundred dollars to sit with me for an hour. I was still giddy about our romantic development. It made me chatty out of nervousness and at one point I stopped to ask if I was talking too much.

"Are you kidding," he said, gesturing to my body. "All this and brains too? Talk all you want." Besides, he said, he talked about me nonstop to his landscaping partner at work.

Lalo was trying desperately to work out the best way for him to move forward. One night we went to the Saxon Pub to shoot pool. Afterward, in the parking lot, he got into a fight with his wife on the phone. He decided then and there he was done. He wasn't going back.

"Can you put me up for a while?"

Uh, no. "We've known each other five weeks, Lalo! This is crazy…I'm sorry, it's way too soon."

He pleaded and I caved. Then, for the next few days, I backpedaled, suddenly aghast at how quickly we were moving. I'd been there before with Charles, and it hadn't worked out well. Lalo didn't waver. In fact, he pursued me even harder, which won me over. The next day I caught a glimpse of us in the mirror doing it doggie style, the image so beautiful to me—his eyes, expression, and sensual movements—it took my breath away. I actually gasped. I was truly in love. I had a boyfriend for the first time in twelve years.

Later that day I met his daughter, Rita. I feared it was too soon for that as well, but Lalo assured me saying, "Rita is different." He hatched a plan that we'd "bump into each other" on the sidewalk on the way to the Zilker Park kite festival. He'd pretend I was just a friend whom he would ask to join them at the festival, but Rita saw right through it. At five years old she was whip smart and damn intuitive. She side-eyed me for a while, but I chatted her up as naturally as I could. By the time we arrived at the festival she and I were fast friends, and when I asked her what kind of temporary tattoo she wanted, she requested one like the starfish on my wrist. Later, on the way home, her dad carried her on his shoulders as we continued talking.

"Rita, how do you like school? Do you have a favorite subject?"

"School is okay. Mostly I like my boyfriends there."

"Boyfriends, *plural?*" I asked, my voice rising to show her I was both stunned and impressed. "You mean you have more than one?"

Rita laughed, pleased with herself. "I have three!"

"In kindergarten?!"

She nodded triumphantly. Then she side-eyed me again, "How many do *you* have?"

"I only have one."

Rita looked at her dad, then back at me. "But do you love him?" she asked, suddenly serious.

"I think I do," I said.

Rita beamed. "That's good," she said, looking me dead in the eye. "I'm glad."

❦

I HADN'T BEEN THAT happy since my early days with Joe. My cat loved Lalo. I sent my mother a picture of him and Rita, and she melted at the father and daughter brown-eyed beauties. Dr. Tina liked him immediately, which gave her hope for our relationship. Lalo was dedicated to working on it with me. Working through the fears we had, our respective triggers, and different ways of doing things. He prioritized fun and socializing. I prioritized producing income and furthering my writing. But we had much in common—he, the reformed drug dealer, me the ambitious sex worker. We were close in age, one year apart. Generation X'ers who'd long relied on our wits to get by. We lived on the fringe and excelled in our respective niches, but we both wanted something better—me, creative and financial success, him, a fun-filled life and close family unit.

If our similarities drew us together our differences contributed to the attraction as well. Lalo had a childlike sense of wonderment, much like Zed, Paul, and Larry had, and before them Joe (who was known as the clown prince of rock and roll after all). My life was strictly structured with a hyperfocus on getting where I wanted to go. I had little time for anything but work and writing, and my days were short on fun and joy. Lalo saw work as a means to an end—a way to earn enough money to get by, while spending as much time as possible watching sports, seeing bands, having sex, hanging out with friends, and meeting new people. The first thing he did after moving in was decorate my patio, adding seating, plants, and a table with a cat bed for Tippy to join us outside, where he quickly ended up meeting all the neighbors I'd not met in the two and a half years I'd lived there.

His biggest fear was being alone. Mine was not having enough time to myself. This was our main point of contention. One night I came home from work, where he'd been waiting for me all day. He'd been working less lately, taking care of Tippy and my apartment, adjusting things to make room for his belongings in our six hundred square feet of living space. I gave him a kiss, put my things away, then sat at my desk in the corner of the kitchen balancing my checkbook, answering emails, and reviewing my calendar for the week. Lalo sat on the couch quietly fuming, until he finally asked if I was ever going to pay attention to him.

"What are you talking about?" I said, genuinely baffled.

"You've hardly said a word to me since you got home!"

"I'm sorry. I had a long day and need time to decompress. I didn't realize you were expecting me to come over and engage with you."

"What do you think living together is all about?"

"How the hell should I know?" I snapped. "I'm not used to living with someone, okay? I'm used to having my place to myself to relax and unwind at night."

"Are you saying you don't want me here?"

"I'm not saying that! But I am saying that after spending eight hours at the club tending to dozens of needy, horny, grabby customers I can't come home to another demanding man who thinks he should immediately be the center of my universe."

We worked through it somehow. Our next argument was about my obsessive-compulsive neatness. One morning, before rushing out the door to our respective jobs, we realized we were both ready ten minutes early, just enough time for a quickie. Standing on the opposite side of the bed I suggested we make it first, then have sex quickly on top of the covers so all I had to do was smooth them before leaving for work. Lalo looked as if that was the craziest thing he'd ever heard.

"You're kidding, right?"

"C'mon, it'll take thirty seconds if we both pitch in." I started pulling on the sheets and comforter, but Lalo just stood there.

"Kristi, that makes absolutely no sense. Why would we make the bed *before* having sex on it?"

"I told you, *so I don't have to make it afterward.*"

"So don't make it afterward!"

"I have to make it before leaving the house!"

Lalo slapped his forehead and dragged his palm down his face. "You do realize this stupid debate is eating up all the time we have for sex, right?"

"Yes! *So, if you would just help me make the bed,* we'll still have eight minutes left to fuck."

Lalo wouldn't budge. He thought my insistence on making the bed before sex—and frankly afterward, considering how rushed we were—was so absurd he was willing to forego sex just to make me see how ridiculous I was being. We spent the next seven minutes yelling at each other about it. I finally agreed to schedule a special session with Dr. Tina so Lalo could confirm with an objective party that he was sane and I was borderline crazy. (Dr. Tina didn't think I was crazy, but she didn't think my bedspread obsession was the sanest thing she'd ever heard either.)

Two days later, I had a meltdown over how little I'd been writing. We fought over my need for space until Lalo agreed to move out while I got my head and schedule together. He was back a week later. I simply missed him too much. We did GHB and had sex for two straight days. Somewhere in that romantic mental haze he asked me to marry him, and I said yes. We'd known each other seven weeks. We'd been an official couple for three.

LALO'S WIFE CONTROLLED THEIR MONEY and cut off his access to their accounts. Lalo was rendered penniless, and I had all kinds of bills coming in, plus expensive pre-cancer skin spots to remove. We found a nearby jewelry store willing to buy all our best stuff. I got five hundred dollars for a three-thousand-dollar diamond ring I'd received in Vegas as payment for a fifteen-minute fuck. Lalo sold his wedding ring for the same amount, then gave me every penny on the spot. I handed some of it back so he could buy track shoes, jeans, and gym clothes. To pay his divorce lawyer's retainer, he sold one of his two work trucks.

His soon-to-be-ex avoided being served papers for ten straight days, until a judge finally signed an order that they could be left on her doorstep. She locked Lalo out of the house and mailbox, canceled his credit cards, cell phone account, and truck insurance, threw out all his clothes and shoes, then snuck over to steal most of the tools from his work truck. She even canceled his satellite radio account and pulled Rita from the soccer team he coached just to be spiteful. She'd harassed my parents and siblings multiple times, finding their phone numbers online and calling them up drunk, in the middle of the night, to rage about what a whore I was. My parents' response was classic, "What our daughter does on her own time is her own business. Please don't call here again." My sister had a newborn baby and was home alone while her husband was stationed in Afghanistan, so one in the morning calls were especially jarring to her.

Lalo's sister was scheduled to testify in his divorce about the time his wife had attacked both Lalo and her in a drunken rage, causing her permanent facial nerve damage. Lalo's lawyer thought my parents' testimony might also be beneficial, so they drove eight hours from Amarillo to support their future son-in-law. When I asked Lalo if he was nervous to meet them he said "yes" so emphatically I jumped. He needn't have worried. My parents adored him immediately, though their presence turned out to be unnecessary. In the end, Lalo and his wife reached a temporary settlement and no one, including me, had to testify.

Lalo was allowed to see his daughter twice a week. One month after we'd met, she spent her first night at my place. Since I didn't have a kitchen table, we ate dinner in the living room where Rita accidentally spilled milk on the coffee table and carpet. Lalo jumped up and chastised her, knowing how much I hated a mess.

"Ignore him, Rita," I said with a wink. "It's just spilled milk and that's what towels are for, right?"

Rita smiled at me, relieved. The next day we took her to a children's concert at Ruta Maya Coffee. All the other kids were dancing but Rita felt self-conscious.

"Do you want me to dance with you, Rita?"

She nodded emphatically, so I danced with her and the other children all afternoon.

During another scheduled visit, Lalo had to work all weekend long. He'd taken Rita to the worksite, but a few hours later called for me to pick her up. Poor Rita had been hot and bored all day, then bitten by ants while sitting in the grass waiting for her dad to finish a big landscaping job. Catching a glimpse of her sullenness in the rearview mirror, I suggested a screaming match in the car, to help her blow off some well-deserved steam. Rita seemed hesitant at first, but quickly got into it. After a long and impressively loud howl, she prompted me, "Your turn! Your turn!"

"I don't know, Rita. I might scare you with how loud I can be."

"Scream, Kristi, scream!" she prodded, delighted by our new game.

"You asked for it," I shrugged, then screamed as loud and long as I could, driving through the hill country, watching Rita fall apart with laughter in the backseat.

Dropping her off at her mom's later, I notice Rita looking sad and quiet. "I don't want to go home," she said. "I want to stay with you and Daddy forever. I want you to marry him and be my new mommy."

My entire life I'd never wanted children but thought I'd be lucky as hell to have Rita for a stepdaughter. I followed her out of the car and bent down to tell her a secret. "I love you, Rita," I whispered in her ear.

She instantly perked up and motioned me back down, to whisper back, "I love you too."

❦

I was learning for the first time how to be in a healthy relationship. So was Lalo. Dr. Tina recommended a relationship book to us, and when it finally arrived Lalo was as excited as if an eight ball of cocaine were hidden in it. We laughed at how normal we'd become. We went to Costco, Bed, Bath & Beyond, Walgreens, and Whole Foods weekly, like an old married couple. (It took three trips to Whole Foods before I learned to walk next to him instead of marching in front, tossing items in the cart as he quietly followed behind, pushing it.) I set him up with his first email account and we synced our calendars weekly. I gave him regular manicures to offset the trashing landscaping did to them. He gave Tippy her meds, did our laundry, and cleaned the apartment top to bottom. He rubbed my aching back daily and I returned the favor most nights. Whenever we fought, as soon as we turned on the radio the song "Love Hurts" would come on—a thirty-three-year-old song I typically heard less than once a year—which we took as a spiritual sign that what we had was indeed true love. I was still working two jobs and trying to write two or three evenings a week. Things were rough but we were happy.

Lalo quit eating red meat and cut way back on pizza without my prompting. He ran and lifted weights and in four weeks lost fifty pounds. His prediabetic blood sugar was down by thirty percent. He looked like the cover of a fitness magazine. My workouts were sporadic at best. I was envious but kept it to myself. I was so proud of him I hardly knew what to say. Especially when he told me he'd quit drinking.

All I'd asked was that he not drink around me, since he got a little cocky after even one or two beers. Since he wanted to be with me all the time, he quit drinking entirely. He went to an AA meeting at the Bouldin house, one block away. He picked up a desire chip and stayed to meet people afterward, then went to another meeting that night. Next thing I knew he was going every day, had a sponsor, and was working the first three steps. He got thirty days sober the same week I reached ten years in sobriety (GHB notwithstanding, but that was just a sex thing, and I didn't believe it negated my sobriety in the least). We went to a meeting together and I spoke about how proud I was of him and his efforts to be a better man lately.

Broke as we were, we had to get creative about dates. We went to strip clubs where I knew the management and could get in for free to watch boxing matches. Lalo found a store for heated massage chairs where they let customers try them out for fifteen minutes at a time. We swung by once a week to lie next to each other vibrating, whispering sweet nothings, and gazing into each other's eyes. We got each other's initials tattooed on our left ring fingers. We had sex two or three times a day.

One day, cleaning out space for Lalo's things, I came across the fifth step "Ideals List" my AA sponsor had made me write. It was a list of dealbreaker traits for my future life mate to have, constituting a framework to help me form healthier relationships than I had pre-sobriety. We curled up and reviewed it together, going over every trait on the list, things like honest, kind, sexy, funny, courageous, etc. Lalo had every trait on my list, though one thing I noticed was that I'd forgotten to put "ambitious" on it. I kept that omission to myself.

Lalo was suddenly putting sobriety and fitness above everything else, which was progress for him, yet a little unfair to me. He hadn't scored any new landscaping jobs; thus, I was suddenly supporting us fully. We discussed flipping houses someday, but his sketchy work ethic worried me. I'd filed bankruptcy three years earlier and had no credit cards to fall back on. I'd lost my condo and moved into a darling, yet tiny, one bedroom apartment in Central Austin. Rent was affordable with two people, but not when one wasn't working, especially since we'd soon need a larger two bedroom, required by the court for Rita's visitation. Yet bizarrely, Lalo decided he needed to quit landscaping to focus on sobriety.

"Yeah, that's not how it works," I stated firmly. "Not while you're living with me, anyway!"

He eventually managed to score a couple new jobs, but only by bidding so low there was no profit left over. I consoled myself with mental lists of everything he brought to the table: love, sex, laughter, companionship, hope, fun. But I was still covering our nut every month and facing a move I didn't want. Worse yet, the prospect of a stepdaughter—if only on weekends—suddenly made me fearful. When was I supposed to finish the two books I was writing? Or my short stories, blog posts, and future screenplays?

Then Lalo got controlling. Strolling down South Congress Avenue one day we bumped into a tattoo artist friend of mine, with whom I'd once had sex, two years earlier. After introductions and a quick chat, we moved on—except Lalo hadn't.

"You ever have sex with that guy?"

"Not that it's any of your business but yeah, why?"

"What the fuck, Kristi?! You can't introduce me to men you've slept with!"

"Don't be insane! What was I supposed to do, ignore him as we passed?"

"Yes! You shouldn't be talking to any man you used to have sex with!"

"That's the stupidest thing I've ever heard. Quit acting like a baby. You're being a jackass."

We fought about that guy for two days. Lalo was also so threatened by one of my former sugar daddies emailing to say hello—a man I hadn't seen in eight years—that I had to schedule another urgent session with Dr. Tina to get him to drop the matter. Another time he diminished my former relationships with Paul and Larry, saying they never considered me more than a piece of ass—as if he knew anything about either man. Another night, he went through my emails when I was sleeping, finding a saved audio recording Charles had sent of us having sex with me orgasming three times. It bothered Lalo endlessly, and after much badgering he finally convinced me to delete it.

Charles and I hadn't spoken in almost a year. He knew nothing about Lalo and called me one day hoping to hook up. Lalo grabbed my phone and threatened Charles's life if he ever called me again. Worst of all, he somehow got me to promise to quit stripping when I turned forty, six months down the road. He wanted me to work full-time as a Realtor, a job I could barely stand to do anymore. From a man who brought in next to no money, the request was infuriating.

It wasn't hyperbole to say that stripping had saved me. Not on one occasion in my life, but three. The first time, when I was a penniless, eighteen-year-old college dropout, freshly clean from meth addiction. The second, as a full-blown alcoholic and crack addict, recently dumped by the rock star love of my life and nine thousand dollars in debt. The third, at thirty-nine, after a six-month dry spell in real estate, without enough in the bank to pay rent or fill my tank.

I'd given real estate my all for seven years, but it had failed me. That's when my strip club customers stepped up. Most of them were white collar gents, though one worked three jobs including delivering Chinese food at night, just so he could afford two lap dances from me every week. These men were my providers; they kept me fed and housed. They delighted in my company and made me feel valued. They appreciated my sex appeal, wit, and intelligence. My strip club customers were more integral to my well-being, self-esteem, and identity than my parents, peers, or past partners had been. If it weren't for them, I'd have been homeless. Lalo didn't have one job, much less was he holding down three in order to be with me.

We fought about it constantly, my work and his lack of it. And though I had righteousness on my side, I could be as shrill about it as my mother had been all my young life. A tone came out of me sometimes I was shocked to hear. This was one reason I didn't win every argument; I'd feel so ashamed of the tone in my voice I'd quickly back down and go along with whatever Lalo wanted.

Our fights got worse when he quit going to AA meetings and refused to do his fourth step. I lost respect for him, which gave his ego a beating. One day, we stopped at a convenience store, where a customer accidentally brushed up against him. Lalo whirled on the man, grabbing him by the throat and pinning him to the floor in an instant. He held back from punching the poor guy, but I'd never seen him explode with rage like that before and it scared me.

Still, we had more good days than bad, and I loved him deeply. So much that it was beginning to irritate me to have customers try to touch me—something that had long been part of the job and, in the past, only bothered me when they tried to suck my nipples or touch my coochie. As bothersome was my constant hip pain and sciatica, made worse whenever a customer tried to grab my hips and grind my crotch on his boner. As if I were a Fleshlight device versus a flesh and blood human. But I still liked stripping more than real estate, where three major deals were slowly slipping through my fingers. None of those sales would close, canceling out a much needed, combined payday of fifty thousand dollars.

One night I came home from a rough day at the club. I'd just done a three-day stint and halfway through day three had barely made a buck. Then another dancer went on stage to Joe Walsh's "Rocky Mountain Way"—a song that transported me to a time when I'd been happy, secure, and in love with a man who took care of me financially. I was on the second stage at the time, a required performance, and thus unable to bail or wait out the song in the dressing room. Being reminded of my former glamorous life while having a shitty day in an empty strip club felt humiliating. By the end of that day, too many men being too grabby for too long added to my sour mood. At home, as soon as Lalo touched me, I recoiled. It surprised me and wounded him.

I was all about income producing but Lalo was all about the relationship. Busy as I was, he still expected me to give him constant attention and engage with the people in his life, from soccer moms to his old friends and new sponsor. He seemed to need much more of a melding of our lives than I did. Lalo was a husband and family man, without a family. I was an extremely independent woman suddenly in a committed relationship. All his life, starting with his abusive father, he'd been made to feel like a disappointment. All my life, I'd entered relationships that mimicked what I had with my own father—a lot of love, followed by the inability to depend on him when I needed him most.

The thing was, Lalo and I were both willing to heal those parts of ourselves, and how better to bring up those feelings so that they might be healed, than to constantly be triggering each other? The triggering part we had down, the healing part not so much.

AFTER HIS DIVORCE WAS FINAL, I finally convinced Lalo to get back on track with work *and* apply for salaried jobs with benefits. We'd been together three months by then. Landscaping the yards of wealthy, horny, Westlake wives he got hit on constantly, but I didn't mind. It only made him hotter to me. And I liked that it boosted his ego and therefore his confidence.

On Memorial Day weekend, Lalo took me to some friends' house for barbecue and my first UFC fight, a title bout between The Iceman and Rampage. Iceman looked anxious from the start, then went down hard and fast in the first round, after opening with a left hook leaving his chin vulnerable. Rampage landed a right directly on Iceman's joy button. Iceman's knees buckled and he hit the mat, arms outstretched, fully knocked out.

Kristin Casey

I didn't know anything about cage fighting, but I knew from experience it did not pay to start swinging without thinking. I knew that imposing your will on the other guy entailed knowing your enemy. And from what I saw, The Iceman's enemy wasn't Rampage, it was fear. Much like fear was mine, one I underestimated all the time. More and more I found myself locking horns with Lalo, swinging willy-nilly—verbally—and otherwise reacting without thinking over deep-seated fears of losing my independence or being taken advantage of by him. I sometimes wondered how much easier my life would be if I tried fighting my fears instead of my mate. At least we were learning to catch ourselves before the arguments got out of control. We loved each other and recognized that fear of not getting what we wanted, or giving up more than we expected, was at the root of our conflicts. We made multiple trips to Dr. Tina that spring and tried to spend more time being sweet to and nurturing each other.

After the UFC fight, we went downtown to see Maxi Priest play. Walking back to my car, at the parking garage at Ninth and Brazos, we stumbled across a block of wet concrete in which Lalo immediately stuck his finger and wrote "Lalo loves"—yet before he could write "Kristi" an elderly security guard appeared, barking, "What are you doing?!"

Lalo looked up innocently, "Just playing."

Nobody moved for a few seconds. Suddenly I got the giggles. Lalo let out a small chuckle. The old man looked perplexed more than anything, then finally wandered off when Lalo promised to stop. Within seconds, of course, he'd snuck back, written my name, then been spotted again by the same guard. We ran to the car and Lalo peeled out, driving down the street before the guy could get to us.

We spent the next two days of the holiday weekend repairing a roof in Barton Hills. Lalo needed an assistant, and I happened to be off of work. In two hours at Home Depot, he taught me about gutters, decking, and Hardie panel. Then, at the job sight—in a touching show of trust, considering my bitchiness of late—he showed me how to use a circular saw, hatchet, and German pruning knife. Mosquitoes ate him alive, despite having doused himself in Deet. I ruined a new manicure with the cheap yellow gloves Lalo bought me, and nearly ruined my favorite Tony Lama boots in the client's muddy backyard, yet it was still the most romantic time we'd had together in weeks. Being in a relationship was like a working holiday every day, I'd noticed.

Mildew, Filth, Tone & Piss

May 25, 2007

Current Location: The Y in ATX
Current Mood: depressed

Wednesday was a tough day at work. The first guy I sat with is a regular who always wants me to climax while dancing for him. (I do climax at work sometimes, but—other than sitting on Lalo's face—it usually only happens if I start grinding on a guy during my Juicy Days when my coochie is extra sensitive.) I'm debating whether to tell him the smell of mildew permeating his laundry and the feel of his filthy, sticky hands isn't quite enough stimulation to push me over the edge. Not an orgasmic edge anyway.

The next guy got more than a few dances but wanted nothing but grind. I don't mind a little grind; in fact, I like it. Not for the stimulation (okay sometimes for the stimulation) but for the response, because erections feel like applause, which in my business is close to extinct. I like the way my customers get all excited like kids at Christmas when they realize I've just positioned myself to swipe their crotch back and forth a few times with my own. What I don't like is when they push me down on it and rock my hips FOR me. Without stopping. Especially on the sofas where I can't dangle my legs on either side like I can on the chairs.

On chairs my body weight rests on my customer. On the sofas it rests partly on the cushions but largely on my hips. And if I haven't made this clear in previous posts, I have thirty-nine-year-old hips that have run thousands of miles over the years and they FUCKING HURT when I'm forced to grind for more than a few couch dances. Which of course is mostly what those fucking dances are—an excuse to grind for four minutes like horny teenagers, except one of us isn't horny, so it's like a horny dude and a girl who just feels trapped.

And pained. And old. And pissed.

The next guy was very appreciative of my dance. "You're really good!" he said after the first one. And "God you're so sexy" during each one after that. *Aw, thanks sweetie, glad you like my style. Glad you like the quality and artistry of my work so much that you got a permanent semi hard-on and then felt the need to fumble around with my hips for the last few dances like a blind man in a maze.* For me that kind of customer response is like driving a car and suddenly having a passenger try to steer it *from the backseat.* (Dude, I got it handled already so just sit back and enjoy the ride before I pitch this thing off a cliff, you fucking dickhead.)

Anyway, while all this fun was being had at the club, Lalo was working like a dog for a friend to pay back the cash she lent him during his divorce. Did I mention his divorce is final? So, after we both had draining days for which neither of us were paid nearly enough, we met at home and got in a fight.

He blames me and I'm not surprised. Whether or not he's right isn't the issue though, because HE thinks he is therefore...well, you know. I'm fucked, basically.

Lalo's changed lately and it's my bad for not seeing it coming. Everyone changes when they get sober. It's a long process with many phases. My sense is that his constant desire to see me happy and efforts at making me so are waning. Not only should I have expected that, but I should've expected it sooner than it happened. Most men last just one month with me and it's not because I'm demanding or a bitch—I'm so fucking accommodating it's sickening. I just happen to choose men that have short attention spans. Quite frankly I was no more emotionally available than they were, and short-term flings worked fairly well in a dysfunctional, desperate sort of way, so I guess that's how I roll.

Until lately. I've craved a deeper intimacy for a long time but once I got it with Lalo, I got scared and tried to push him away. He wouldn't let me, and that's probably when I fell totally in love with him—seeing him fight for me when I was pushing him away with all my stupid fear. Because relationships, as much as I used to crave one in my single days, scare the LIVING SHIT out of me.

                                    Kristin Casey

In the beginning I really did believe that Lalo was just another one of those flings. He fit the bill perfectly as a seriously hot, married alcoholic. Match made in heaven, sure to last less than six weeks—my usual. Except he turned out to be different. And so, I let myself trust him.

He hasn't been to an AA meeting in weeks and quit working his fourth step. Which is when most people stop working the steps permanently. Which not coincidentally is when their emotional healing and spiritual growth cease. I'm not saying he's definitely one of those people, but I used to live in Vegas, and we have a term for that there. We call it *pretty fucking good odds.*

In the middle of our fight yesterday he says he thinks he wants a woman who's better at "coping" with life. There's so fucking much wrong with that statement I can't address it all here. Suffice it to say his THREE visits with MY psychologist of the past SIX YEARS probably don't qualify him to make it. Nor do his TWO MONTHS of sobriety compared to my TEN YEARS. Nor does his working of 25% of the twelve steps compared to my completion of all twelve and the full integration of them into my daily life.

I'M JUST SAYING.

Though the worst part of this tension really is my fault, and I don't know how to fix it. I'll talk to Dr. Tina next week but in the meantime if anyone knows how to keep a girl from turning into her mother, bottle it now, sell me lots, then go on to make a fortune overnight. Godspeed, man, seriously. Because that IS my problem and while I'm stuck with it for now, Lalo doesn't have to be. He almost left me yesterday (not the best example of a person knowing how better to "cope with life" but whatever). I don't blame him really; when my mom took that same tone I used on Lalo yesterday, I wanted to walk out too. Unfortunately, I was an infant, toddler, or otherwise without a driver's license at the time.

At seventeen, I left home supposedly to go to college but really to get away from my mother's tone. I can still hear it in my head like it was yesterday. Unfortunately, often when I CAN'T hear it—that critical, chastising, condescending tone—is when it's coming out of my own mouth attacking Lalo.

CHAPTER 6

June 2007

THE CRIPPLING LONELINESS I'd lived with since my breakup with Joe Walsh, had been, for a time, enough to make me actively suicidal. Since getting sober the pain had muted, so that I merely fantasized about killing myself, on a daily basis. For the first five years of my sobriety, it had been a multiple-times-a-day thing. Antidepressants helped, but I still had suicidal ideation more days than not, until, at nine and a half years sober I started stripping again, taking control of my life in a way I hadn't for a long time, which seemed to do the trick. The suicidal ideation went away, but the depression I lived with hadn't. Antidepressants had made it manageable rather than eliminating it.

Four months into my relationship with Lalo, I learned I was losing the health insurance I'd been able to get through my parents' business. Without insurance Wellbutrin cost seventy dollars a month, which equated to four lap dances at Perfect 10. As hard as I was working—all but one day of May and June—I simply couldn't justify the expense. I made the decision to wean myself off it.

Once I got down to the lowest possible dose I started having scary spells of mental and emotional darkness, like someone would randomly turn off the lights in my head and heart throughout the day. I'd go from feeling normal and stable to suddenly awash in doom, gloom, and despair. Each spell lasted for an hour or more and I called my therapist in a panic. "I can't go back there," I sobbed. "I can't go back to living in that darkness! Please help, Dr. Tina."

She told me to be gentle with myself and have Lalo help me. When the darkness came over me I was to relax in his arms, letting him stroke and soothe me any way he knew how. Bubble baths, candles, music, comedy shows, or whatever might lift my spirits, calm me down, or help me feel secure somehow.

"Try it all," she said. "Make this your top priority right now."

We did and it helped. I'd curl up and try not to think about anything other than being safe in his arms. The spells started passing quickly, and two months later were hardly to be found.

I never did understand the errant brain chemistry behind my lifelong clinical depression but was certain drug and alcohol abuse had made it worse. Also, that the trauma of my breakup with Joe and ensuing suicidal years had compounded whatever was broken in my brain, making it profoundly entrenched. I'd also come to believe that falling in love with Lalo had sparked a dopamine flood to beat all floods. And that whatever was broken in my brain somehow got rebooted or just plain washed away. Because once I got fully off the antidepressants, I was no longer clinically depressed. I considered it a miracle, coming to believe that Lalo's love had saved me—literally saved my life—and that to leave him for the "crime" of flailing financially would be a greater crime itself.

I promised to be the best girlfriend and fiancé possible. I not only felt I owed it to him to stay in the relationship, but I wasn't about to give up all the fun, love, and great sex. It was not only the best sex of my life but the only time I'd ever had incredible sex at my fingertips—literally any time I wanted it. We were still doing it multiple times per day, though maybe just once on days we were fighting.

One day, postcoital, we lay together on the bed, his smooth brown limbs entwined with my fair, freckled ones.

"I don't know where you begin and I end," I murmured.

"That's how it should be," he replied. Because to Lalo that was the ultimate goal—total enmeshment. I only agreed during the afterglow of sex, the rest of the time I struggled to maintain some sense of autonomy.

The following week we fought over money for two straight days, then made up. Again, I felt I'd be crazy to break up with such a sexy, fun, loving man, considering how long I'd been alone in the past. Lalo was approaching ninety days sober and was doing an amazing job landscaping the home of a new real estate client, enabling me to list it at top dollar for her neighborhood. Hard as I worked, I had more fun in any given week with Lalo than in the entire year before he came along. I wasn't ready to give that up… and for what? I'd be covering all my monthly bills either way, right? I vowed to give Lalo more time to get his shit together.

Some days I'd sit back and watch his every move—driving, polishing his glasses, toweling off, walking across the room, or sitting quietly—thinking he was the most exquisite creature God ever created. His chiseled, upside-down trapezoid torso killed me. I was the luckiest woman I knew.

Lalo told me my body was perfect and sacred. Too sacred to be shared with strip club customers or blog readers. No one, including myself, had ever considered anything about me sacred, and it eventually won me over. He convinced me to delete three of my blog avatars that showed side boob or nipple. Then he convinced me to quit stripping entirely. I cleaned out my locker at Perfect 10 with more ambivalence than I'd had about anything in years. I so wanted to make him happy—to repay him for healing my broken heart and brain. I understood he needed to feel like my protector, since he'd not been able to step into the role of provider yet. And I loved the way he cherished my body; despite the way it subtly made me feel like it was no longer entirely my own. After all, I'd been sharing it with strangers for as long as I could remember. Maybe it *was* time for me to take it back now…not just for myself but to share with Lalo. I didn't really know; it was all so confusing.

❧

For a while, things improved. One day we found a pocket of time for some seriously amazing lovemaking. We'd both been working hard on my new listing for a few days in a row, and Lalo's stellar landscaping work helped me sell it in record time. I was thrilled and decided we should spoil ourselves by spending all Sunday morning in bed, naked, watching ass porn. One thing led to another and when my phone rang in the middle of everything, I picked it up with my free hand with the intention of turning off the ringer and putting it right back down.

What happened instead was that I turned off the ringer and put it right back down *on the answer button*. Meanwhile there were plenty of subtle sex noises coming from me, Lalo, and Jasmine (the unofficial reigning queen of ass porn), yet it still took me a long moment to respond to the voice in my head saying, "Check your phone, check your phone, check your phone!" Which I finally did, only to discover a very sweet Realtor on the other end patiently waiting for me to say "Hello." Which I didn't. Instead, I hung up and went back to what I was doing.

So my phone was ringing daily with real estate business and my bells were ringing daily with Lalo business, and even though I'd had almost no time off in weeks I was happy and in love…most of the time that is. The rest of the time we were fighting, sometimes badly enough to make me pull away. And on one occasion badly enough to make him pull away.

The time had come to move to a two bedroom in the back of the apartment complex, losing the downtown skyline view I'd come to love. My leasing manager had asked for a final confirmation on the move, which I'd given reluctantly and against my better judgment. In my heart I knew I should ask Lalo to move out and get a two bedroom on his own for him and Rita. That I was giving up too much of my autonomy and freedom. That we should slow things down and be a couple who lived apart for a while, and Dr. Tina didn't disagree. But ever persuasive Lalo had other ideas, and once again I caved.

He promised me he'd handle the entire thing—packing, moving, unpacking. But when the day of the move arrived, nothing was done. Most of our things still weren't boxed up and Lalo's friend never showed up to help lift furniture. I was incensed, and Lalo seemed to be in a weird sort of trance and was doing nothing to fix the situation. By midafternoon I was panicked, and we had a screaming match over it. He disappeared and I jumped in my car to hire homeless workers off a street corner. But my furniture was oversized and heavy, so the homeless men gave up halfway through. When Lalo returned he laughed at the situation, payback for yelling at him earlier.

I started crying. I'd really fucked myself now. Committed to a much pricier apartment with a man who was failing me at every turn. What was I thinking? And where did I go from here?

My tears moved Lalo enough to kick him into gear. He somehow managed to move my king-size Tempur-Pedic—the biggest, heaviest wet noodle imaginable—across the entire complex and upstairs to our new unit, all by himself. With his back problems it was quite a feat. Still, the fighting returned and escalated within minutes. He called me demanding. I called him a loser. He put me down. I retorted with something about his personal insecurities causing him to fetishize white women. I didn't realize how much this little truth bomb would upset him.

He snapped, chasing me out of the new unit, down the stairs, and across the entire complex (relatively small and empty on a weekday afternoon). I escaped into the old unit, still with half my belongings in it. Lalo barged in to find me cowering by an empty bookshelf. In the blink of an eye, he grabbed me by the throat with one hand—his signature move. The one that immediately disabled his opponents. He'd told me about it long before, that by cutting off their air supply it rendered people immobile. It worked as well as he'd described. To thrash about or fight back at all would've raised my heart rate triggering an immediate need for more air—air that had been cut off entirely, as I basically dangled, wide-eyed and frozen, from Lalo's grip. He stared me down until I was just about to pass out, then let go. I dropped to the floor gasping for air, and he walked out.

Later I found him in the new unit, stuffing his things in a duffel bag.

"What are you doing?"

"What does it look like?"

"You can't leave me here all alone!"

"The fuck I can't. It's what you want anyway."

He moved from the bedroom to the bathroom where, in a blind panic I cornered him. Suddenly, all rational thought was gone, and pure survival instinct took over. To allow the man who'd saved me from almost fifteen years of depression and abject loneliness to disappear from my life was impossible for me, despite all his failures that day and the days preceding it.

He tried to squeeze past me, and I cracked. "No!" I cried, clinging to his waist.

He marched on, as I slipped downward, falling to the floor to clasp onto one of his legs. He was stronger than me and would've wrested free if I hadn't wrapped both my arms and legs around his one leg. Try as he might, he couldn't cross the bathroom that way. He looked down at me as if I were crazy. As if I'd become someone he'd never seen before.

I was sobbing like my life depended on him because in my heart somehow it did. As if I would shrivel up and die without him or simply cease to exist. Through huge, gut-wrenching sobs I begged him not to go. Over and over, I pleaded, as he inched forward, casting puzzled glances down at me, looking frustrated and torn. In that moment, I was probably closer to the enmeshed partner he'd always wanted then I'd ever been—despite the fact that something had irretrievably broken between us the instant he'd grabbed me around the neck. All I knew was that something terrible was taking place and I refused to let him go. He was my life preserver, my oxygen, my father.

Back in Vegas in 1993, when I'd made the wrong choice to leave Joe Walsh for an abusive, jobless drifter named Majid, my life quickly spiraled beyond even the crack-fueled existence I'd been living in LA. When Majid lost control, one day, beating me up for the sin of trying to break up with him, cops threw him in jail and my father sent friends to help get me on an airplane and fly home. But months later, back in Vegas, I'd continued spiraling with alcohol, and at some point my father simply gave up on me. My mother had set hard boundaries about when I could call home (only when I was sober), but on the rare occasion I managed to abide them, my father would never get on the phone. By 1995, I'd decided to drink myself to death, and by 1997 came within a hair of doing it. And my father turned a blind eye. The last four months of my drinking I don't think he spoke to me once. He didn't try to help, fly out to talk sense into me, offer to put me in rehab, or tell me how much he loved me. He just…checked out. Because as much as my father loved me—which was tremendously, I fully believe—he was the last person to stick his neck out for people or get mired in any sort of controversy. It just wasn't who he was. He didn't understand addiction or mental illness. And my father, just like Joe, was nothing if not nonconfrontational, so instead of trying to muddle through in my best interest, he simply looked the other way. He was more inclined to resign himself to losing one of his five kids than to stir up tension by flying to Vegas to convince me not to kill myself. And honestly, I never blamed him. I was as averse to confrontation as most people. But to say that I didn't experience genuine trauma over his complete emotional abandonment when I needed him most and my life might've literally depended on it, would be to cover up for him shirking the duties God gave all fathers.

As for Lalo, something was suddenly different between me and him, but I didn't care; I couldn't let him go. I couldn't let him leave our new apartment. He stopped inching forward and leaned against the wall, talking me down—promising he would stay—until I let go. Five minutes later he left anyway. I sobbed on the bathroom floor for an hour, then curled up with Tippy for the rest of the night, fully spent and hollowed out inside.

Grass Not Greener

June 18, 2007

Current Location: up a tree, without a Lalo
Current Mood: shattered

This will be my last post for a while. Things aren't going well. They're going so badly, in fact, not even writing can help me now.

My sweet Tippy has sores—bumpy, scabby bites from fleas in the grass at my old apartment. Lately she'd enjoyed venturing outside almost daily, a habit she quit two years ago when her arthritis got bad. But my household of late had been such a happy place that even my aging, invalid kitty had been venturing outside the bedroom. She'd join me and Lalo on the couch after dinner, and most mornings take a stroll outside to soak up the sun and nibble a few blades of grass.

Thanks to those vicious fleas, though, she's now rife with discomfort. And it's just so ironic…that this renewed vitality of hers made her vulnerable to their sneak attack.

We live in a new apartment as of yesterday, two stories up with a slight greenbelt view, but no grass outside the door and not much happiness inside it. Sweet Tippy has been crying, scratching herself, and wandering in circles, making horrific noises like I've never heard from her…full of confusion, pain, and fear. They break my fragile heart and flatten my soul. And I'm ashamed to say that these noises, well…I think she got them from me.

It doesn't matter anymore because since this afternoon we're both sort of dazed and silent. Tippy and me, alone in the big, new apartment with trees and privacy all around. Big, green, beautiful trees that taunt me because the one who loves trees most—the one who taught me to look up, see their beauty, and feel their splendor—is gone.

I used to worry that my independent streak would be hard for a man to live with. I used to worry that the pain from my unhealed wounds would surface at all the wrong times and scare off anyone who got close. I used to worry that I'd been single for so long I'd never manage to meld as a couple. And I used to worry that to venture outside and bask in the sun would leave me vulnerable as fuck. That I'd end up with wounds even more painful and bloody than what I already have.

I don't worry anymore; I was right all along. Small comfort that, as I huddle with my Tippy, resigned to the silence, licking our wounds together in the dark.

CHAPTER 7

Summer 2007

Lalo returned the next day, silently moving the rest of my things into the new unit. When he was done, he asked if he could stay. I said yes, of course. We would never be quite the same, but I was as dependent on his love as I'd ever been. I couldn't go back to the emotional isolation of life pre-Lalo—the crippling loneliness, sexual frustration, and agonizing insecurity that I was inherently unlovable.

That night I lay on the sofa watching *South Park*, with Lalo on the floor next to me. The events of the past twenty-four hours had me so spent and discombobulated I started giggling at the TV show and couldn't stop. Lalo didn't quite get the joke but found my laughter contagious. We lay there laughing together in a way that felt mildly bonding but also indicative of the fact that we were still on separate pages. He didn't get it—didn't get what it meant to be a dependable, reciprocal partner to someone who'd just given up her most profitable job and an apartment she loved *for him.*

Dr. Tina saw him privately, then told me he was really trying to make it work and that he absolutely truly loved me. Neither of us told her about the throat grabbing thing. Above all, Lalo craved loyalty and devotion. I craved security and freedom. I wanted so much to believe those weren't incompatible needs.

Lalo threw himself into finding steady work and I helped him write a résumé. He told me he was terrified of losing me, especially to Joe, with whom I was still in contact. Joe had lent me some money the previous month, despite Lalo's insistence that I not take it. I'd borrowed from multiple other friends first, but it hadn't been enough. Joe had offered even more money than I took from him, but I didn't tell Lalo that.

I tried to be empathetic. Lalo had grown up in the barrio of McAllen, Texas. His father was a boxing instructor who'd thrown a twelve-year-old Lalo in the ring with eighteen-year-olds and punched Lalo himself on occasion outside the ring. Lalo's father had convinced him he'd never amount to anything. Lalo had made a success out of drug dealing, but he'd never attempted to go mainstream before. I knew how hard it could be. In my first mainstream job selling credit card processing, I'd had anxiety attacks before every sales call. No one had been there for me, which made me want to be there for Lalo all the more. I'd been completely on my own for fourteen years. So starved for love and affection I was willingly living with a jobless man who'd once gripped my neck and cut off my oxygen supply for calling him out on his shit.

❧

I focused on my writing, taking my laptop to Ruta Maya Coffee during the day because our new unit had too few windows and felt claustrophobic. Ruta Maya made me wistful for the funk dancing I'd done there over the years, but I tried not to be sad or miss that part of my life too much. I was working too hard at real estate and writing to have energy for my favorite bands anymore. And my dedication was paying off. I received two encouraging rejection letters from highly regarded literary magazines, stating that they loved my writing and specifically requesting I send more of my work. Then I got my first short story accepted! The *Foliate Oak Literary Magazine* accepted a short story about me and Joe at Joshua Tree titled "Dry Docked." I was speechless.

I sold the listing Lalo had worked on—in under twenty-four hours. My client was delighted, and the commission was enough to pay all our rent and bills, plus repay the friends who'd lent me cash the previous month (except for Joe, because he didn't seem to care one way or another). I finally felt like I could take a breath, which is when I got another notice from the IRS. They'd already audited me for two previous years (after which I owed them nothing, both times), and now they were claiming I owed nine thousand dollars for an entirely different year. I didn't know why they kept coming after me. When I called my accountant about it, he said it was surely a mistake and he'd handle it. *Oh, and by the way, while you probably don't owe nine thousand for 2004, you do owe ten thousand for 2006.*

Ten thousand in debt overnight, with barely enough money in the bank to get through August. If I didn't sell a house that month, I'd have to start stripping again in September. I decided not to mention it to Lalo.

❧

He thought we should try a hot yoga class, considering how much back and hip pain we were constantly in. I found a Bikram studio in Westlake, and we loved it. After our first class, the best student there asked if I was a dancer.

"Of sorts," I replied.

"It shows," she said. "Your form is fantastic already."

We threw ourselves into it, going every other day. Lalo came up with enough money doing odd jobs for two monthlong class passes. One day after class, after everyone else had left, we lay on our mats, turning our heads to look at each other.

"Marry me," I said, surprising myself.

"Can't," he joked. "Not practical."

I laughed at the role reversal. In truth we were toying with the idea of eloping soon or having a small wedding in six months, on the one-year anniversary of the date we'd met. In my heart I didn't really expect it to happen. I loved him as much as ever, but my faith in his ability to step up as the man I needed was thin.

He got a job at Gold's Gym as a trainer, but the pay was pitiful, and he quit shortly thereafter. I didn't blame him, but we had to do something. He went to Dallas to work for his dad for a week, pouring concrete, and I discovered that for the first time I didn't miss him. Back in Austin, he continued looking for work without success. Still, he found time for daily two-hour workouts and runs on the lake where four or five women per day waved at him.

Meanwhile, I lived in constant fear that I wasn't getting enough done. The feeling never left me. I needed more time to write. I had so many stories crammed in my head I feared the fragile ones might suffocate before I could get them on paper. Sometimes they pounded on the backs of my eardrums and eyeballs, and I feared too much time away from the inspiration tap would decrease their flow.

I also had little time to work out, and when I did my energy was low. I was weaning myself off caffeine and Adderall and starting to feel it. It was necessary though. My adrenals had been fried for as long as I could remember, and none of the many medical doctors I'd seen had been able to help me. I'd recently found a reputable naturopath, but I couldn't afford to keep seeing her or buy the supplements she recommended.

I needed to sell more real estate, which made me cringe at the thought, flashing on Annette Benning's miserable character in *American Beauty*. I interviewed with a new downtown broker about joining her team as a buyer's agent. She seemed befuddled and displeased by my aversion to nightly networking parties, stating with pride that she left her ten-month-old baby at home every night to attend promotional events in service of her big-name company's new office, where they sold overpriced condos to swarms of tech bros flocking in from both coasts. She was as stressed out and bitchy a Realtor as I'd ever met.

I didn't get the job. Walking to my car, I wondered how fast she'd trade her nightly networking events for the party I had in bed with Lalo every night. Or if she felt concerned at all about working sixty hours a week while a nanny raised her kid. I also couldn't help wondering what it would feel like to have a life partner, like she did, who was supportive and shouldered fifty percent of the burden.

❧

My attraction to Lalo was waning in lockstep with my respect. He reminded me of Majid. Both Lalo and Majid were dashing, sexy men who lived off the women in their lives and expected that to be fine with them. Both could kill a man with one hand but not earn a decent living with both.

I took care of Lalo in ways he'd promised to take care of me. He barely worked and when he did, he didn't pay taxes. He'd promised to get a job with benefits so we could both have health insurance. He'd promised to stay sober, get a decent car, and find steady work—none of which happened. I'd also come to suspect he'd been lying about having a college degree. He also didn't see enough of his daughter, which was a major sore point between us. Meanwhile, I'd kept all the promises I'd made him. I quit stripping, quit yelling, worked out more, moved into a large apartment, and embraced Rita as my own.

My overriding feeling every day was abject disappointment. The problem was, at my core, I didn't believe I could do better.

One day we had a fight while driving down the freeway. Lalo was belittling me and treating me like a child in my own car—a helluva nice Lexus LS400. After that, I hardened toward him. Still, I initiated sex in the hopes of bringing us back together. He was game but would rush it every time lately. Foreplay had gone out the window and I didn't know why. I did a lap dance for him in our living room. Before the song was over, he was inside me, fucking me.

Then he said, "Pinky swear you'll never dance for another man."

"Just ensure I never have to," I said. All I got was a blank stare. It was like he didn't understand that it was entirely within

Kristin Casey

his power—his and no one else's. Otherwise, I had no problem returning to stripping. I was at a crossroads awaiting a sign. Night after night I dreamed of houses and escorting. As an escort I felt secure, empowered, and appreciated for my work. The dreams of houses were of situations in which I felt trapped and uninspired. In one, I lived in a beautiful community where everyone had a lush garden except me because my watering hose was broken.

At the end of August, six months into our relationship, Lalo still didn't have steady work. My Free Will Astrology horoscope said it was time to say goodbye. His said it was time to go home.

Strength & Flexibility

August 11, 2007

Current Location: Savasana
Current Mood: determined

After my first class back at Bikram yoga, I received praise on my form from a woman with ten percent body fat and the flexibility of a Cirque du Soleil performer. The 105-degree heat and sixty percent humidity are almost unbearable halfway through each ninety-minute class (I'm Nordic for God's sake!), but afterward I'm totally energized. The instructors praise my full locust and rabbit poses, but I often skip the second set of camel, which they say is the one that makes you feel the most vulnerable (go figure). The hardest of all is triangle. I can get into it fine; I just can't hold it. I lack strength, dammit.

I'm flexible. Always have been. It helps, considering how many hardcore addicts I've dated, disagreeable customers I've tolerated, and severely depressed mothers I was stuck with (just the one, but she was a lot). You've got to roll with the punches, bend over backward, twist without breaking, and kick high (and hard) when all else fails. As a child the kicking part came naturally. The people-pleaser backbends came later.

I did backbends on stage at Sugar's when I first started stripping at eighteen, not coincidentally the same time I first threw out my back. Getting out of bed one morning, searing pain shot through my lumbar. I collapsed on the floor and stayed there, unable to call for help. I spent thirty minutes crawling to the kitchen phone. My best friend's mom brought soup and got me settled on the couch where I stayed for two days. Every couple of years it happens again. The last time was after the Bonnaroo Music Festival.

Some friends had set up camp backstage and invited me along, but by day two the temptation to take X with 70,000 dancing, tripping, rolling kids in that massive Tennessee field was stronger than me.

It scared me and I left the festival early. At home I took a shower, mulling over the realization that I was conflicted about what kind of lifestyle I wanted. Reaching for a towel, it happened. I hit the floor in excruciating pain. Two days later my kinesiologist, knowing nothing of the above events, commented casually that the area of my back in spasm correlated with the part of my emotional body conflicted about where I fit in. Huh.

Aside from that day at Bonnaroo I've hardly desired drugs since getting sober, but I've struggled with the temptation to isolate for as long as I can remember. To curl up in child's pose and turn off my phone all day...maybe forever. To rest my shaky foundation and not feel so vulnerable and off-balance. Panting and sweating at the peak of Bikram's standing series, I'll glance at Lalo next to me getting stronger and more flexible daily. He always mouths something encouraging to me to keep me going.

I haven't thrown out my back in over a year, and now that I have no insurance to pay a chiropractor, I'm hoping yoga will increase my core strength and reduce spasm events. My instructor says the yoga studio is a microcosm of the macrocosm of one's life. I'm surprised when I manage a pose exceptionally well and equally shocked when I don't. I never know when my flexibility will rise to the occasion and sustain me, or when weakness will appear to topple me.

When class begins, the instructor tells beginners to "just stay in the room." If the poses become too much or the heat is unbearable, *above all, stay in the room*. If you do, you'll get the full benefits. When class is over, they tell you to come back tomorrow. Stay, then keep coming back. It's the best way to keep from becoming sore—to keep building strength at your core. Go figure.

CHAPTER 8

September & October 2007

We drove to Amarillo so Lalo could work for my dad's property management company, fixing up homes and whipping Dad's lazy work crew into shape. Lalo drove, got a speeding ticket on the way, then as soon as the cop pulled away, started speeding again. I knew he was acting out, but I was so happy to have a work break while he brought home the bacon for a change, I didn't complain about it.

Our first day in Amarillo, we hiked around Palo Duro Canyon with my folks. Later that day, they remarked that they'd never heard me laugh as much as when I was with Lalo. "Your mother and I have never seen you this happy before and we love it," Dad said, beaming.

Once we were back home, Lalo's ex continued harassing us, making multiple drunken phone calls. One time she called me Big Head McNasty, which I found so funny I actually liked the crazy bitch for a moment. She told Rita to tell Lalo not to let me around her anymore, but Rita refused to abide her demands. Then she sent Rita over with a family photo album, hoping to make Lalo nostalgic for their life together. I flipped through the pages.

"You guys look so happy. I thought you said you were miserable with her."

"Kristi," Lalo said patiently. "I *was* miserable. These pictures? We're drunk as fuck in all of them."

The next week his ex called drunk again, slurring that she would never get over Lalo. "You fucking bitch, you stupid whore… you're everything to him," she slurred on my voicemail.

Lalo looked at me and shrugged. "I been trying to tell ya."

❧

WE HAD AS MANY good days as bad. We broke up at least three times in September and October. One time he chucked the TV remote at me from across the room, missing me but almost hitting Tippy and breaking both the remote and the glass on my favorite Vargas poster—a two-hundred-and-fifty-dollar expense. That was the last straw. It was only a matter of time after that. I was stuck in an expensive two-bedroom apartment I couldn't afford on my own, but as soon as my lease was up next year, Lalo would be out on his ass. Till then I made the best of a bad situation.

I made him a cake for his thirty-ninth birthday. It was a somber, tense occasion. He told me I'd broken his heart more than I'd ever know. That he was pondering suicide again.

"Lalo, please stop," I sighed. "I haven't kicked you out yet, so you have a lovely apartment to live in *and* two new landscaping jobs. What's the problem?"

I pulled further away from him. Holding an open house (for another Realtor) in a McMansion near Zilker Park, I gazed out the window, watching thousands of tourists walk down Barton Springs Road on their way to the Austin City Limits Music Festival. Hundreds of couples who'd pooled their hard-earned money to take a vacation together and dance to live music all weekend. I deserved that, too, I thought, and right as I started wondering if I'd be better off single sooner rather than later, Lalo showed up. The open house being over, I locked the door behind him and took him upstairs to have sex on the master bathroom counter. The mechanics of our sexual chemistry were still stellar, but emotionally I felt nothing for him throughout it.

My horoscope said to "set a clear intention that you won't sacrifice material security for emotional intimacy, or vice versa." Lalo's horoscope said it was time to begin a phase of bright beginnings. Instead of dumping him permanently though, I took him back three times in a row. Dr. Tina said at this point it would be best if we lived apart. Lalo owed me fourteen-hundred-dollars in missed rent and bills but was finally contributing a little here and there, so I let him stay. I was biding my time, living my life, practically single in my head, stripping for a living again.

I received a third encouraging rejection letter for yet another of my short stories, handwritten high praise with pointed requests to submit more of my work. Never had so much love been shared for pieces no one planned to publish, the last one so glowing that the editor actually wanted to publish it but said I could do better than her little online magazine (*Swink*) and recommended I tell Will at Nerve.com that she sent me. The piece was a personal essay—as personal as I'd ever written. Whether *Nerve* published it or not, I was over the moon to be recommended to them.

I'd sold three homes in three months and was showing property all over the hill country, but real estate was in a slump and prospects for more sales anytime soon didn't look good. Besides, I missed stripping—the sexual hedonism, music, atmosphere, and all that wonderful cash. I auditioned at Exposé on South Congress Avenue.

Exposé was smaller than Perfect 10, got fewer white-collar customers, and had no bottled sparkling water for me to drink. But it was a ten-minute commute versus almost sixty to Perfect 10. Smoking was prohibited, and—far as I could tell—the building wasn't riddled with mold like Perfect 10 was. My respiratory issues of the past six months had cleared up completely in the ten weeks I'd been away, and I was thrilled to not have to breathe toxic air to make a living anymore.

After handing in my application, I got a skeptical look from the dayshift manager, Dennis. "You started stripping for the first time six months ago, at thirty-nine years old?"

"No, I've stripped for ten years total. What are you talking about?"

He pointed to the section where I listed my previous three jobs. Two of them were real estate brokers.

"You didn't ask for the last three clubs I stripped at. You asked for the last three jobs I had."

He shook his head like I was a little nutty but told me to get changed, then talk to the DJ about cueing music for my audition. As soon as I took the stage, I saw Dennis freeze and watch transfixed until I'd finished my set, dancing to Melody Gardot's "Who Will Comfort Me" and Dusty Springfield's "Son of a Preacher Man." Before I could exit, he approached and tossed a ten at me. "You're hired," he said. "And thank you."

"For what?"

"For coming to work for me."

It was nice to be appreciated. By the end of the day, the general manager had also thanked me, said I could leave early anytime I had real estate business, and went over the club rules with me, something that had almost never been done at any of the twelve clubs I'd worked at.

At almost forty, I was the oldest stripper there, though most customers guessed I was in my mid-thirties. A few other girls there were actually that age. One was working on her PhD, one had a second job as a Realtor, like me, and the third was a housewife bringing extra cash into the household. The club had more diversity than those I'd worked at in the past, with fifty percent being black and Latina ladies. Most of the girls were young and pretty, though quite a few were out of shape. I'd noticed that millennials weren't nearly as concerned with physical fitness as Generation X, and at most clubs this cut into their income, though I'd yet to tell if it made much difference at Exposé. While I quickly became the top

earner on my shift, the flabby girls seemed to have their fans…
though in time I realized most were just sitting with their drug
dealers and pimps.

A couple weeks in, one day in the dressing room, as I was doing
some real estate business on my cell, another dancer was talking so
loudly to herself that I had to put my colleague on hold and ask her
to please be quiet. Her response was to pause briefly, as if confused,
before shouting at the ceiling, "It's called speed, sister!" and clanging
a couple of empty lockers for effect. Two hours later I overheard
her on her cell begging someone to bring her more drugs. I politely
resisted the urge to clang a locker or two, mostly because I was
pretty sure she wouldn't get it, but also because I hadn't clanged a
locker since I was a twenty-one-year-old, obnoxious, drunk stripper.
Overall, my coworkers didn't bother me so much as they made me
concerned for the reputation, and thus profitability, of my new club.

At the end of my first shift, I went home with three hundred
dollars and a huge bruise on one knee from an uneven light fixture
in the stage floor. I'd need to nearly double that income to make
the job worthwhile, but once I developed new regular customers it
wouldn't be a problem.

One of my first regulars was a CPA named Randy, who offered
to review my 2006 tax return as soon as I told him about it. Based
on my expenses that year, the $9,600 bill sounded unreasonable
to him. Randy was a sixty-something, exuberant, tousled good ol'
boy. We immediately clicked and I spent two hours dancing for him
and his dentist friend. By the time he left, Randy was professing his
undying love to me.

His dentist friend was more reserved, but a nice guy who told
me an interesting, and oddly familiar, story. Apparently he'd met a
stripper in Vegas twelve years earlier at the Crazy Horse Too. She
worked the afternoon shift, a pretty strawberry-blonde from Austin
whom he'd drank shots with and made plans to party with after
work. Unfortunately, he said, she passed out in the dressing room

before her shift ended. He'd never seen her again and called it one of the biggest disappointments of his life.

After the shock wore off, I told him that in 1995 there was only one strawberry blonde from Austin working mid-shift at the Crazy Horse Too—me! We laughed our asses off about that before he graciously accepted my apology for passing out on him twelve years ago. (When he suggested I still owed him that date, I claimed the statute of limitations was up, not to mention the fact that it was him who'd gotten me drunk in the first place.)

Not all my Exposé customers were as delightful. One night, three separate customers reeked of a weeklong meth binge. The third wore damp clothes and had a bonus scent of vomit on top of everything. Later that day, I sat with a clean-cut forty-year-old who placed a call to his dealer right in front of me, then freely admitted he'd been doing meth regularly since he was eighteen and that he'd started shooting it up in recent years. He had twin toddlers at home who were three years old.

With my three shifts per week, I developed a stable of regulars almost immediately, but only two or three really good ones. In fact, the club frequently had as many dancers as customers, in a fucked-up ratio that made it hard to bank any night of the week. Still, Exposé offered not only a fresh source of income but a reprieve from the stress at home, an escape from the claustrophobic tension between me and Lalo that had gone on for months. My customers were sweet, complimentary, and interesting. Laborers of all kinds, but also pencil pushers, lawyers, tech guys, and one filmmaker. Most were less grabby than my customers at Perfect 10, but they didn't come in every week or stay long when they did. Nor did they tend to spend hundreds on me in the VIP section. I worked hard and was never idle. If there was one man sitting alone at Exposé while I was there, I worked him until his wallet was empty. I tried to be strong and just roll with it all, as Exposé seemed to be my best option for income at the moment.

Awkward Through the Fog

September 11, 2007

Current Location: hovering unsupported over invisible furniture
Current Mood: worried

Today my Bikram yoga instructor asked if she could use my awkward pose as an example to the class. I obliged, as fifteen semi-strangers watched me sit, arms outstretched, with an almost perfectly straight back, in an invisible chair. Why awkward pose is one of my best I don't know, especially considering I've spent most of my life with an arch in my back.

I'm out of money. Real estate's slow season is officially here, made worse by the fucked-up loan market crisis. What's weird is not even the best brokers in Austin seem to think our local market is vulnerable. Bring it up in any Tuesday morning sales meeting and watch a room full of Realtors suddenly do more awkward posing than a packed Bikram yoga class.

Speaking of awkward, I just told Lalo I'm going to start stripping again. He handled it well, which is to say there were no unkind words or raised voices. No one threatened to move out. He told my folks last week that we're planning to marry. My dad asked him if he knew what he was getting into. I suspect he was only partially kidding.

Lalo had a birthday recently. I'm dieting, so he alone ate cake while I ate my words—the ones written here a week ago stating I no longer strip for anyone but Lalo. They were bitter and hard to swallow. Awkward going down, you might say. Which I'm expert at, right? Supporting my weight in uncomfortable positions, back rod straight, arms tense and trembling. Yep...I'm flexible enough to undo all the good quitting did for my relationship in the first place. Flexible enough to do what needs to be done. Which, for starters, is come up with $9,600 the IRS is demanding I pay.

I'm also stronger by the day. You should see my quads in awkward pose—solid as rocks. I execute a decent toe stand, no longer struggle with camel, and get better at triangle every day. I do well in the spine strengthening series. I have a strong back, capable of carrying heavy loads and trudging steadfast through hardship, despite the wear and tear on my lumbar. My main struggle is in the standing series, where my glutes give out sooner than my classmates'. When it comes to my personal support structure and the subtleties of maintaining the body in ideal postures, I am lacking. People with good core strength learn to identify and activate the muscles needed to accomplish various tasks. I'm working on it. I probably would've benefited from doing Jane Fonda's *Buns of Steel* more than three times in my twenties, but regardless, I'm strong enough to do what I must. I'm just not smart enough to figure out why I still must at my age.

My birthday is in six weeks, at which point I'll be a forty-year-old stripper. And while there's nothing wrong with that in and of itself, it's an awkward position to be in right now—in a relationship while nearly naked on display for a club full of horny men. I have three days to find a way out if there is one. That is, if I truly want one.

Bikram instructs students to get out of yoga poses the same general way they got into them. He also says, "lock your damn knees" and "don't think too much in Savasana." I have no idea if any of that applies to my situation. I know Bikram is a multi-fucking-millionaire who never had to grind on strangers' laps to keep a roof over his head. Though he did clean a lot of toilets once upon a time, he now charges $10,000 for his instructor training and certification. That's four hundred dollars more than the IRS is taxing my labor, which is, once again, bending over backward for a club full of strange, horny men.

CHAPTER 9

November & December 2007

EVERY NOW AND THEN Lalo did something seriously endearing. One early Monday morning, around two o'clock, I was awoken by a trio of young people in the parking lot below our second story bedroom window.

"Hey," I shouted at the two men and one woman yammering inanely within hearing distance of a dozen bedroom windows in our building. "There are people trying to sleep in here."

"Shut the fuck up, bitch."

"Motherfucker," I muttered, and sank back down into bed.

In the streetlight coming through the blinds, I saw Lalo's eyebrows furrow. "What's going on?" he asked, sleepily.

"Nothing, just some dude outside calling me a bitch."

Lalo opened his eyes and sat up at the window. "Hey, man, what did you just say?"

"I said, 'shut up, bitch,'" the guy replied, extra pleasantly since he was buzzed and having fun with it. His friends chuckled at his antics, spurring him on. "You got a problem with it?" he added, stupidly.

Lalo, wide awake now, answered back evenly. "Stay right there, dude." He put on his pajama pants and slippers and walked outside. I sat up at the window for a better view. The threesome continued their slow stroll across our lot, likely waking more tenants with each window they passed. The girl said something in a concerned voice, but the loudmouth of the bunch assured her that their friend—the other guy—had his back. I could tell by his voice he had no idea Lalo was headed his way or that the man he'd pissed off was built like a UFC welterweight champion.

Tippy joined me at the window and together we watched Lalo catch up to the trio at their car.

"Which one of you is Billy Badass?" Lalo asked, his tone emotionless and even.

That got their attention. None of them moved or said a word for a moment, then the loudmouth stepped up, telling Lalo to calm down, while reaching out to touch his shoulder.

"Do not fucking touch me," Lalo practically growled.

The guy backed up. Suddenly the girl became remorseful as hell, apologizing profusely and telling Lalo they'd leave right away. Unfortunately, her friends had had enough to drink that they didn't back down right away. The loudmouth started defending himself, saying it was all my fault. That they were minding their own business when I rudely, for no apparent reason, called him a motherfucker. Then his friend stepped toward Lalo and puts his hands on him for real, pressing on his chest in a way that suggested Lalo should back off. Instead, in the blink of an eye, Lalo pulled his signature move, clamping his fist around the guy's throat. The guy froze, unable to breathe, just like I had when Lalo had done it to me. At that point Tippy lay back down to sleep but I stayed at the window, highly entertained.

With his hand around his friend's throat, Lalo looked at the loudmouth guy and said calmly, "Apologize." But the guy refused to, so Lalo squeezed his friend's neck a little tighter and then suddenly both the loudmouth and the girl started begging Lalo for mercy, apologizing repeatedly.

"Not to *me*," Lalo sighed. Jerking his head in the direction of our bedroom window, he said, "To *her*."

The loudmouth looked up to the window and in a clear, contrite voice, said, "I'm sorry for calling you a bitch!" Lalo dutifully let go of his friend and quietly strolled back upstairs, while the trio of drunk idiots jumped in their car and peeled out. I was so turned on by the time Lalo crawled back into bed that I dove between his legs and sucked his cock until he came.

One of the most powerful epiphanies I'd ever had in session with Dr. Tina was a year or two earlier, immediately after describing yet another of my mother's tirades against me that had been particularly degrading. Dr. Tina had asked where my father was during all this.

I'd shrugged. "Next to her on the couch, I guess."

"And what was he doing?"

I looked at her blankly. "I just told you…sitting on the couch."

"Yes," she'd said patiently. "But what was he *doing*?"

"Again, *sitting*. On the *couch*."

Tina sighed. "Doing and saying…what, nothing?"

I shook my head no, shrugging again. What the hell was she getting at?

"So, he wasn't coming to your aid or trying to calm her down in any way?"

And that's when it hit me. Twenty-five years after the fact. My father hadn't come to my rescue during any of Mom's verbal abuse. That while, until the bankruptcy anyway, he'd been a competent provider, he'd never been my protector in those situations I'd most needed him.

Lalo standing up for me, flexing his muscles, and making that verbally abusive asshole apologize to me, was the single most romantic, and flat out masculine, thing any man had ever done for me. How was I supposed to kick out a guy who did something like that?

❧

In Amarillo, weeks earlier, Lalo had worked hard, swinging a chainsaw up in tall trees for half the day and commanding my father's slipshod crew the other half. I'd stayed home in my parents' dining room working on my how-to book for strippers. One day I got swept up in anxiety over it and Lalo sweetly talked me down, assuring me the book was going to be great and everyone would love it. I'd never had anyone believe in my writing like that, much less take time to soothe my writerly insecurities when they flared up.

Then, the day we got home to Austin, Lalo got drunk and acted like a brute, bitching about my stripping and saying he knew I thought he was a loser.

"I don't think you're a loser, Lalo," I told him. "But I think *you* think you're a loser and *that* is our biggest problem."

Because of all this, though my parents and therapist had faith that Lalo would turn his life around any day, my friends were beginning to think I was crazy for allowing him to stay. Much like my three-year affair with Charles, my time with Lalo had run its course while I was still stupidly hanging on. I just couldn't help thinking that he needed me now. That no one had been there to support me in early sobriety, and that while Lalo was no longer sober, he *had* changed his whole life to be with me. Sometimes I wondered if the reason I drew a man like Lalo to me was because I'd never forgiven myself for being an alcoholic, drug addicted fuckup. That maybe I was healing that wound inside me by loving Lalo through his hard times. I went back and forth over it daily. Because I also felt like I'd done my time—ten hard years of sobriety! I wasn't sure I wanted to go through Lalo's with him, especially when it didn't feel very healing for me lately.

One night, he came home drunk again, then blew up at me for emailing a customer about a potential business opportunity the customer had extended—selling racing boat technology. "It's none of your damn business!" I screamed. "I'm trying to generate income. Meanwhile, all you've accomplished is to *drive drunk* twice this week!"

Two days after that he scrounged up enough money to bring home flowers, swordfish steaks, and carrot cake. He grilled the fish and sliced me a big piece of cake afterward. "Did I provide?" he asked me sweetly. Yeah, I thought. One dinner, big deal.

The next day he sent me an email that swept me off my feet.

Honey, I feel like I need to say a few things about yesterday, the past two weeks...hell, the last year and then some. First, I truly am sorry for completely stressing you out. Your time is precious, and it's wrong of me. I won't do it again. I didn't sleep last night because I was thinking about us, my options, your options, your future, your career, my work, etc. It's overwhelming. I've never felt so uncertain and vulnerable in my life. Yet the last nine months with you have been the most satisfying time of change and growth I've ever experienced. Hell, the sex alone...I mean, what can you say about that? Other people would never understand. It's truly making love, which I've never done on that level EVER!! Thank you for all of it. Your patience, love, financial support, encouragement, and enlightenment. I don't know what the future holds but am still willing to strain toward it together. I hope you feel the same. I really do. I'm sorry it's been so rocky. I don't know how much we must do until our luck changes, but let's be strong and not quit on us now. I LOVE YOU!!!! ~Lalo

We spent the weekend making love and watching movies, football, and porn. We went to a dinner party where Lalo charmed every one of the other guests. A few days later, I was tearing my hair out again, wanting to kick him out on his ass. One of the landscaping jobs he was supposed to have done was for our yoga instructor. Because he never finished it, she never paid him. "What the hell have you been doing for two weeks?" I asked. He had no logical explanation and I started to wonder if he was visiting strip clubs during the day or maybe sleeping with his ex-wife again. She'd called to ask me how long Lalo had been shaving his pubic area.

"Lalo, how does your ex-wife know you started doing that for me?"

"Dunno," he shrugged. "We were just talking, and it came up in conversation."

I dropped the subject, realizing I didn't give a rat's ass if he was fucking her. What I cared about was that my mental pro/con lists on him were becoming very one-sided. On the pro side, I got great sex and companionship. On the other hand, I had extra rent and grocery bills, less time to write, a psycho ex-wife to deal with, and daily complaints from Lalo about my stripping. I was fed up with his drinking and driving, inability to earn, jealous streak, and violence. He'd pawned most of his tools and thus couldn't take many of the job requests he got, and I suspected he might be doing some small-time drug dealing while I was at work.

Somehow, we muddled through. After a long discussion about whether we were compatible anymore we decided to try again. Neither of us were ready to go it alone. For Thanksgiving we met up with my entire family at Disney World in Orlando and had an amazing time. It was the first time I hadn't been solo among my four married and partnered siblings in fifteen years. And Lalo shined around other people. He was never more of the man I wanted him to be than when he was with my friends or family. We joked that if one of us would just win the lottery all our relationship issues would be over. He could take care of the house while I wrote all day and we fucked all night, neither of us expecting anything more of the other.

During one of our fights, we'd broken up for two days, and while I'd felt a sense of relief, a weighty pain had settled into my heart, and quickly. As if it were waiting right outside my window all along, waiting for us to break up. Before meeting Lalo, I'd lived with a sick, empty, anxious feeling every single day. One that made me break down sobbing all the time. Sometimes it made me beat my stomach with my fists. Daily it made me question everything about myself and my choices, made me dread my future and hate my present. Made me cry myself to sleep at night and dance like a woman possessed every chance I got. I wasn't ready to go back there.

Besides, I still loved him. Loved his humor, his touch, his sensibilities. The way he talked to people, walked across a room, protected me, and was so affected by me. I loved his moods, his sense of wonder and curiosity. His dangerous side, his vulnerabilities, his romantic ways. Sometimes he'd walk up behind me and just stand there, breathing on my shoulder, letting me feel his body heat until two seconds later I melted. That was one of Lalo's favorite ways of seducing me. His sexual energy was so strong, all he had to do was stand behind me, breathing. I'd instantly get weak in my knees and wet in my pussy.

Late in November, he finally applied at Whole Foods like I'd been asking him to. He also went to work for a loan shark, beating up people who owed money. Suddenly he was talking about keeping a gun in the house. "My house?" I snapped. "Like hell you will."

One day, he showed up at home with ice packs on his head and no money to show for it. When he wouldn't explain why he hadn't been paid, I wondered if he was working off a drug debt. I decided to think of him as my lover instead of my boyfriend. It made it much easier to live with him and not care about the shit he got up to.

One day, I called him from work, and he sounded high. When I asked what he was up to, he said, "Waiting on a dope deal."

"What?!"

"Waiting on a dope deal," he repeated.

"What kind of dope?"

"Just dope."

"What are you on, Lalo?"

"C'mon…"

"Seriously, I can tell you're lit. What the fuck are you on?"

Click. He hung up on me. I called Sprint and had them freeze his line, then left work early to go home and take the phone from him completely. We fought for two days. I told him he disgusted me. He said I was overbearing. I told him the drinking and drugs had to stop. He said he didn't really want to be sober; that's not the kind of life he wanted to live. Then, in a bizarre twist, he finished writing his résumé, typed it up himself, and sent it out to employers. Then he went to an AA meeting. Go figure.

Meanwhile, I went to work and had a good day at the club, making money and meeting fun, interesting customers. One in particular.

"You're really attracted to me, aren't you?" he asked.

"Yes," I said, surprising myself, though not surprising him. He was used to it. A tan, tousled blonde with a fit physique and sparkling blue eyes, wearing a western shirt and jeans, he had the kind of boyish charm women loved and strippers took home to fuck for free. He said his stage name was Bobby.

"Let me guess. Your real name is Thor."

"No, it's *Thorn*."

"Funny, my real name is Rose. Clearly we're meant for each other."

I sat with him for an hour. He said I seemed like someone who created magic. And that since I was a writer, he bet I could manifest things just by writing about them. It sounded like a line he'd used before, but I didn't care. I liked talking with someone who understood longing and manifestation. I liked flirting with a man who thought life could be managed and manipulated to serve me, instead of Lalo's attitude that life was out of our control and that we'd "always have to work" to get by. That our life together, though filled with love, would materially always be about just getting by. Most of all I liked the idea that the universe was sending me a sign that I could attract an entirely different kind of man.

After work I went home and wrote about Bobby in my journal. That night, Lalo snuck into my dresser drawer and read it, then started a fight about it. But this time was different. I refused to get defensive.

"Look," I told him with a shrug. "If you don't want to lose me to men like Bobby then maybe you should learn to be more like men like Bobby."

Lalo thought the less he needed out of life, the stronger he was. I thought the more I manifested for myself, the stronger I was. Our perspectives were utterly incompatible. But it was Christmastime, and we had a two-week trip to Amarillo planned, during which Lalo would work again for my dad while I worked on my writing projects. We drove through freezing rain and black ice for nine hours—Lalo with his eyes on the road, gripping the wheel precisely at ten and two the whole time, while I read to him and Tippy from *The Austin Chronicle* and a two-year-old *Penthouse* magazine I'd bought on sale at a truck stop. Once there, Lalo worked incredibly hard, delighting my folks and making me proud—which made me hot for him again finally. When things were going well like that—with him working, me writing, and us fucking—I could pretend everything was fine and we still had a chance at a happy life. Amarillo was a small, flat, boring city but, for us, it was like a honeymoon every time.

When we got home, I reinstated his phone line then listened to his voicemails, a few of which were from other women, though nothing directly incriminating. I looked at his November phone bill and found other calls to and from more women—some of whom I knew and others I didn't. Though none of it was proof that he was sleeping around, it certainly seemed possible, and a part of me wanted to be outraged and disappointed. But in truth I didn't care much and blew it off.

While it would've upset me greatly to discover Lalo had been seeing other women during the first six months of our relationship, now that we weren't getting along it hardly mattered. I believed in temporary fidelity for certain situations, but we weren't currently in one of them. Lalo and I were at our best in the early stages

   Kristin Casey

of falling in love, soothing each other's loneliness and matching each other's sex drive perfectly. As much sex as he had to give in those first six months was the same amount I craved. Neither of us had any leftover sexual energy to give away. Those first six months we were healing each other's traumas through our intimacies, emotional, physical, and sexual. Monogamy tended to work for me, and most people, early in a relationship. I'd felt the same when first dating Joe. It was only over time, when I needed more sex than he could give me, and Joe needed more variety than I could give him, that we both resorted to "cheating." Were Lalo and I capable of lasting the same six years Joe and I had, there's no doubt we'd have become consensually non-monogamous at some point, for many reasons, not least of which being the adventure and connection with a variety of people that I felt made life worth living. But a relationship that long with Lalo simply wasn't going to happen. Meanwhile, I was living in the present, assuming our time was coming to a quick end but not actively doing anything about it.

A couple days after the new year, Lalo got a full-time job at a reputable landscaping company, with benefits. Just my luck, I thought. I've got one foot out the door when he finally gets his shit together.

Deep Metaphor

February 3, 2008

Current Location: today
Current Mood: content

In yoga class yesterday I realized that I could hold triangle pose (finally!) for the full minute if I don't go too deep into the posture. I have no idea if this is a good thing, but I'm going with it for now.

It made me wonder if I shouldn't *apply that policy to the rest of my life*.

I'm a woman of extremes, less so now than in my youth, but always the kind of girl who figured that if one is good, ten is better (laxatives being a notable exception, but I digress).

Before I quit drinking at twenty-nine I was consuming a hundred cocktails a week. I smoked two packs of cigarettes a day, more when I was on cocaine, and up to three packs a day on meth (in my teens). Upon quitting smoking, I ate everything in sight for a year, including entire cheesecakes for breakfast until I slowly got my eating disorder under control. When I got my first job as a Realtor, I immediately launched into an eighty-hour work week. My broker adored me (well duh), and though I hated the long hours I didn't know any other way to do things. During that same time, I was marathon training, running forty-five miles a week *and* lifting weights at night. When I finally cut back, I had time to check out the best thing Austin has to offer—live music—and proceeded to go dancing two to seven nights a week for five years straight. I quit that lifestyle the year I returned to stripping in 2006. Three months later I met Lalo. He moved in with me five weeks after that, and we decided to get married one week later.

I think it's fair to say *I tend to push myself into the deepest expression of every posture I assume.* And that it's time to give myself a break.

In yoga, form is more important than depth, and I think that applies to most of life, including relationships. Staying in the present moment—the only one that exists—is a lifelong challenge for most people and I'm no exception. I'd probably do well to stop stressing out about what I'm experiencing and simply focus on my breath.

Balancing stick is a ten second posture but gets my heart rate higher than any other. It's strenuous for sure, but what doesn't help is that half the time I come out of it red in the face and dizzy as hell, then realize I've forgotten to breathe through it. Funny how that works.

CHAPTER 10

January & February 2008

In late January, I called a psychic that an Exposé customer had told me about. Sean Harribance was an East Indian man raised in Trinidad, whose abilities had been studied and proven in multiple clinical settings over forty years. He lived in Houston but did a reading for me over the phone.

"Hi, Sean. This is Casey, your one p.m. appointment."

"Yes, one moment," Sean replied in a thick accent, followed by a long silence. Then, "Your love life is a catastrophe. Why you let men ruin your life, all your life?!"

I didn't know how to respond to that other than to chuckle at his boldness and sigh at his accuracy. He told me it was bad enough I'd quit college for my first love (Joe) but that now, with Lalo, I was putting too much effort into the relationship and not enough into my career. "You could've been a senator by now!"

He went on. "You're very independent and should've gotten your master's degree. Writing, especially drama, could be a living for you."

He said I should pursue the how-to stripper book and write a memoir. And that I would do well to write another how-to book about sex for women. He told me he could see that Lalo was a great lover, that I was tons of fun in bed, and that he (Sean) was impressed with my blowjob abilities. (If I had any doubts about Sean's psychic powers, that comment alone wiped them out.)

He said I was an amazing dancer who could've made a living in Hollywood at it, including small acting parts, which would've come easily to me. That I was very talented, and my parents messed up by not helping me become more of a success. He said I'd do well to open my own strip club, something I'd long fantasized about doing. Also, that Lalo and I would do well flipping houses, though it wasn't what I really wanted to do.

"Mostly," he said, "you tend to partner with the wrong kind of men…confused men who need guidance and hold you back in life."

He said I was the best thing to happen to Lalo and if he was ever going to change only I would be able to make it happen. That Lalo could be a success with my help, but it would require Lalo working hard at it, and working hard to support me while I spent my time writing. Only then would we be happy. Otherwise, Lalo would always hold me back.

"The problem is," he said, "Lalo doesn't like to work for anyone but himself. He only takes orders from you because he loves you— so much that it makes him cry sometimes. If Lalo didn't love you as much as he does, he would've left you by now because you're hard on your men! And yet every man you've ever been with still thinks about you. Even that rock star from before. He still loves and misses you. But he also worries you're wasting your life away."

Sean told me all of this without knowing one thing about me. I'd even given him a fake name so there was no way to Google me (not that my blowjob skills were anywhere on the Internet). And while some of what he said was news to me (any kind of success in Hollywood for me was especially hard to believe), most of it affirmed what I already knew. That Lalo would hold me back for the rest of my life and that it was long past time for me to throw myself fully into my writing.

The next day, Lalo took me to see *The Diving Bell and the Butterfly*, a movie about Jean-Dominique Bauby's life after a massive stroke, when his body became a diving bell, his imagination and memory a butterfly. Throughout the movie, all I could think was that writing was my butterfly and real estate my diving bell. And that if Lalo had his way I'd be confined to the bottom of the ocean, enslaved to selling houses for the rest of my life.

At Costco, before diving into our monthly shopping, we often liked to stop and gaze at the huge flat screen TVs and jewelry displays near the entrance. One day, weeks earlier, I'd told Lalo I had an idea for what to do when we finally saved a little money. He replied, "Buy a ring and get married?"

"Uh, actually I was thinking we get a new forty-two-inch TV to watch UFC on."

Lalo sighed and shook his head, muttering something about role reversals.

Days later, he commented that unrestrained ambition was the bane of many a relationship. That same day, I received an email from a successful writer friend, who, in commenting on my packed schedule, said *there's nothing wrong with ambition*. Lalo's position angered and offended me. My friend's nourished and encouraged me. I'd been postponing the inevitable for months. I'd called a psychic to confirm what I already knew and to ease feelings of guilt I harbored over the breakup that was coming any day now.

THE ANNIVERSARY OF THE DAY we met was January 29. I was scheduled to work at Exposé that day but stayed home with my first ever allergy attack. When the club called to tell me only one dancer had shown up by opening time, I agreed to come in anyway. Once there, I ended up dancing for two hours for a makeup-free, bi-curious woman in a pink flowered skirt, modest T-shirt, and sensible shoes. Now, I'd dated or bedded a dozen women in my life and fallen in love with two of them; it just happened to be quite a long time ago, and I'd lost all romantic and sexual desire for women since. Because of that, I had an aversion to lap dancing for women.

 Kristin Casey

I simply felt nothing doing it, whereas dancing for men—no matter their age, attractiveness, or body type—always felt highly erotic to me.

Whatever. A buck was a buck, and she and her husband were lovely people. Once it was over, I forgot about her completely, though that evening when Lalo asked how work had gone I mentioned it.

One week later, frustrated about being overloaded with real estate work for which I would likely only be paid a fraction, I decided to splurge on a gift for myself—a lovely little silver jalapeño for my charm bracelet. I'd told Lalo months earlier that I wanted one to represent him, my own personal sexy, spicy vato. When I called to tell him about it he sighed. "Guess I'll go return the one I already bought you for Valentine's Day."

We laughed about it together. Before hanging up he said, "I love you and can't wait to see you tonight." I expected to see him that evening after work, but he didn't come home for hours. Instead, he called me drunk, saying he was at his new house. "What are you talking about? Your new house *where?*"

"South," he slurred.

"Lalo, you're not making sense and I refuse to deal with this right now," I said, and hung up.

He finally came home, stumbling drunk and for some strange reason hurling insults at me along the lines of "lesbian slut," "whore," and the like.

For all his faults Lalo had never spoken to me like that. And for good reason—there was no way in hell I'd tolerate it. A screaming match ensued. It didn't last long because I demanded he leave, and since his name wasn't on the lease, unless he wanted the police to haul him out, he eventually had to go on his own. The moment he did I called my leasing manager with an emergency lock change request. As soon as the locks were changed I threw everything Lalo owned out the door onto the patio. It took multiple trips, and in the middle of it, Lalo's friend Ted, three doors down, peeked his head out. Ted was a good guy and didn't want to get in the middle of things but did text Lalo to let him know what was up. Lalo picked up his things the next day, and that was that. Eleven months after letting him move in, I was free again.

And so was he. Because up to that point Lalo would rather let me stifle his true self—the irresponsible, semi-employed, party boy he really was—than live without me. He loved me that much. He'd made himself miserable to be with me. My horoscope said it was time for me to "do my own life." To either perpetuate my childhood—keep recreating the unreliable relationship I'd had with my father—or kick it right out from under me, which in breaking up with Lalo I finally had. Lalo's horoscope said it was time for him to "control his own time" and attain greater freedom. I knew he'd miss me terribly but would land on his feet.

All the ladies loved my Lalo. He'd slept with more strippers—for free—than any man I knew. He'd had affairs with wealthy Westlake housewives, after their husbands went to work and they'd approached him while landscaping their yards, all shirtless and sweaty. Baby girls were captivated by him, while toddlers and young girls tended to follow him around at parks, restaurants, and grocery stores. Grown women did it too. Strippers followed him into parking lots, runners on the trail waved at him daily. One day, while he was walking alone down South Lamar Boulevard, two separate women pulled over to offer him a ride. All the thirty-something single women at my apartment complex giggled and blushed every time he smiled or said good morning. I knew he was heartbroken over losing me, but also that he would be just fine.

He started hanging out with Ted on a regular basis, I suspected to keep an eye on me and anyone I might bring home. There was no one else in my life yet, since I was still too busy with my two jobs and writing pursuits to find time for dating. I emailed Joe a few days after the breakup and said that I'd love to see him if he were up for a visit. He wrote back and was incredibly supportive. He said he sincerely thought I had done the right thing, that I'd been trying to make it work because I loved Lalo, but it simply wasn't working. He said the Eagles were going on tour and rehearsals started in a week. He'd planned on being in Austin for a solo gig but due to the Eagles tour (a short notice decision), he now had to be in Europe.

Besides, he said. "Guess what—I'm in a relationship…trying to make it work. You and I have the worst timing, don't we? But you can email me whenever you're having breakup blues."

I was more upset about Joe being in a new relationship than I was about me being out of one. I told him to let me know if they broke up. Also, if they got engaged so I wouldn't have to hear it on the radio. I asked Lalo to stop hanging around the apartment complex and pool, but he ignored my request. He liked being close to me and wanted me back, but I made it clear that was never going to happen. When he offered to help me with rent anyway, asking nothing in return, I softened. At first I told him no, that it wouldn't be right to take his money when he wasn't living there, but I soon changed my mind, simply because I needed the extra cash to get through the month. In exchange, I let him keep my spare cell phone—temporarily, I said. "As long as you're working I want you to have it."

That minor act of generosity would come back to bite me in the ass.

❧

THREE DAYS AFTER THE BREAKUP, Lalo disappeared for an entire weekend. We'd never gone that long without talking, and, despite being broken up, I was concerned for his well-being. Lalo was prone to suicidal thoughts, even during good times. When his ex-wife called me from his phone I didn't know what to think. I didn't call her back but couldn't help wondering why he'd given her his (my) cell phone, and if he hadn't, how did she end up with it?

The full story was packed with the exact kind of drama I'd come to expect from Lalo's ex. I got the details from Lalo upon his release from jail, where he'd spent the weekend.

Lalo had gone to her house to spend time with his daughter. Couch surfing as he was, he couldn't have Rita over, so his ex's house was the only place he could see her. His ex-wife, though, had refused to leave and spent the entire afternoon haranguing him about me. Apparently things escalated to yelling, and then she lashed out at him physically. I had nothing but Lalo's word to base this story's authenticity on, but I knew about his ex's violent history and so I tended to believe it was true.

Lalo said he knew better than to stick around when she got like that, so he took off, jumping in his truck with the ex-wife on his tail. Before he could peel out she'd reached into his truck and swiped my phone from it. Lalo said he drove off rather than fight her for it. Unfortunately, she called 911 claiming domestic abuse—saying that Lalo had hit her. The cops found Lalo, pulled him over, and arrested him on the spot. I didn't know if drinking was involved but it was certainly possible. I didn't ask because frankly Lalo's problems weren't my problems anymore.

I wanted to feel bad for Lalo—three days in jail sounded like a nightmare—but I also thought only an idiot would allow himself to be around her at all. Once I found out she still had my phone I called the police to report the theft and gave them her name and address. They retrieved my phone and asked me to come down to the station to pick it up. When I did, they told me that Lalo's ex had gone through all our text messages and was intending to use one of them to fight Lalo's custody arrangement.

Apparently, Lalo had not deleted a single text from me ever, so the ex-wife had our yearlong history of private exchanges in her possession. One in particular she planned to use as evidence that Lalo was back on cocaine. The text in question was a one-month-old joke between him and me. I'd texted him from the dressing room one day to say I'd picked up a scratch-off on the way to work and won ten dollars. "We're rich!" I'd said. "What should we spend it on?"

"Let's buy a bump," Lalo joked.

"Lol, right," I replied.

Sitting with the detective who'd retrieved my phone, my jaw hit the floor upon hearing this, right before a hard eye roll.

"Maybe you should go ask one of your buddies in the vice department if there's such a thing as 'buying a bump,'" I said. "Because there absolutely isn't."

"Tell me more," he said, interested.

"A bump is such a small quantity of blow, no one would ever bother to *sell* it! A bump is something you bum off a friend or a friend offers you as a gift. And what's more, Lalo's ex-wife is fully aware of this. That text exchange was us joking around at the absurdity of buying drugs in the first place. For starters, Detective, I've been in a program of recovery for ten years. And if Lalo was going to do a bump, not only would he not tell me about it, but he'd also probably buy a quarter ounce, not a measly fingernail full."

The detective thanked me for my time and gave me back my phone. He promised to not to pursue any charges or an investigation into Lalo's supposed drug use.

Surprisingly, I barely missed Lalo when it was over. My entire life, I'd never really felt complete as a person unless I was in a relationship or dating one special guy. I was hardly alone in that sentiment. Most people partner up specifically to feel more whole and complete, because the partners we're attracted to tend to embody qualities that we ourselves are missing. We do the same for them; that's what attraction and chemistry are about. Ideally, we date a lot when we're young, then use those partner connections to bring out all our various sides and "shadow selves" so that we can integrate them into our personalities. Then, by the time we settle on a life partner, we're much closer to "whole" than we once were. The problem is that instead of using our partners to inspire us to develop our missing qualities within ourselves, we get lazy and come to depend on *their* presence to integrate those traits into our lives on a daily basis.

Lalo brought a sense of childlike wonderment into my life. He was someone who prioritized fun and friendship—something I hadn't done my entire sobriety, to my detriment. Similarly, his attraction to me was surely (though perhaps subconsciously) a need to embrace more structure and discipline in his life—traits I embodied strongly, as did his (crazy or not) tech supervisor ex-wife. Lalo felt lost without that kind of stability in his life (whether he'd admit to that or not), otherwise, he never would have been attracted to women like us. I had to admit, I felt just as imbalanced without his joyous energy in mine. But I was smart enough to know I could bring joyous energy into my life on my own. Whether I *would* remained to be seen.

What I did know was that I'd become a far more authentic person in the year I'd been with Lalo. Someone who stood up for herself and her deepest needs, who believed in her value as a person and partner. Someone who'd given up people pleasing in relationships, who no longer tolerated poor treatment or overly controlling behavior. Someone who prioritized her vision for her own best future and who planned to nurture and protect those ambitions with healthy, appropriate boundaries.

Salome, Hemingway, Nature's Way

February 10, 2008

Current Location: my way
Current Mood: contemplative

Dostoyevsky said, "Hell is the suffering that comes from being unable to love." I believe this to be true. I know that Lalo's love healed me, and that by enabling me to love again he rescued me from a hellish fate.

Hemingway said, "When you love, you wish to do things for [them], to sacrifice, to serve." I think Lalo sacrificed a lot to be with me. I just don't think his idea of what needed to be done, and my idea, were anywhere near each other.

Harville Hendrix, PhD, in *Getting the Love You Want*, states, "…you must *be* [not just choose] the right partner. As you gain a more realistic view of love relationships, you realize that [it] requires commitment, discipline, and the courage to grow and change; [it] is hard work."

Most people say that trying to change your partner is wrong and futile, but I disagree. In fact, I think that's what relationships are all about! Good relationships turn both parties into better versions of themselves. Humans are not only fully capable of change, but changing in positive ways is our sole (soul) purpose.

It's only *human nature* that cannot be changed, and we should probably thank god for that.

What I know about human nature helps me understand my customers and clients. Understanding their motivations helps me intuit what they want and need from me. And not just me but all of us—dancers and erotic entertainers worldwide. There has always been a place for us, a deep-seated and positively motivated need for women like me…since the beginning of time and throughout history.

In that way, at least, customers will never change, and I *thank god for that*. Lalo saved me from the hell of crippling loneliness and my customers will save me from the hell of once again flying solo.

Part 3
CUSTOMERS & CLIENTS

(ambitions & boundaries)

Kick & Charge

December 12, 2007

Current Location: Final Spinal
Current Mood: determined

I've been thinking a lot about the yoga room as the microcosm of the macrocosm of life.

On days I lack strength in some personal situation—say, agreeing to pay more than my share of rent and bills *again* or tolerating beer drinking instead of job hunting—I'll find my poses harder than usual to execute and maintain. My standing leg will shake in balancing stick, or I'll completely lose my balance in standing head to knee.

Likewise, on days I'm being inflexible—impatient with loved ones or stubborn about something stupid—invariably my flexibility in class will be lacking. Suddenly camel pose won't be a simple backbend like I've been doing since I was six, but instead will feel like I'm Jennifer Jason-Leigh suspended between two semis in *The Hitcher*. And standing head to knee with stretching pose will be like a hot poker jabbing into my hamstrings.

Days when I make decisions based on self-respect and healthy detachment, I'll go to class and perform like Wonder Woman. But even on my best days, one thing I always struggle with is stamina. It's partly a lack of core strength and partly about balance, I think. In standing bow pulling pose, most students fall out before the sixty seconds is up, me included. I can, however, usually stay in for forty-five seconds, kicking well over my head. In fact, the kicking is the easiest part for me, *and therein lies the problem.*

The key is to kick and charge equally. Now, I can kick high, hard, and in any direction I need to, including straight up—always could. It's the charging forward I'm not good at. It doesn't come naturally. I must remind myself to do it, even while my back leg is kicking over my head.

If you're going to be out of balance, it is better to overdo the charging versus kicking. My instructors all say that if you fall out of the pose you should fall forward, proof you were charging harder than kicking. It makes sense that in yoga, as in life, if I'm kicking all the troublesome shit to the curb but not charging forward toward bigger, better things, I'm still standing in the gutter, am I not?

CHAPTER 11

November 2007–February 2008

SIMULTANEOUS TO THE MONTHSLONG back and forth breakup with Lalo, a lot else had been going on in my work and writing life. I signed up for the Writers' League Agents and Editors Conference in hopes of scoring an agent there. I'd made progress on both books I was writing and multiple short stories I'd been working on for months or even years. Feedback on Zoetrope.com had been so encouraging that I'd submitted a new short story to multiple literary magazines. One wrote back praising my writing but requesting a more powerful ending. I sent them a different one instead, about the first time I'd ever exchanged sexual services for cash, which they promptly accepted for publication—my second short story credit! The success so buoyed my self-esteem I started querying literary agents about my stripper blog as a potential book. It never came to anything, but whatever. One of my book ideas would take off someday; I was sure of it now.

Work at Exposé continued to be hit or miss. Overall, I was earning sixty percent of last year's average, and the money was gobbled up by bills the second I got home. December was exceptionally slow, but by January I acquired enough regulars that, one day, five of them walked into the club at once. In February, between real estate and stripping, I worked twenty-seven days of the month, just like the previous year. Some days I met nothing but assholes and perverts at the club. Other days mostly kind, generous customers. Some days my fellow strippers were delightful and encouraging. Other days sloppy, rude, and disparaging.

One night, an unstable—and probably high as fuck—dancer climbed a radio tower behind the club, then hung upside down by her knees for fun. When twelve emergency vehicles showed up—ambulances and cops, all flashing their lights—business understandably came to a dead stop. The neighboring restaurant had to close for the night costing them four thousand dollars in lost revenue. I probably lost out on two or three hundred myself. The girl was blackballed from every strip club in town and cursed by every stripper at Exposé who'd been screwed out of her rightful earnings that night.

One week earlier, a fellow dancer broke into my locker and stole my new cell phone—a six-hundred-dollar expense. Thankfully she'd dropped it on the dressing room floor before making off with nothing but my clothes. Everyone knew who'd done it but since my manager couldn't prove it he couldn't fire her. Sensing my frustration, he begged me not to quit. He even let me skip paying his tip out that night, so I promised him I wouldn't. Afterward, the thief took every chance she got to kiss my ass and suck up to me, which was almost as annoying as the robbery.

One day at work, I was bombarded with compliments from customers, such as "You are, by far, the best one in here" to "Oh my god, you're amazing!" and "You move like no other dancer I've ever seen, with unparalleled grace and sensuality!" One of our best dancers told me how much she loved to watch me on stage every day, marveling at how I could dance to any style of music "and always be so sexy and graceful." Six weeks later, the subject of my age came up in a dressing room conversation with three other dancers. One of the young girls offered sweetly that forty wasn't "that old." Another chubbier girl with two of the worst (round, hard) implants I'd ever seen, scoffed, "Well if forty isn't old than what the hell is?!" I ignored her and took the stage, only to be approached by a handsome twenty-eight-year-old customer who tipped generously and told me I was the "hottest one in here. These younger girls got nothing on a cougar like you."

I questioned my value in regard to romantic relationships every day, but my confidence as a stripper was unshakable. The pervs and assholes only got to me because I knew I deserved better than to deal with them. One day I'd do twenty-five dances for one customer, raking in an easy five-hundred-bucks. The next I'd sit with three addicts in a row, or some pedophile rambling on about his love of kiddie porn and how he'd once fucked his fifteen-year-old sister. Working at Exposé was an adventure, and I rolled with the punches because, while it was hardly the upscale level I'd grown used to in Vegas, there were plenty of worse clubs I could've ended up at in Austin.

The real test came at the end of February, when I made a hard-earned five hundred and fifty dollars one day—a typical sum twelve months ago—by doing "extras" (any activity beyond the local sexually oriented business ordinance) for all my customers, and I mean every single one. It wasn't a good omen. The economy was tanking and despite what outsiders seemed to believe, strip clubs were not recession proof at all.

Some days I wondered if it was pure insanity to believe I'd ever have a life of lasting security, happiness, and ease. Other days I saw the universe conspiring to help me embrace abundance and attain my goals through one of the high paying job offers coming my way.

I'd toyed with the idea of moving into commercial real estate but eventually determined it would be a pointless lateral move in a field I was already sick of. My license was coming up for renewal and I intended to let it lapse for good. I thought I could supplement my stripping income with lap dance seminars, which had been suggested to me multiple times by customers, strippers, and friends who'd said they'd love to learn to do for their boyfriends and husbands what I did for my customers.

Even better, though, I'd had offers from customers to work in sales. One from a guy who invented some kind of racing boat technology. The other from a political consultant named Kenneth "Buddy" Barfield, who was working a deal to bring a new private airport to Austin. He needed someone to sell plane stalls for him. He said I'd meet a lot of celebrities and movie people and earn up to two hundred thousand dollars a year.

One night, one of the owners of Exposé asked me to dance for a friend of his. Afterward, chatting about relationships and marriage, he seemed surprised to hear I had a low opinion of the latter. "That's too bad," the owner said. "Because you're a catch, and from where I'm sitting it seems high time you find a great guy to take care of you for the rest of your life." Months later it hit me: he'd been trying to fix me up with the friend of his I'd danced for.

It wasn't that I was opposed to being taken care of. It's that I understood the tradeoff. Men who supported their partners expected to be taken care of in return. No one knew better than sex workers how needy men in their fifties and sixties could be. And unless I was in love, taking care of a man's wants and needs sounded an awful lot like a full-time job. One I couldn't walk away from if it proved to be suffocating. When things had fully spiraled south with Lalo, I'd been able to kick him out and change the locks because it was my name on the lease. If I lived with a man who controlled all the money, what was to stop him from doing with *me* as he pleased?

...& one bonehead

March 15, 2008

Current Location: doughy
Current Mood: crushed

Monday night at Exposé, a customer I'll call Mr. Grouch sauntered in like he does most nights around five. He grumbled about how much his workday sucked, then asked me if I was happy to see him in that rhetorical way he does most nights around 5:01 p.m.

He always says stuff like how he's the only customer who really "gets" me, because apparently no other customers could ever possibly "get" me like he does. I told him *yes baby, you're my favorite 'cause you really get me, plus you really turn me on, and I don't have to fake it with you like I do with everyone else.* I told him all this shit just like I do most nights around 5:03 p.m.

The thing is this—though I rarely slip into that typical stripper bullshit—I happen to know that this is the exact fantasy Mr. Grouch comes in for. Because Mr. Grouch (unlike some other customers who live in complete denial about their dis-likability) is fully conscious of the fact that he needs to pay someone to be nice to him.

Then Mr. Grouch gets three dances in a row, grinding hard and pushing my hips down firmly on his rolling pin-sized boner (painful yet impressive, I admit) so that forty-eight hours later I'm still sore around my bikini line. Also, a tad fearful that one day I'll be in the dressing room changing to go home and pull down my thong only to see my two, soft special doughy places flattened like pie crusts and hanging to my knees from rolling-pin-man maneuvers.

Really, there is no amount of cash for which I will oblige that. Just none. I guess what I'm saying is, if you really want to you can steamroll my honesty for the right amount of money, but please do not ever rolling pin my coochie.

CHAPTER 12

March & April 2008

My horoscope recommended forgiveness. To "find redemption in an influence that has broken your heart." When Lalo suggested we be friends with benefits, I hesitated momentarily then jumped in with both feet. Two weeks after we'd broken up my Juicy Days started, so turning down reliably great sex simply didn't compute right then. I'd also just worked twenty-nine of the last thirty-three days and needed to cut loose—which we did, having the kind of hot, frenzied, primal sex that left us disheveled and dazed and looking like a *Life* magazine photo after a Midwest tornado strike. Two weeks later, he broached the idea of being *monogamous* friends with benefits and I immediately bailed on the entire thing. I had no use for monogamy, especially with him. How would that be different from the dead-end relationship I'd just extricated myself from? Besides, monogamy made no sense to me. I looked back on my marriage plans with Lalo as pure folly. I was forty years old. I'd been having sex for twenty-five years and, God willing, would have it for at least twenty-five more. The idea of sex with the same man for twenty-five years was somewhere between hilarious and horrifying to me. Yeah, no. Not happening.

But we managed to remain friends. Not that I had much choice seeing as he texted me all the time. (Of course, I had a choice; I just didn't see it clearly at the time.) It wasn't easy because he was still really struggling—doing odd jobs to pay for the crappy studio unit he'd finally secured and trying to see his daughter while hitting blockade after blockade from her mother. One time, he called to ask me to speak up for him in court to help secure a better custody agreement. Instead of simply declining, I snapped at him for presuming I had one hour of free time, much less an entire afternoon.

I started pulling away from the friendship as well. But I didn't see how to do that either, so days later when he texted to tell me about a new woman he was seeing, a photographer he called the "coolest, kindest chick ever," I blew a gasket. I emailed him a page-long screed, calling him selfish and self-centered for rubbing my nose in his ability to replace me so quickly. For making note of her artistic success, knowing how hard I struggled to get noticed for my writing. For implying I wasn't as cool or kind as I could be. And mostly for doing nothing more than sharing some happy news and treating me like the friend I'd agreed to be in the first place. Part of me wanted to be happy for him. A bigger part hated his guts right then.

It was that strength versus flexibility thing again. At work I juggled the perfect balance of give and take. In my personal life I either bent over backwards or lashed out and changed the locks in the blink of an eye. When I first broke up with Lalo, I'd had flying dreams, sailing on the winds of freedom. Soon afterward, I started having sex dreams and orgasming in my sleep. I missed physical intimacy terribly but didn't trust myself to fall for a new guy. I was hesitant to even go on dates yet, not quite grasping how to date in a way that honored my needs and boundaries. After experiencing the joyous early months of falling in love with Lalo, I wasn't terribly interested in dating emotionally unavailable or married men again. (Dr. Tina had helped me see that it wasn't a healthy habit, and not because I owed anything to their wives, but because I deserved more from a partnership than someone who couldn't truly fit me into his life.) Nor was I interested in another committed relationship when I had other all-consuming passions rolling around in my head. If there was one thing my failed relationship with Lalo had taught me, it was that I was long overdue to quit seeking a man to fill a void in my life and to instead take ownership of it myself. To focus on achieving my biggest dreams and highest goals for financial security and writing success. I simply wasn't capable of doing both at the same time.

As for attention, validation, and connection, it was easier to get that stuff at work. In a safe, controlled environment where I called the shots, and my "partners" desired me so strongly that they happily turned the reins over to me. Over and over and over.

❧

THAT SAID, A SUPER-HOT GUY had been flirting with me. I'd met him downtown one night and saw him around on occasion. Recently we'd exchanged email addresses and he'd been sending flirty emails, asking me out regularly. Like Lalo, he was a year or two younger than me and ripped. I'd also never seen him without a cigarette and beer in hand because hot guy was also party guy, and I needed another party guy in my bed like a hole in the head. But I'd hardly had sex in eight weeks and my resolve was wearing thin.

I finally agreed to go out with him. I shot a decent game of pool in a cute sundress and high heels, and though I missed a lot of combo shots and scratched on the eight ball, I looked damn good doing it. We took a two-minute ride on his '77 Kawasaki, then made out in my bedroom for the same amount of time before I called it. He was sweet, funny, respectful, sexually skilled, and surfer chill. But in the end, after the intense emotional and sexual intimacy I'd shared with Lalo, casual sex suddenly seemed boring as hell.

We lay in silence on our backs on my bed, staring at the ceiling while I absently massaged my breasts. He glanced over at me.

"Are you giving yourself a breast exam?" he asked, bemused.

I laughed. "Yeah, I guess I am."

That's when he realized I wasn't into him. We made small talk for another thirty seconds and then I walked him outside. He climbed on the bike, lit a cigarette, offered up his cheek insistently for a kiss goodbye, and then rode off.

The attention had been nice, and it was fun to shoot pool again, but I had no idea when I'd go on another date. I figured I'd leave it up to fate, who was hopefully better at complicated combo shots than I was.

❧

SEAN THE PSYCHIC had said that if I'd just go out a little I'd have great dates right away and be in a solid relationship within a year, but in recalling all my dating mistakes pre-Lalo I feared going through that learning curve all over again. My horoscope said to seek out erotic experiences at three times the norm. It did not say why, and who the hell had time for that sort of thing anyway? My relationship with the ever-playful Lalo had taught me I desperately needed to incorporate more fun and connection in my life. But I had no desire to go out. I skipped a big UFC fight at Exposé because it made me miss watching UFC with Lalo. I walked to the Reggae Festival at Auditorium Shores, then turned around and walked home, feeling like an outsider among all the happy hippies and relaxed stoners there. I'd been invited to multiple parties, none of which I attended because I was a clean and sober introvert who disliked socializing with people who were drinking. I'd thrown great parties in my late teens that had all ended with a bunch of strippers and their partners playing drunken topless chicken in the pool. Fun stuff. But I was younger then. I didn't have the weight of the world and my extremely precarious future on my shoulders then.

What I did love to do was go dancing to live bands, which felt like the opposite of socializing in that it energized me. I could ingest the energy of great live bands and regurgitate it through my body, giving it back to them in a cycle of energy that, night after night, had once sustained me. In the months before meeting Lalo, my dancing and sexual adventures had severely dwindled, but the excitement of our new love and incredible sex had temporarily filled the void. Passion had always sustained me. It was my happy place, where I felt the most grounded *and* in touch with the divine. It facilitated spiritual growth and emotional healing, and I still needed it in my life.

The smart move would've been to take partnered dance classes—something I'd always wanted to do—to learn salsa, two-step, and swing. To meet new people and especially new men. To be led by a strong partner around a dance floor week after week. But at the end of the day, I was exhausted from dancing and socializing for eight hours at the club or showing property to clients who never bought anything.

I missed my regular Bob Schneider shows and those of my other (semi-local) favorite, Ian Moore. Ian typically played a dozen shows a year in Austin, Bob probably ten times that (and more, including his occasional shows with The Scabs). For five straight years, I'd caught most of Bob's shows, and all of Ian's, in Austin, Dallas, and Houston. Bob and Ian's music put me back in touch with the part of me I liked most—the expressive, feeling, passionate part—while temporarily relieving me of the identity of an overworked, underappreciated laborer. Their music made me feel ageless and weightless and as far from a Realtor as could be. It was my vacation and my therapy. One of the few things I thought made life worth living. Their music put me in touch with all the sorrow, grief, remorse, rage, and yearning I'd suppressed over a lifetime. It brought up all that shit that I could then dance out of my body, pounding and shaking out my traumas somatically on a cold, hard dance floor, purging my body and psyche of the pain and turmoil I'd held onto for too long. Their music was the most cathartic thing I'd ever experienced.

I tried to explain it to Bob once. We'd bumped into each other in the parking garage across from Antone's, like we did almost every week. He'd just returned from a long tour, and I was so happy to see him play every Tuesday and most Fridays in Austin again that I decided to tell him how much his music meant to me. I told him that I'd originally discovered him in early sobriety, after a long, dark, painful period in my life. That things had been so difficult, and I'd been isolated for so long, that his music had literally saved me. Because back then, no matter how bad things got during the week, all I had to do was remind myself that on Tuesday I would get to dance my ass off to him at Antone's, and that for those two hours, at least, everything would be okay. He seemed genuinely moved by that and told me it meant a lot to him that I'd shared it. Two weeks later, I was pulling out of the same parking space, about to drive off, when he pulled up and motioned me out of the car to give me a few homemade CDs he'd been working on in his studio.

Bob's music could be as fiery and funky or as raunchy and hilarious as anything I'd ever heard. It could also be deliciously dark and twisted. The first time I saw him play with The Scabs I thought, *This is my tribe, the one I must have been kidnapped from as a child.* I knew of no other band like it and I thanked God I lived in Austin where I could experience his music live almost any time I wanted. I'd made a promise to myself in 2002 that I would never allow real estate to keep me from either an Ian Moore or Bob Schneider show. And while I was only a part time real estate slave these days, I was also slaving away at my writing and working hard at the club three days a week. And so, I was craving Bob and Ian again. And not just their music. I missed Bob's devilish laughter, Ian's long hugs, and their band members' endless flirtations and creative inspiration.

Austin's unparalleled live music scene was like a living, breathing, almost omnipotent thing. A thriving, vibrating mashup of both musical and sexual intensity. It was the exact hotbed of creativity and connection I'd needed in early sobriety. Because of that, I even missed some of the fucked-up flirtations and interactions I'd had with men from the scene that had felt more like embarrassing face-plants than genuine intimate connections. But still, they were attempts to connect that I eventually felt proud of, if only for the courage it took to put myself out there in the dating world at all in early sobriety.

The music scene had been my second home from 2002 to mid-2006. In that time, every two years my guitarist friend Jeb would give me a surprise kiss, then—while my romantic expectations revved up on overdrive—avoid me for days afterward, as if he'd sobered up and thought better of it. My drummer friend Chad and I spent months emailing sexy scenarios to each other, followed by an endless indecisiveness on my end that made him finally give up pursuing what could have been a spectacular connection. I crushed on my young singer-songwriter friend Luther for a year, then hesitated too long the one time he opened the door for something to happen, losing my chance at yet another intimate connection. I struck up a flirty email exchange with visiting poet Nick Flynn, then got too aggressive too fast, scaring him away in an instant. I looked back and cringed over those miscalculations for years, until finally realizing that, for me, it was one, big, important lesson. That it was almost always better to take a shot and misfire than to never take a shot at all.

I'd once flirted endlessly with my dear friend Bruce. Five straight years of a flirty friendship that had yet to go beyond suggestive comments and sexy looks. Soon after meeting him, it hit me that he was everything I wasn't and desperately wanted to be—the epitome of cool, for starters. Intense in a good way yet utterly breezy about it. Not just talented but exceptionally skilled. And despite his many bandmates and high-level collaborators, Bruce was just as incredible as a soloist. Justifiably confident he was also courageous enough to be vulnerable, trying out new material weekly at an eastside coffeeshop, back when I could barely put pen to paper *in secret* for the roiling fear of failure that consumed me. Bruce was my muse and inspiration. Watching him navigate a music career taught me how to be creative—to *become* a creative. And he had swagger. I'd never seen a more delicious and authentic swagger than that man casually crossing Antone's concrete floor… not on the big screen, not on TV, not in James motherfucking Dean. Maybe that's why I couldn't consummate our chemistry; I was far too intimidated to be vulnerable with him emotionally or authentic with him sexually.

Other flirtations from that time panned out only marginally better. My sexy neighbor Glenn and I danced around each other for a few weeks before finally having sex, but at the time I was so depressed and he was such a seemingly normal—together, stable— guy I couldn't overcome the incompatibility in my mind and the connection quickly faded away. My newly sober, promoter friend Chevy reminded me so much of myself in early sobriety—lost, struggling, vulnerable—that it brought out my nurturing instinct, which of course expressed itself sexually. Unfortunately, our chemistry was off and over the years we finally quit trying to make it work (but not before he gave me one of my favorite compliments ever when he said, *I love how elegantly dirty you are*). I also finally hooked up with Mason Ruffner, the sexy guitarist who'd been the opening act on Ringo's first All Starr Band tour, back when I was Joe Walsh's girlfriend and secretly crushing on him. I never made myself available for a second date because being with him reminded me too much of Joe, and how I still, to my chagrin, missed Joe almost every day. None of those connections ever came to anything, but they did provide the training ground for every future successful connection I eventually made. They helped me overcome the debilitating self-consciousness of early sobriety and helped me develop the courage I needed to embrace the inevitable ups and downs of dating.

Above all I missed the genuinely successful romantic adventures I'd experienced. The year before meeting Lalo I'd had a short fling with Okkervil River's Patrick Pestorius—two months' worth of pure, sweet tumbles in the hay, before our tryst ran its course. Before him I'd been in a brief relationship with The Lucky Strikes singer and guitarist, Craig Marshall, who'd treated me like a princess for three months, at which point, fearing we were too different to ever really get each other, I'd—rather presumptively and carelessly—broken up with him. Craig was the only man I ever opened up to about the stressors in my life who didn't tell me to relax more. Instead, he told me that I shouldn't have to work as hard as I did. He validated my frustrations and left it at that. He was the most thoughtful partner I may have ever had and great fun in bed. But we weren't in love, and I was only thirty-eight at the time. And with no desire to have children, perhaps even then I knew deep in my heart that there was no need to commit to one man full-time. That monogamy wasn't my path in this life…not at that young age, anyway. Not with so much left to explore, so many men left to meet, and so much life—including a sex life—to live. (I'd gotten a little off track with Lalo soon afterward, swept up in the love and dopamine rush. Had I kept *him* at arm's distance, we surely would've had a far easier and longer lasting romance.)

Ultimately, to me, flirting, and the sex it sometimes led to, was the most fun way to get to know someone (the sexier ones, anyway). Limiting myself to one person to have sex with would be like limiting myself to one person to socialize with. It simply made no sense.

❧

I COULD TELL most of what I needed to know about a man by the way he had sex. Just like a person's yoga practice, a man's sexual style was the microcosm of the macrocosm of his approach to life. Take Charles, for instance. As my lover for three years, Charles had always been completely immersed in the moment, utterly present, bizarrely talented, and far more skilled than he gave himself credit for. Often the smartest person in the room, he could be arrogant and insecure in equal measure. But sex and music got him out of his head and in those moments he was a god like no other. My favorite memory of him was sneaking into a neighborhood pool off Oltorf Street, right next to the train tracks. We'd gone skinny-dipping in the middle of the night, and Charles went down on me as I gripped the edge of the pool behind my head, floating face up in the water. Just as I started to come the train roared by blowing its whistle, deafening us both and drowning out my cries as I orgasmed. I think the man was part amphibian.

As successful as Larry was, he was a lost boy at heart, sensitive and in need of validation. He didn't trust his instincts or trust that they would be appreciated by his partner, so he could be hesitant about sex, even evasive. He needed to be embraced and accepted, and until then would fly under the radar, getting what he needed—in sex and in life—by being subversive.

Rob suppressed his passion. Technically speaking, he could do no wrong in bed—and it would seem life—but he never felt safe unleashing the full force of his will on me, which would've been welcomed and reciprocated gladly. I think he deferred to other people a lot, especially the women in his life. I don't know if he didn't trust his own strength or simply had a healthy fear of it. All I know is that if he'd led more with his heart than his head he probably would've gotten more of what he wanted.

Christian was scared to engage fully. He forever danced around the perimeters in a way that felt safe to him and didn't require full exposure, since full exposure would trigger his fear of failure and perhaps also fear of success.

Paul had been through hell and back in life but was sober for many years by the time I met him. He took the reins in bed, taking into consideration his partner's needs and concerns, but ultimately moving forward as if he knew best. He followed the important rules, but plenty of others he wrote himself. He liked to push the edges. He adapted as needed, turned on a dime, and kept right on going. That's how he stayed a success in the music business, during its changes from plentiful session work to the digital age. While other session musicians lost most of their business, Paul forged successfully ahead.

Zed was as playful and in touch with his inner caveman as anyone I'd met. Unrestrained and making his way based on how he felt in the moment. He was the epitome, to me, of how sex should be had, and maybe how life should be lived. It was just unfortunate for him that despite being happily married he wasn't satisfied sexually, since his wife wasn't much of an adventurer. Rules applied to her in ways they didn't to him, in life and in bed, so he found a way to get his needs met without hurting her. Until one day he reached a place where he was finally ready to commit. That said, even after he got sober and ended our affair, I ran into Zed more than once at strip clubs around town, so how satisfying his marriage really was to him is anybody's guess.

I HEARD A FAMOUS divorce lawyer say once that people should start asking themselves what exact problem marriage was meant to solve. Just like me, he questioned what possible romantic or spiritual purpose marriage really served to most couples. I understood loneliness and the desire to secure a permanent partner to stave it off forever, or as long as possible before one person demanded their freedom again by filing for divorce. I just didn't see the point of marriage unless a couple planned on having kids. Marriage for couples with children was just as much of a trap, if one with a temporary justification. But even then the "till death do us part" thing seemed excessive at best, deleterious, and a step much too far. I knew countless couples who'd broken up and just as many who'd gotten divorced, and it was definitely the latter who were the bitterest I ever met. Marriage for childless couples especially was nothing more than a way to make it as complicated and painful as possible for a person to leave, no matter how miserable and stagnant the partnership had become.

Before meeting Lalo, I craved the intimacy of a committed relationship, the kind that could evolve and deepen over time until our two souls were fully bonded in like-minded partnership. But now that I'd had it I felt satisfied to a degree, like, *okay I know what that's like now*. It was nice having the security of one guy in my life every day for a while. It healed the broken part of me from when my father and Joe abandoned me. But I wasn't broken anymore. I found the necessary strength within myself and didn't need commitment or fidelity to make me feel whole and safe. I didn't need one man to be everything to me and I didn't need the pressure of having to fulfill all of that one man's needs. The disappointment that led to was untenable. I shuddered to think of how close I'd come to marrying Lalo, and how exhausting the process of divorcing him would've been. No thank you.

Besides, I missed the days of dating multiple men. Every man I'd ever partnered with brought out a different side of me than the guy before him. With Larry, I felt grounded and self-assured compared to his adorable neurosis. With Paul, I was a rock and roll chick again, but unlike with Joe I had my shit together, making Paul and I rock and roll peers in recovery. With Zed, I felt more playful, young, and carefree than I'd ever felt with anyone, including as a kid! With Charles, I was in mutual awe. He was in awe of me sexually and socially and I was in awe of him creatively. These men, just by their presence in my life, reminded me who I was in a more complete sense than I'd been able to cobble together without them. Little by little, one at a time, they'd started making me whole again so I could move forward in the world and in my life without them.

But oh, how I missed male sexual energy. And the way it brought out my feminine sexual energy. I wasn't surrounded by dozens of hot, sexy musicians anymore. Whether it was because I was truly too tired to go out and socialize most evenings, or I'd lost faith in the entire process—or lost faith in my ability to thrive in that process—I simply couldn't bring myself to do it. During the day, I was surrounded by needy, horny, married strip club customers. I gave them every bit of energy and attention I had. I understood their loneliness, too, the loneliness of someone who felt trapped. My work was draining and fulfilling in equal measure. But as tiring as it could be, it was still easier than potentially striking up something personal that was real and deep and long-lasting—something to help me continue healing, growing, and evolving the way my past relationships had—only to end up feeling used and disappointed in the end. I didn't feel strong enough to go through that again. So, I shortchanged myself by not even trying.

Don't Fear the Reaper

April 4, 2008

Current Location: 1972
Current Mood: listless

"It's cold in here," he says, sinking into the wingback chair, his hoodie bunching and gathering around his neck. He smooths his salt-and-pepper mustache a few times then puts his hand down only for it to rise again automatically. He sees me watching and stops fidgeting.

I grab his arm for leverage and pull, rolling my chair closer to his, knocking armrests. "Here," I say, kicking one leg up to rest on his lap. "Have some body heat."

He traces two rough fingertips around my ankle, hesitating near the clear plastic shoe strap. I think he's shy, afraid to touch my leg any higher. "You must be cold too," he says, his accent more apparent now that he's using complete sentences. When I first came over, he'd responded with one-word answers—"no" (he wasn't waiting for anyone), "sí" (I may sit down), "no" (he'd never been here before), and "sí" (he'd like a lap dance).

"I have goose bumps," I point out. "See?"

They're all over my leg. It's a good leg—sinewy and strong. But he still doesn't touch it. His hand hovers over my calf, then disappears into the front pocket of his sweatshirt. He laughs like a little boy. He's nervous and it's cute. I can see his wheels turning as he searches for something to say. "What do you do for fun?" he asks.

"Well, I work a lot, so...not much, actually."

"Are you single?" he asks.

"Yes." I don't elaborate. I usually say more—that I was single for fifteen years, dating lots of men casually, and then I had a boyfriend whom I loved, but we broke up. I don't say any of that. It's two hours before my shift ends and I'm out of conversation. I silently wait for the song to end so I can dance the next one for him.

He sits up and twists to face me. We're practically side by side and he wants to look directly into my eyes. "Are you lonely?" he asks.

"Yes," I say, surprised by his boldness. "I am."

He nods and settles back into his seat. We both stare ahead at nothing, listening to "(Don't Fear) the Reaper" by Blue Oyster Cult.

I angle my body toward him. I throw my other leg over his lap, crossing them at the ankles. "And you, are you single?"

He nods. Married once, for five years, he says. They had three kids, all boys. He's early fifties tops—almost old enough to be my father, but close enough in life experience so that we understand each other. He wears a gold crucifix around his neck. It's big and flat with little flourishes. I have a similar one tucked in the back of a jewelry box. Mine is silver, but otherwise like his. Old-school style; more cross than Christ. It seems strange that a Mexican Catholic of his generation would be divorced. I wonder if he's a widower but decide not to ask.

The song is winding down, but I don't stand yet. I turn to him and give his arm a squeeze. I have to ask. "Are *you* lonely?"

He holds my gaze and nods. "Yes," he says and turns away, still nodding. I'm nodding, too, though he doesn't see. We sit silently for a moment. I feel his hand on my leg. The song has ended, and another begins.

I look at my customer and smile. "Ready?"

He smiles back. "Yes."

I kick my feet to the floor and drop my sweater on the chair. Goose bumps up and down my arms. This is the part I still love. Even cold, drained, and weary, I almost never tire of the dancing.

The fleece of his hoodie is soft on my belly. His neck is warm on my face.

CHAPTER 13

May & June 2008

ONE OF MY EXPOSÉ REGULARS was a local film producer named Fred. I'd given him a link to my stripper blog and the following week he told me that I had talent and should write a screenplay. Also, to jump on it soon because the second biggest contest in the country—an Austin-based screenplay competition—had an entry deadline six weeks away. I knew instantly I would do it. I'd write my first screenplay in the amount of time few professionals could manage and enter it into the Austin Film Festival competition. It took me two weeks to secure a cheap version of the necessary software, but once I had it I wrote the screenplay—*Speed Punk*, based on the novel turned memoir I'd been working on all year—in exactly four weeks.

It was good. Really good. And it had to be, because it was up against four thousand other scripts, many by experienced writers who'd worked for months or years on theirs. If I didn't make the top ten percent my entry would be meaningless. If I broke into the top ten percent, I'd get noticed and possibly an offer of representation by a Hollywood agent.

When I was done, I went back to revising my memoir and writing the stripping how-to book. I'd brought in one of my oldest stripper friends as a collaborator and we'd come up with the title *Secrets of Successful Strippers*. With a combined thirty-five years of experience, we were now contributing equally to the book, except that I was doing most of the actual writing. The extra labor cut into my work hours while she was able to work at her club all she wanted. It was frustrating and I was considering asking for a larger percent of any book advance we got down the road. We'd signed up for the Agents and Editors Conference in June, a networking event where I would pitch both my projects in the hopes of landing representation or a book deal.

In preparation, I signed up for a memoir pitching class given by a *New York Times* bestselling author. Suzy Spencer was a smart, warm, witty woman who kept her students engaged, writing and presenting pitches and giving feedback to each other. At one point she told me I could literally step in and teach the class because I really knew what I was talking about. Also, that my pitches were the best in the class and I had star quality. At the end of the day, the other twenty students agreed that I was the most likely to "make it." The day before, I'd received an email from my writer/producer friend Jack Hazzard, a man with far more artistic success than I'd had. He'd told me my writing was compelling and honest, with a high level of self-awareness.

All that encouragement boosted my confidence right when I needed it most. The closer the date of the conference got the more anxious I became. I needn't have worried. By the end of the weekend, I had one editor and three agents requesting samples of my work, including Michael Chabon's big shot agent, Mary Evans. She'd been impressed with my pitch and even brushed off the conference moderator who'd come in to tell me my time was up. "Leave us," Mary had said. She wanted to hear more about my book. Then, when I was done, she told me to send her the first fifty pages when they were as good as I could get them. "I won't read any submission twice," she said firmly. "So, only send me your best."

On top of needing to focus on polishing those fifty pages to a Michael Chabon level of "good," I had to learn how to write a book proposal for agent Abby Koons for the how-to strip book. Suzy, who happened to know Abby, told me that Abby definitely wanted to represent me but needed that book proposal first. My writing partner wasn't capable of that kind of assignment, which in the end took me two months to complete.

I was slowly learning to take more risks and be more present. To be vulnerable in a good way—by accepting the possibility of rejection while committing to act with empowerment. To stay out of the past or future, while harnessing all my inner strength for the task at hand.

Regulars and Newbies

May 4, 2008

Current Location: working my ass off
Current Mood: somewhere between content and *are you kidding me?!*

As much as I have on my plate lately, I'm super pleased with my success at the writer's conference. And while real estate is as big of a drag as ever, I'm still selling properties in a tough market (one which looks like it might become a full-blown housing crisis any day). Exposé income is becoming more of a challenge, too, but with an expensive apartment move, doctor and dental bills piling up, and annual Realtor fees due, I have no choice but to keep plugging away. Thankfully, after switching up my schedule recently to include Saturdays, I'm delighted to discover more middle-aged businessmen at the club on weekends than weekdays, which lately have been full of young wannabe gangsters spending more time staring at their cell phones than the nearly naked goddesses on stage.

My first customer yesterday was a regular who likes to buy me lunch, and while it's not wild caught, they do serve a damn tasty piece of salmon at Exposé—not to mention one less piece I'll pay six dollars for this weekend at Whole Foods. Anyway, Gil is a sweetheart who never fails to tell me he's "had a lot of lap dances in my life but never one as good as yours." He's the kind of customer who is a regular fixture at his favorite table, has a favorite waitress and tips her well, considers the crew at his local strip club to be his friends, and throws an annual party that many of the girls attend. I, too, consider him "safe," meaning he doesn't ask me out, knows his place, and appreciates the dancers' hard work—which is why we appreciate the hell out of him.

Then I sat with Bill, a stocky cancer survivor visiting from a small town, who'd dropped off his wife and daughter at the mall while he spent a couple hours with me. He was incredibly complimentary in that way I find exceptionally annoying, by which I mean rote and repetitive. So much that I eventually stopped saying "thank you" altogether when it became detracting from my performance. Still, I liked Bill, with his big heart and endless good intentions, sharing his recent experience with radiation, chemo, and his newfound lust for life (and the total lack of it for his wife of forty years). He had endless trivia on Napoleon's war tactics and unerring pride in his sixty-two-year-old boner (Bill's, not Napoleon's), which I found mildly interesting and hella cute respectively.

Then I sat with Clint, a thirty-four-year-old bartender/actor who always reminds me of skater punks from my youth, which is to say he has a shaved head and is cute, sexy, and slightly hyper. As usual he wanted to cuddle like a puppy until "just the right song" came on for the sole lap dance he can afford per visit. I didn't mind this time, because once I got him to stop kissing my neck and shoulder (too intimate for me, sweetie, sorry) and redirected his energy into a back and shoulder massage, I was in heaven. The kid is incredibly sensual, and at the same time as happy a person as I've ever met (which makes me wonder if he's on X every time I see him). His compliments, though sometimes also repetitive, are always genuine, and when I grind on him we sometimes get into this zone where I feel like we're dry humping in a dark corner at a high school dance or something.

Later I sat with Moe, a small-framed, late thirties, electrical engineer from Italy. Anyway, the poor man *just* found out that his wife (a stunner—I saw pics) lied to him about being previously married (twice before!), so we had a lively discussion about honesty, romance, and his utterly broken heart. Moe, (unlike Gil or Bill but exactly like Clint) did ask me out yet handled my rejection well. And though he came to Exposé solely to drown his sorrows, when I told him I only needed three more dances to meet my goal and go home, he bought one. I then accidentally kicked over his beer (because it was on the floor) right before he offered to let me *move in with him.* He then told me all about his mom, including how often she visits and how she worries about him being single at his age, and how much *she'd surely like me.* Such a sweet thing to say...and, incidentally, a major clue as to how he ended up married to a woman he knew precious little about.

My all-time favorite regular JJ came in yesterday, a handsome man with gorgeous eyes and a super fit body that meshes perfectly with mine, which is partly because he knows how to sit just right, as in not too slouched, nor too rigid. On that note, it's a little shocking how few men figure out how to adjust their posture once I start dancing.

It's like this. If I'm doing a body-slide and our crotches don't meet up, relax a little and push your hips forward an inch or two (*duh*). And if I'm straddling your lap with my legs thrown over the armrests and our crotches aren't meeting up, *sit the fuck up* a little. Honestly, I have to wonder how some guys manage to execute halfway decent sex in a bed if they can't even figure out how to properly align our bodies for a simple lap dance in a chair (but I digress).

Anyway, JJ is a favorite for a lot of reasons, but partly because he knows how to touch me when I'm dancing. His fingertips trace my skin everywhere like perfect unbroken feather strokes—my arms, neck, back, legs, etc. He's incredibly sensual and never pushy (which makes me want to be pushy with him), plus we have chemistry. Unfortunately, sometimes we also have humidity to deal with, which means by the third or fourth dance my skin starts to feel sticky. Because the club is too cheap to invest in a proper AC system—one that manages not just temperature but humidity too—it happens to all of us on muggy days and there's nothing to do but take quickie sponge baths in the dressing room sink. I must've had five today—one after every stage set (a daily must) plus two more to ensure smoother body-slides.

Another one of my favorite semi-regulars came in this weekend, but sadly the humidity ruined what should've been his usual string of lap dances in the VIP corner. I only did two, because by then we were both sticky, with Tommy's whole head flushed and damp, and my entire body covered in a thin, clammy film. But even though I only danced seven minutes I still ended up with a permanent wet spot in the crotch of my favorite lavender thong. Because not only is it ungodly humid in Austin, my Juicy Days are here in full force so it's also hella humid in my coochie and thong (heh).

Normally, this would be the best time to dance for Tommy, because the way our bodies matchup is a perfect crotch-to-crotch dry hump for however long he feels like workin' it. That's the best thing about him—he does the work and all I have to do is straddle, relax, and enjoy. Which is not something most customers should try (almost no one gets it right actually), while this guy has real talent for it. Style, stamina, and form to beat all—seriously I can only imagine how hot he is in bed. Alas, the humidity ruined it for both of us today (heavy sigh).

Still, I had a wet spot the entire shift, which I didn't bother to do anything about other than flash it from stage, doing the splits on my back ten times over the course of the day.

Another favorite regular is Red. I like Red for the same reason I like JJ. They're both cute, smart, super sweet, and most importantly, *know how to touch me*. Today, Red traced his fingertips all over my arms, back, legs, and neck, as I lap danced *and* the entire time I sat on his lap talking. The only time he doesn't do this is when his wife joins him at the club. They're swingers and as happily married a couple as I've met. When they come in together we get a whole party going at their table with three or more other dancers joining me there. Red and his wife are generous, fun, and intensely likable—so much so that I've taken to sitting with them whenever I run into them at Ian Moore shows around Austin.

Which brings me to my last customer today, Michael. No angel him, nor speck of charm in his devilishness. It all started with his jarring and just-plain-weird initial instruction (you read that right) to sit on his lap for the worst back rub of my life while simultaneously scratching his hairy legs from ankle to thigh (he actually demonstrated how I was supposed to do it) followed by an absurd attempt to dance for *me* to "get me in the mood" (wtf?) which became one horrifying moment after the next. At one point, without any warning, this six-foot-five hairy ass monster, crammed his knee between my legs, rubbed it into my crotch (again, wtf??), then *sat on my lap* reverse cowgirl-style and proceeded to *grind*. (I screamed, he stopped, enough said.) The absolute worst though, was a request early during my first lap dance, as I straddled *him* (the way God intended) gently grinding, when he said that I "should go ahead and cum" because he might "lose it in a minute too." Just...ugh.

Though I really do understand that some men are that stupid, what really pissed me off was his expectation that I hang out and chat for free once his two ten-dollar dances were over. Because no one is that stupid. Many men *are* that entitled though, and I was having none of it. I sent him straight to the ATM and then spent the rest of our time together making money and instructing *him* on how to behave in a strip club, which (shocker!) doesn't include lap dancing for your lap dancer *or instructing her on anything*.

CHAPTER 14

May & June 2008

Between the spiraling economy and onset of summer, business was scarily slow. Most days, I got to the club at eleven in the morning, dressed quickly, then spent up to an hour at the bar watching a *Las Vegas* rerun on TV. Our DJ would play some of the best songs of the seventies and eighties, from the Allman Brothers to Toto (oh shut up, you like them too), until the first customer finally strolled in, sometimes as late as noon. When it was my turn on stage I would dance to modern rock, adult alternative, or favorites from my earliest days stripping at Sugar's in the eighties, like "Danny's All-Star Joint" by Ricki Lee Jones, Deep Purple's "Hush," or a selection of Bad Company and Three Dog Night tunes. Sometimes there were customers to hustle dances from when I got off stage, and sometimes there weren't. For the first time in a decade, I had no suitors in my personal life, so the only "men in my life" now were club customers. And while those "relationships" were nothing if not fleeting—lasting the length of three songs versus three weeks or three months—I found our interactions often moved me in ways that taught me valuable life lessons, especially in regard to my abilities with patience, forgiveness, and boundary setting.

One day in early June, I struggled through a slow lunch and afternoon crowd doing no more than one or two dances for anyone. At the end of the day, with an hour left to my shift, I'd met a mere two thirds of my goal—a goal I'd already been lowering every six months as the economy worsened and the club's lunch crowds (for

lack of a better term) shrank even farther. Three songs before I was
due on stage again I spotted a small, crabby old man in a wingback
chair by the DJ booth and knew immediately he needed me.

He was stiff, sullen, uncommunicative, and completely
transfixed by the sight of my tiny schoolgirl skirt and lacy bra.
I liked men like that because it meant I didn't have to bother with
the usual pleasantries. I could just get down to business with guys
like him, leaning in slowly until my breasts became a big warm blur
in his face, then twisting my neck to whisper in his ear, "You want
some of this…baby?" (It was rhetorical, really.)

He cleared his throat, looking suddenly much less sullen, and
stiffening in an entirely new way. "Yeah," he said. "Let's do it."

He opened his knees so I could position myself between them,
and as the next song began I did my thing. Peeling, dropping,
sliding, rubbing, whispering, stroking, grinding…all the moves
I knew and loved and that turned me on just for executing them,
regardless of the withered old man I was doing them for.

The song ended. "Want another?" I asked. He nodded firmly
and I did my thing all over again.

Then it was over, and I was due on stage, my DJ having cued
my music already. "Honey, I hate to rush off but I'm due on stage,"
I tell the man.

"Okay," he said, without reaching for his wallet.

"I need to collect for my dances," I further explain.

He looked frustrated, as if I was putting *him* out. Meanwhile,
my song continued to play as my DJ looked to me expectantly.

"Sweetie," I said to the old man, "you still owe me forty dollars."

He shifts in his seat. "I'll give it to you later."

"Yeah, that that's not how it works," I explained. "You need
to take out your wallet right now, extract forty bucks from it, and
place it in my hand."

He grudgingly took out his wallet, and I immediately reached
out and helped myself to everything in it—fifteen measly dollars—

                                                    Kristin Casey

before pointing out the ATM, unfortunately located right next to the front door. I would've walked with him, but I knew he wasn't going to use it. There were no credit cards in his wallet except a Texaco card. *I've lost this one*, I thought.

As I walked onto the stage the DJ, Jason, asked if I was alright. "Yes," I say. "That little old man rushing out the door just stiffed me for twenty-five bucks, but I'm fine."

That's when Jason, God love him, rushed right out after the little troll.

By the time my set was over, Jason had returned to tell me the man had gotten away. He'd jumped in his little truck, and though Jason caught up and knocked on his window yelling at him to come back inside and pay me, the old man drove off. Jason was incredibly complimentary to me over the mic for the rest of the night and refused to accept my tip-out when I left.

A week later I was on stage early, before the lunch crowd again, with only three customers in the whole club. A handsome gentleman with cropped salt and pepper hair and a glowing tan approached the stage. A silver and gold James Avery cross peeked through the neck of his Tommy Hilfiger shirt. He kissed his fingertips and shook them together in the air—another Italian, obviously. Enamored with me, it would seem (though with Italian men I always got the sense it was really *themselves* they were enamored with). Anyway, he tipped me three times during my three-song set so I headed straight over when I was done.

He was a corporate attorney from Dallas who had just walked off a case because, he said, the corporation was robbing people. The look of disgust he made seemed a little well-practiced to me—a typical lawyer trick—but whatever. I was there to believe what he wanted me to believe.

We talked and cuddled in the corner for an hour as more dancers hit the floor. Eventually, there were twice as many dancers as customers (ten tops), so I stuck with the drunk lawyer who, after three beers and three dances told me he'd gotten out of rehab three days ago. He was staying with his mom in Fredericksburg and living on his corporate cards until the company got smart and cut him off. That's when I figured it was time to collect for my dances, which he gladly agreed to, *as soon as he used the ATM.*

My heart sank. Somehow I knew he'd already been cut off.

He tried them all, I could see from where I was sitting. Back at the table he was no longer enamored with anything, especially me, because I told him he needed to pay me regardless.

"We've had fun and I like you," I said. "I understand you're going through a hard time, but I can see you're a good man and I know you don't want to stiff me."

"I'm sorry," he says, this time without bothering to hide that he's lying because by then he was only sorry for himself.

I put my arm around his neck, feeling for the silver chain I'd seen earlier. I soothed his anger, saying "Everything will be okay. You'll get back on your feet in no time. Meanwhile, I'll just keep this until you can pay me what you owe me." I showed him the silver and gold James Avery cross I'd just taken off his neck. It rested in my palm, but he didn't snatch it back. He wouldn't have made it if he'd tried. I'm quicker than any drunken corporate lawyer you ever met.

I left him and found the manager, Dennis, who handed the bartender his eyeglasses then promptly threw the sad little lawyer out. The guy had the nerve to put up a fight, but the bartender, manager, and DJ all closed in on him and it was over in seconds. They told me he yelled in the parking lot that he was a lawyer and would sue. The DJ laughed at him. Dennis said I could skip paying house fees until it compensated for how much I was stiffed. When that day came, I planned to give the cross to Dennis if he wanted it. It was nice…I'd always liked James Avery.

Weeks later, near the end of my shift (in what was becoming a disturbing trend), I'd made barely half my goal. The huge bachelor party of European rugby players filling the VIP room had bought no dances from anyone at all. However, there was one terrifically entertaining customer sitting at the stage—an aging hippie biker dude dancing around and tossing money on stage as he tipped all the girls, one by one. True to form, he did the same thing when I got up there, dancing around and tossing me a few singles and one twenty, right before reaching for his phone, pointing it at me, and shooting.

At that point I dropped elegantly to my knees, thanked him sweetly, scooped up the twenty-three dollars, and then just as deftly confiscated his phone. I walked across the stage and told the DJ what happened, who called for the manager.

I placed the phone on my skirt behind the curtain and returned to the main stage, but drunk hippie/biker's drunken female friend took it upon herself just then to join me up there and demand I return the phone. That's when I decided my stage set was on hold. Dennis hadn't arrived so I went to find him, then returned to finish my stage set. The DJ said I didn't have to but why not? I was a professional after all. Also, I didn't have anything better to do.

Dennis finally arrived and erased the pictures hippie dude had taken of me, which turned out to be mostly black space and colored lights. Then he gave the phone back to the customer with a stern warning about going to jail next time. The customer apologized profusely, both to Dennis, then me. I forgave him, because really, how big of a jerk can a guy be who tipped one dancer twenty-three bucks on stage?

Customers like him were harmless enough. What I hated were the guys who stiffed me. The main reason I quit full-time real estate was all the unpaid labor it forced me to do. If the stripping industry came any closer to mirroring the real estate industry, I didn't know what I was going to do.

❧

AROUND THAT TIME, my neighbor Richard reached out to me for a favor. He knew an older couple with a thriving new business in town. They were looking to invite a young woman into their sex life on occasion in exchange for financial support. They'd asked Richard if he knew anyone who fit the bill, and while Richard didn't, he figured that since I was a stripper I'd know a plethora of ladies for them to choose from.

My financial situation was dire, and I wasn't getting any younger, so I emailed him a one sentence reply: *Will I do?*

He agreed to forward a few of my pictures to the couple, who promptly got in touch and invited me to lunch at The Driskill Hotel.

Sam and Kate were indeed older and successful. They were also rather attractive. I guessed them to be close to sixty-years-old but in excellent shape, with good energy and high spirits. Sam was a tall, broad-chested man with salt-and-pepper hair and a beard. Kate was petite and athletic, with wispy blonde hair and a dainty, raspy voice I found both sexy and comforting. Sam's voice was deep and booming, and he spoke candidly about everything, including their plan to find a young woman to join them in bed on occasion.

"We originally envisioned a college-aged woman we could compensate by paying her tuition," Sam said. "Until seeing your pictures, we hadn't considered someone your age, but you seem to be everything we're looking for."

One thing they were clear about was wanting someone who'd never done this type of thing before. They didn't want a "pro," Sam said. I didn't tell them I'd done it more times than I could count.

The first time, I was eighteen years old. I'd been stripping for a couple of months when my manager introduced me to a distinguished, elderly man known in the club as "old man Robert." I was still learning the ropes as a stripper but certainly earning enough to get by. I'd probably agreed to go home with him as much for the experience as the money. I'd been fascinated by prostitution, especially the high-end kind, since I was a kid. My date with Robert was an uncomfortable experience, but not for any reason other than my own mental baggage. Robert couldn't have been kinder, cleaner, or quicker. And once it was over I left his place three feet off the ground for the surge of power I felt—a sense of being wanted in a way that was stronger and more intoxicating than any I'd ever experienced.

From then on, I accepted paid dates from strip club customers roughly half a dozen times per year—whenever the guy was enjoyable company and his offer was good. Back then, that meant two hundred fifty dollars for an hour of my time, which was a lot of money in 1986. I'd quit this kind of "moonlighting" after falling in love with Joe in 1988. I started up again after we broke up and I returned to stripping. After getting sober, I was instantly able to command five hundred dollars an hour. So, I proceeded to moonlight in that fashion twice a week until moving back to Austin, one and a half years into my sobriety. I hadn't taken money for sex since then—not for ten straight years. But with the economy in the toilet, a recession on the way, and my financial situation more precarious all the time, I saw no other way to get ahead.

Sam and Kate seemed to like me, and I left our lunch praying to hear from them again. I'd not had sex with a couple since a handful of awkward threesomes with Joe in the nineties. And I had no interest in sex with women, not since breaking up with my last girlfriend in my teens. But Kate and Sam were special. She was down-to-earth and sweet as could be, but also regal in a way, and Sam was definitely her king. They reminded me of Kurt and Goldie. And who would turn down a threesome with Kurt and Goldie?

I couldn't imagine a more perfect couple to relaunch me into a line of work that had always felt easy and natural. Kate and Sam seemed fun, respectful, and trustworthy. If they called me, I knew I'd be in good hands.

They called me.

We met at the Hilton downtown, in a suite Sam had reserved. They each had a drink—wine for Kate and whiskey for Sam—and poured me a sparkling water with lemon. We chatted about trivial things and then got down to business. Sam had firm ideas about what he wanted and what turned him on, which was mostly doing it doggie style with me. Kate wanted to watch, which she thought might turn her on a little but in fact turned her on a lot. Me being sexual with her was less important to them—at least this time—which I was glad for. Yet somehow Kate and I ended up fooling around a little anyway. How could I not? She was simply delightful—feminine, sexy, and beautiful, and impossible not to play with. We kissed and caressed each other's breasts while her husband fucked me, but it didn't go much farther than that until our second date, when she went down on me.

I could tell they'd talked things out thoroughly beforehand. After the sex we were all more relaxed and hung out talking for an hour. They asked about my life like they were truly interested, then gave me great advice on things like whether to post nude pics on my blog and how to make the most out of my writing projects. Before it was over he'd mentioned a "next time." She talked about "going slow" but also about having me out to their ranch soon and maybe going to Belize together someday. All very good things. A win-win-win, I'd say. They even paid my Vegas rate of five hundred dollars an hour (versus the going rate in Austin, which for some reason was only three hundred dollars an hour, barely more than Austin's rate twenty years earlier).

So, I was devastated when after only two months of seeing them they stopped calling. I reached out and we arranged one more date before they stopped calling again the next month. Around that time, I accepted a paid date with one of my favorite strip club customers, a tech geek named Derek, who had a shaved head and wore horn-rimmed glasses. He came over once a month for three hundred dollars. I also agreed to have sex with my new accountant in exchange for him fighting my $9,600-dollar IRS bill. From there I started accepting other "moonlighting" offers, which were few and far between but helped keep me afloat until I could figure out my next move financially.

Empowerment, Vulnerability, Presence

June 8, 2008

Current Location: triangle, camel, and standing head to knee poses
Current Mood: contemplative

My two least favorite poses in Bikram yoga used to be triangle and camel. Triangle still is, probably because it engages every muscle at once but especially my glutes, which aren't as strong as they could be. Plus, my hamstrings, while looser than they once were, are still tight enough to hamper me. I'm not sure how it correlates to the macrocosm of my life, but I'll continue giving it my all and hope it gets easier in time. If a plant doesn't need to understand photosynthesis in order to grow, let's hope I don't either.

I usually want to understand everything I'm going through though. Whether that's a control issue or healthy quest for self-awareness, I don't know. But I seem to evolve faster when I understand why I'm struggling.

I used to hate camel because it's such a vulnerable pose. But I think my real problem is that it's *actively* vulnerable. Meaning you can do the backbend by resting your weight on your ankles, but you're not supposed to. You're supposed to push forward through your chest and hips, exerting power throughout the most vulnerable posture—seemingly a contradiction in terms.

How that relates to the macrocosm of my life? I realize that being vulnerable without engaging my strength is a lazy way to live... the exact way I lived before getting sober, in fact, letting life lead me around by the nose, never taking a stand or making a hard decision about anything. I'd find something compelling or thrilling—the punk scene, booze and drugs, promiscuous sex—then dive in and let it take over. I didn't carve out a workable niche within those arenas. I let them take me for a ride, carried down a creek of increasingly dangerous rapids straight to a thousand-foot waterfall, without so much as an oar or lifejacket. Vulnerable as hell. Empowered not at all.

Once I got sober, I changed things. Carving out niches in the densest of places, like real estate, where I've beat my head against a wall for nine years. Never relaxing long enough to be open to what else life might offer. Like the way I dated for years after getting sober—with conveniently married men or long-distance partners I knew couldn't hurt me by getting too close. Vulnerable barely at all. Empowered only in the vaguest sense, because eventually something's going to give, be it the wall or my head.

I think the trick is to be open in life, let people get to know me, or even get close, all while maintaining healthy boundaries and making conscious decisions about what I want. I take more chances with my writing these days, being more revealing about the good, bad, and ugly of my past without getting mired in maudlin self-pity. I'm more likely to let men chat me up (on the rare occasion I go out), more myself while we're talking, and less likely to care what they think. Now *that* is a freeing experience—vulnerable and empowered at the same time.

Likewise, I don't seem to mind camel pose lately. It still makes me dizzy but it's not the torture it used to be, and when it's over I sometimes get a rush. As for triangle, I don't know what I'll have to go through in the macrocosm of life to finally improve there. I don't know where the correlating challenge is regarding inner strength but I'm sure life will show me soon enough. Maybe I won't have to understand it in order to grow, but most likely I'm too analytical for that. Most likely, I'll have to learn by going through some shit. Some *more* shit, I should say...sigh.

I'm weaning off caffeine again. Successfully in that I've bypassed the headaches, sluggishness, and lethargy of the last few times I've done this. (Yes, I'm stupid enough to put myself through this more than once—I'm an addict; sue me.) It's slowed my metabolism, but since I recently dropped under my ideal weight it turned out to be a wash.

The bigger deal is that not only are the "workout supplements" I was taking full of caffeine, but they also have ephedra—an effective metabolism booster that's terrible for my adrenal glands, which have gone through enough for one lifetime. Over the years I've spent thousands of dollars on health care practitioners, supplements, and other therapies to support my frazzled adrenals. Healthy adrenals are vital for managing stress. Continuing to take something so hard on them makes no sense.

I have so much going on right now that it's hard not to get stressed. Last Thursday I did, becoming grumpy and anxious in class until thirty minutes of hot yoga hell had passed. That's when my teacher instructed me to go further into the pose. I was in standing head to knee, already standing on one leg with the other kicking straight out, bent over and grabbing my foot like a stirrup, while bringing my elbows below my calf. I wasn't up to putting my head to my knee just then (most students don't) until she said to me point blank, "You're too good to not go all the way."

Ah, the metaphor of yoga. I've been super negative lately, about finances, workload…you name it. Frankly, I was on the verge of collapse from the weight of it until her words hit home instantly.

I'm too good to not go all the way.

I mean, what else do I have to do? Why not plan to go all the way? Without ephedra if possible, which screws up my breathing in class. Which brings me to another yoga-as-life metaphor. If you're not breathing right you're not technically *doing* yoga—you're just sweating to death in a room full of other half-naked people (and as fun as that sounds, it's kinda not).

In Bikram yoga, we do the same twenty-six posture routine in every class. That on one day your triangle sucks but your locust rocks, yet the next day the opposite occurs would seem odd…but isn't. Because people's lives tend to change from day to day, so you may be stronger one day, weaker the next, flexible one day, inflexible the next.

For example, it's no coincidence I was hyper-flexible my first day ever in yoga. I'm that way in life…bending over backward in areas where I really should stand my ground. All last year during my relationship with Lalo, I struggled with Bikram's strength poses. Likewise, with Lalo himself I spent most of last year learning to hold my ground instead of bending to his will (because that man could charm every ounce of strength out of me with one sly smile or sideways glance).

These days, my biggest challenge is regulating my breathing, which correlates to mindfulness. To not letting whatever *just* happened drain me of energy I need for what's *about* to happen. In 105-degree heat, at sixty percent humidity, it doesn't matter whether I can maneuver into tricky positions and hold them for extended periods. If I'm not breathing calmly, I'm too stressed to be "present."

I've lived my life letting my heart rate control my breathing. Stress has dictated my state of mind as long as I can remember. In class, we're taught that by controlling our breathing we slow the heart. It's about gaining control over your life—empowerment, in other words. So, it was gratifying today to find more control over my breath.

Now for the macrocosm. Before the Agents and Editors Conference, I'd started stressing out so much I lost a week of sleep pondering every bad choice I may've made with my writing projects. But as soon as I attended my first workshop—and got instantly present—everything was fine. More than fine…phenomenal.

Then, after a five-day break from yoga, I finally returned to find better than ever control over my breathing and heart rate. I'm in control of my feelings, stress level, and performance, remaining fully present and ready to handle whatever comes next.

CHAPTER 15

Summer 2008

In July, I learned the job selling private airplane stalls, that Buddy Barfield was to help me get, had fallen through. The film studio construction planned for East Austin had been scrapped, so the need for a new private airport was no more. The racing technology sales job offered by another Exposé customer similarly disintegrated. I tried to see it as a sign I was meant to pursue my writing.

I went to a book reading by Sarah Katherine Lewis, a former stripper and sex worker who'd written one of my favorite memoirs, *Indecent: How I Make It and Fake It as a Girl for Hire.* We knew each other from our respective LiveJournal blogs and had a lovely chat after her reading at BookWoman. She signed my book: *With love and working girl solidarity to a gorgeous smarty pants uber vixen.* I was beyond touched. Also enlightened, because in chatting about her book tour and proceeds I was coming to understand how challenging it would be to ever earn a living as a writer. Sarah's book was better written than almost anything I'd done and certainly my novel-turned-memoir in the works. Also, arguably sexier, being largely about the sex industry while mine was about the punk scene and drug addiction. Sarah's second book, *Sex and Bacon,* was just as wise and witty as her first, but she was clearly eking by as an author.

I wasn't anywhere close to sending super-agent Mary Evans the pages she'd requested. And in September I heard back from Abby Koons and Brooke Warner, the agent and editor most interested in my *Secrets of Successful Strippers* manuscript. They loved my book proposal and completed pages, but in the end determined that its readership would be too niche to turn a profit for them. They strongly encouraged me to self-publish. Instead, I abandoned the project altogether, when, by chapter five, it became obvious that my writing partner and I had vastly differing perspectives on exactly "how to" succeed as a stripper. I gave her everything we'd written, including my notes, and wished her the best should she decide to pursue it solo.

I'd become friends with my pitching instructor, Suzy, who'd asked me to read her new manuscript, *Secret Sex Lives*, and give notes. It was a fantastic personal account of her journey into the world of alternative sex practices (kink). In witnessing her eventual success with it, I had to wonder who would give a shit about a dark little memoir detailing my self-destructive crystal meth experiences twenty-five years earlier.

My stripper blog, on the other hand, was becoming popular. I got a write up on Glamour.com followed by a lengthy interview in *The Austin Chronicle*. The *Glamour* comment section was full of disparaging remarks about strippers in general, but I didn't care. Non-stripper women didn't always understand me, and I'd come to accept that. What mattered was that my writing was getting noticed. I had two short stories published by then, plus multiple poems and essays. *$pread*, an award-winning magazine by and for sex workers, had asked me to write for them. My first article was called "The Age Edge," about how stripping over forty could be an asset versus deficit. My next article, "Stripping in a Slump," was about the challenges faced by the strip club industry in a recession. In late September, I got a call from the producer of a morning talk show in New York City, needing a stripper guest to share secrets about what went on in our VIP rooms. She asked me point-blank if sex was happening in there, and since it wasn't at my club I said no. Then I raced out to buy a new dress and shoes for the taping, only for them to find a different stripper to appear who claimed that yes, strip club VIP rooms were chock-full of sexual encounters.

I sold my last home in September, then quit real estate entirely, letting my license lapse when it came up for renewal two months later. Not everyone needs to be fulfilled by their work, but as a single, childless woman, work was all I had, and thus I very much did. I couldn't have been happier to be done with real estate, though quitting effectively eliminated any financial backup plan I had. How much longer could I continue to strip? I had no idea, but for my sanity I knew I couldn't be a Realtor any longer.

I read a quote by novelist Haruki Murakami about the need to prioritize one's time. About how people often get mad when writers don't have time to socialize, but how his priority was always his readers and making each book better than the last. It gave me strength to continue doing the same, no matter how many of my friends were pressing me to spend more time with them. One of them expected me to take a day off work to hang out while he was in town from Chicago. I was incensed! The guy was a doctor who should've known how hard it had become for me to keep my head above water as a stripper. (I blew him off and didn't speak to him again for ten years.)

Then my friend Weasel died. He'd been the bouncer at Sugar's Gentlemen's Club, where I'd first started stripping in the late eighties. We'd been friends and lovers and, back in the day, part of a larger Sugar's family. His death reminded me of how much I'd always loved the strip club business, which until recently seemed to love me back. I still had days when I felt like I was doing what I was meant to do, but there were forces against me that made it hard to imagine doing it much longer—my age, the recession, customers who expected more "extras" every day, and coworkers who refused to maintain the healthy boundaries that helped the rest of us feel respected by our customers.

❧

Kristin Casey

ONE MORNING THAT SUMMER, I hit the floor at Exposé by eleven fifteen and settled in at the bar watching the Olympics with two other punctual girls. Half an hour later, two customers wandered in, ordered lunch, then turned toward their nearest TV to also watch the Olympics. On both screens impossibly flexible gymnasts twirled Hula-Hoop-type things, performing bizarre and beautiful acrobatics including spinning on one toe in the standing splits. We were all entranced, but as a dancer (of sorts) myself, I was particularly humbled.

I was wearing my trusty sweater, which just that morning another dancer had pronounced "sexy," probably because it cinched at the waist to accentuate my shape and opened at my cleavage where rounded flesh spilled proudly from my favorite black lace pushup bra. Still, a thick cardigan hardly showed off my best assets compared to the other girls who, freezing or not, had theirs on much better display. *Fuck it*, I thought…*today I choose comfort.* Most days, by noon, enough warm bodies arrived to chase away the chill. That day, we had no crowd at all and therefore no warmth, so my sweater stayed on.

I went to sit with the two businessmen. The younger one was buying his friend a birthday lunch. They were friendly enough, yet my witty, sexy banter alone didn't immediately hook them. They needed visual stimulation beyond a small peek of cleavage. I again debated removing my sweater, but since I was almost due on stage I figured I'd wait and wow them from there. Unfortunately, right as I hit the stage their lunch arrived, leaving me ignored for most of a three-song set as they shoveled in food, conversing in grunts and nods perfected over years of rushed business lunches. I resisted the urge to stomp my foot at the edge of stage to get their attention. I was professional, danced well, and was finally rewarded in the last ten seconds as one of them looked up and caught a glimpse. Guy #1 nudged Guy #2 who nodded back as they grunted in approval. *Bingo*—I was in.

I exited the stage and moved in for the kill. Birthday boy was ready for a dance, so I took him to my favorite corner. Afterward, he made a long exhale and said "Wow!" Returning to his friend, he sent him over to me with instructions to "just get the dance, trust me…don't ask questions." Birthday boy's friend had a similar reaction and as he paid me said it was the best dance he'd ever had. My anxiety about what looked to be a terribly slow day alleviated…a little.

Pretty soon the customer-to-dancer ratio was evenly matched—ten of each, which was where it stayed for most of the day. A few lap dances took place sporadically as hours passed. I did none, however, and a gnawing anxiety overtook me. Four hours into my shift I'd still done only those first two dances. I'd frequently heard other girls complain about that happening, and on rare occasions it had happened to me, but I never let it eat away at my confidence like it did that day. When a fellow dancer asked me what was wrong, I nearly burst into tears.

Considering I'd been writing a book about successful stripper tactics I was suddenly as embarrassed as I'd been stressed. So, I brushed it off and called one of my semi-regular customers who promptly showed up to save the day, or at least make it half as terrible as it would've been otherwise.

The next day was better. My favorite regular, JJ, arrived for our usual string of mutually pleasurable lap dances. Immediately after he left, a waitress informed me that Barry, a customer I'd met a week ago, was back to see me. He'd told me that he would be, but I'd forgotten because customers say that all the time yet rarely follow through. After six dances in a row, I wrapped up with Barry and promptly spied David, another new customer from last Friday who'd also said he'd be back. I cleaned him out in no short order with four quick lap dances before he promised to return to see me soon. And so it went. I was hardly idle for a moment all day, surpassing my daily average by midafternoon. Around then I met

Jorge, who tipped me on stage, too shy to look me in the eye, yet able to state in a serious tone and near perfect English that he'd "like to count all my freckles."

"That could take a while," I said. "They tend to move around when you're not looking." Jorge thought that was delightfully funny. Once off stage I went to sit with him.

He was a cute twenty-five-year-old who'd moved to Austin from southern Mexico a mere two months before. The friend he'd come with was paying for their beers because Jorge had no money at all, much less twenty dollars for a dance. I chatted with him anyway, needing a breather from the fast-paced day. I asked how he liked Austin and about his family back in Mexico. I also wished him luck at his new job and complimented his skin, a beautiful golden brown that was silky soft and almost hairless. "My favorite," I told him. As I was leaving I said, "Once you're settled in your new job come back and get some dances." Then I moved on to another customer.

During my next stage set I saw Jorge again, approaching less shyly this time. So not shy, in fact, he asked me out on a date, to which I replied, "I'm flattered but I can't."

"Why not?" he demanded, furrowing his brow.

"I'm too busy with my three jobs but thanks for asking."

It wasn't enough for him and Jorge persisted, but I had no time for it and got straight with him right there on stage.

"Sweetie, I'm flattered but I'm forty, old enough to be your mother."

Jorge didn't care. "Age is just a number," he insisted.

I started laughing. "You're sweet. I have to go."

I could hear him pleading behind me as I walked off the stage. Next thing I knew, Jorge was trailing me all around the club. He even approached me sitting with other *paying* customers. I excused myself, pulled Jorge to a corner and sat him down for a talk. I was in a good mood and was gentle with him.

"We have nothing in common," I said. "You're too young for me."

"I'm mature," he countered. "I'm going to make something out of myself; you'll see."

"It's great that you're so driven and disciplined. But I'm sorry, I'm just not interested."

He repeated that he'd never met anyone like me. I told him Austin was full of lovely young women who'd love to be with a smart, handsome, loving man like him. He seemed so hurt and maybe it was silly, but I wanted to let him down gently. I told him I need to be with an older, more established man, one more settled in his life and career.

"You mean you need your bills paid? But I can do that," he cried. "I will pay your bills for you!"

I realized these acrobatics had tumbled completely out of my control. Also, I was bored with the display. "Jorge, I'm going back to work now. Thanks for the ego boost and good luck with your new job. You'll make some lovely young woman very lucky one day. Goodbye now."

He followed, still pleading, so I darted into the dressing room. I'd had a great day and decided to go, changing clothes and rushing to my car before Jorge spotted me.

Alas, days when I would bank like that were becoming rare as could be. Two weeks later, I walked into the crowded dressing room at noon. A new girl was explaining loudly to another dancer why she always placed a small towel underneath her wherever she sat. "I'm big on hygiene and like to protect myself from where other half-naked women already sat and left traces of their ass juice."

Another girl and I giggled about that for five straight minutes before I hit the floor. First I sat with Robert, a club regular who didn't buy dances but occasionally tipped a girl for her time. The first time I ever sat with him he'd given me one hundred dollars for letting him brush my hair. Afterwards he said, "I've had an erection four times in the last ten years and the fourth was just now brushing your hair." He always said he liked me best, which I suspected was in part because we were both recovered alcoholics. Also, I didn't hit him up for money with sob stories like the other girls. That day alone, he told me, one waitress said she needed dental work, so he'd give her one hundred dollars. And one dancer told him she needed a new tire and he'd given her fifty.

I didn't tell him about the $1400 in dental work I needed. He was starting to avoid the sob story girls and I didn't intend to be one of them. But since I had nothing better to do, I chatted with Robert for an hour that day, listening to his WWII stories. Before he left he gave me most of what he had left in his wallet, twenty-five bucks.

Next I sat with Stan, a Vietnam vet and former tank commander who was in the club every day. He also never got dances but paid certain girls for their time if he could see their tits. He was half cocky, half crotchety, and it didn't bother me at all. It was an act I had to get past to find the real him—like a scavenger hunt for clues to solve a bigger puzzle. I usually sat with him for twenty minutes for twenty dollars, but sometimes he only had five dollars and I'd leave after two songs. I hadn't had time to crawl around inside his head until now, and finally learned enough about him to know where to begin asking questions—Vietnam. *What's it like inside a tank? Did you lose friends? Were you injured? How many times? Is the shrapnel still in your chest?* In the end, I learned how to operate a tank (sort of) and made thirty dollars. And he was sweeter and less crotchety by the end of that hour than I'd ever seen him.

Around five in the afternoon, I zeroed in on the bachelor party. They'd been there over an hour and were starting to settle in with a few rounds of drinks and sporadic lap dances. The first group of strippers to sit with them were young and rowdy, doing their job of making the boys feel masculine and rebellious, before moving on. At that point, some of the men were individually glancing around at the rest of us…looking for the best fit for one-on-one dances. Of the younger men the hottest was a ruggedly handsome Joe Rogan-type, who was clearly a gym rat. He'd been checking me out in my shiny turquoise bikini with a sparkly, macramé butt wrap (not the *best* ass juice protection, but sexy nonetheless). He (like any good gym rat) complimented my low body fat, but unfortunately had no cash to spend. I chatted up the groom instead, discussing romantic love and our favorite skin care regimens. He was complimentary yet disinterested in the lap dance thing, having come to the club for the benefit of his buddies. I eventually left the table only to be called back ten minutes later. Rugged gym-rat guy had borrowed twenty bucks from the best man and wanted a dance…and that's how I finally broke one hundred dollars and allowed myself to go home.

As I tipped out Dennis a too big chunk of that day's too small earnings, I couldn't help but remark, "Anyone who thinks the economy isn't hurting the strip club business has their head up their ignorant, juicy ass."

THE SCABS WERE PLAYING at Antone's that night, and I hadn't seen them all year. Next to great sex, which I'd had none of lately, there was nothing I'd rather do. It was great to see my friends in the band (though Charles rushed by with the quickest of hellos, perhaps because the last time he'd called me Lalo had threatened his life), but in the end I danced for only half the show, then left early, still exhausted from a long day at work. Outside the club, I ran into Zed who'd just played a gig down the street. After a long hug we caught up on each other's lives. He was still sober, still married, and happier than ever. He asked about Lalo, and I told him we'd broken up. I said I spent my free time writing now, and that I, too, was happier than ever.

I'd kept copious journals since getting sober. My entries over ten years had slowly morphed from daily investigations into how

                                        Kristin Casey

much I meant to other people, to daily investigations into what my life could be for *me*, who I was in my own eyes, and what value my relationships brought to me versus solely to my partner. In some ways I missed the simpler days of plugging away all day at real estate, then going dancing every night…dancing, flirting, trolling, fucking. All the fun things I did before throwing myself into my writing. But I was probably misremembering those days somewhat. Omitting the heartache and anxiety that accompanied me downtown every single time. The crippling loneliness I'd felt suffocated by for most of it. The vague empty hole in my gut I forever tried to fill with the attentions of every hot musician I met back then. The wounds I alternately wore like a badge or tried to hide from everyone I cared about.

I wasn't nearly as lonely or insecure these days, but my future was still incredibly precarious. All I knew was that, finally, at age forty, I was living life for me and no one else. Right or wrong, I felt at home in my little corner of the sex industry, writing my brains out in whatever free time I could find. I had meaning in my life, and not just regarding my writing. I helped countless married men in search of their misplaced masculinity, lifting their spirits, as they, in return, kept me fed and sheltered. I was important to my customers, as a good listener, sounding board, and pseudo therapist. I deduced what was missing in their lives or making them feel bad about themselves, then provided as much approval, affection, and arousal as they could take. I made them feel understood and appreciated because I did understand and appreciate them. While fleeting, some of my strip club interactions were the most open and honest relationships I'd had. Also rewarding, because as manly as my attention made them feel was as attractive and feminine as their desire made me feel. Not exactly a 401k, but it was something. I was satisfied and fulfilled at the end of the day because a handful of men left my company feeling better about themselves and their lives. Until I could use my writing to help men be more understood and appreciated, I did it in a strip club. Either way it was an honor to be in that position.

Maybe my writing would take me somewhere. Maybe I'd meet a special man again. Two massively huge maybes. But I had nowhere else to go, and frankly felt like I was supposed to be there, right where I was. Maybe I should be further down the road—further along in my writing career—but ultimately I was meant to be on that same road. My days consisted of writing, stripping, and fucking for money, and despite that I should've been doing all of that at a higher level, I enjoyed most of it. Anyway, I had no choice but to plug away, day after day, hoping and striving for something better. What shape that took, I didn't know exactly. But something having to do with writing and sexuality, certainly.

Early in September, I received notice that my screenplay, *Speed Punk*, had made "second rounder" in the Austin Film Festival contest. That was the top ten percent of thousands of entries. I'd never gone to school for it, or even taken a workshop on screenwriting. I'd heard about the contest six weeks before the deadline, read two books on screenwriting, then spent four weeks writing my first script ever, feeling like it was the most natural thing in the world. I was proud of myself, and while I unfortunately wouldn't advance any further in the contest, it gave me the confidence I needed to consider pursuing it as a career. There was more money in screenwriting than book writing and it came far easier to me. Plus, I had an idea for my next script—a love story between a former drug dealer trying to go legit as an MMA promoter to win the heart of the woman he loves, a high-end escort and stripper in Las Vegas. They always say write what you know, and I knew those lead characters inside and out.

Silicone versus Skill

July 31, 2008

Current Location: *Still here, bitch*
Current Mood: accomplished

As an exotic dancer, I allow my audience to witness my celebration of sexuality as I perform on stage. For the right price I indulge them in that same heady experience by way of a lap dance. What I don't sell to my customers is my *actual sexuality.* Only the right to temporarily participate in the celebration of it.

If I fake it with a customer—manipulate or deceive him into believing he *himself* has sparked my arousal, or that he has a genuine shot with me outside the fantasy world of the club, then I've sold that customer a piece *of me.* I've auctioned off a valuable chunk of my feminine sexual energy for a couple of measly bucks. And that gives him power over me, which is degrading and a huge problem in our industry.

Yesterday a blog commenter remarked that bigger breasted dancers can "get away with telling the truth better," implying that flat-chested girls must be manipulative to make a living. This perspective—that lies and manipulations are either necessary or acceptable operating procedure—is problematic to me. It makes the customer a target and every interaction adversarial. The customer becomes the enemy—a mark needed to be conned in order for the dancer to win "the game."

Sure, some customers *want* to buy into the fantasy that their favorite strippers are truly "into" them. Not just indulge in it but to invest in it fully. And? Does that mean *I* have to entertain the fallacy? How degrading!

Please. I make a living off guys with heads based in reality. Maybe my *short-term* cash flow is occasionally affected when I don't play "the game" but retaining self-respect and a positive attitude ensures a stream of income from future customers. Call that karma or basic economics, but the less I behave in ways that make me bitter and hard, the more I attract quality customers.

Besides, honesty doesn't equal full disclosure. I don't tell my customers everything but neither do I mislead them. Though it's tempting to take advantage of men who seem to be asking for it, I could no more justify lying to compensate for my age or B cup breasts than I could push real estate clients to purchase homes that aren't right for them.

There's another way to make big bucks, and that's showing customers genuine affection and attention. I shower them with emotional and erotic labor as they shower me with twenties and hundreds. Back in Vegas, I looked at every customer as "my next victim" thinking, "How much does he have and how quick can I take it from him?" Whereas in Austin, I go into every interaction thinking, "What does he *need* and how can I give it to him?" I had the same (high) degree of success in both cities, but my mental health is a thousand times better now than it was then.

My job is to immerse customers in the fantasy *of the moment* so they forget about some fantasy future date with me. It takes skill (a lot, frankly) but since when does anyone get rich without a few fucking skills? I spent twelve years learning mine. Also, seven in therapy, eleven in recovery, and forty experiencing life on this planet. I've negotiated all kinds of interactions and I use those lessons to make win-wins out of every one of my strip club transactions.

Yes, some customers won't take me to VIP unless the possibility exists to fuck me outside the club. If I were thirty instead of forty, or had DD's instead of B+'s, would they take me to the VIP anyway? Maybe. But if I can get that first dance the argument is moot. One dance from me, and tit size and age lines cease to exist. My brains, class, wit, and sex appeal get me in, then my lap dance skills transcend any remaining resistance.

I've seen so many strippers unable to connect on a sensual level and be clueless how to get inside the heads of their customers for what they need emotionally, much less do half the lap dance I can do. Instead, they fake attraction and availability to make a one-time cash grab before jilting or ghosting the guy and losing him forever. That's not how you instill loyalty. That's no way to make regulars or generate good karma.

There is a difference between erotic labor and emotional labor, and erotic labor may sell *faster*, but alone it does not sell *better*. The key is to do both—open the door with the former and then keep it open with the latter.

CHAPTER 16

Fall 2008

WHILE WRITING A SCREENPLAY had felt like second nature, the business of screenwriting was utterly alien to me. So, I decided to attend the Austin Film Festival Conference in October at The Driskill Hotel downtown. On day one, I competed in the first round of pitch competitions, where over one hundred amateur screenwriters pitched their scripts to big shot producers in a public setting. Even with my crippling phobia of public speaking, I managed to do quite well but just shy of advancing to the finals.

I spent the rest of the weekend attending panels led by successful Hollywood writers, directors, and producers. During the lunch break I chatted up Hollywood icon Robert Townsend, actor/comedian/writer/director/producer, who couldn't have been warmer and more encouraging. Later, I listened to writer/producer Polly Platt describe her writing process, which I was delighted to learn was in most ways just like mine. Hour after hour, it was confirmed that what I already instinctively knew about the craft of screenwriting was spot on. I merely needed to learn how to sell my work and break into the business, which revealed itself to be far more complicated and unlikely than I'd expected.

I'd studied the publishing business for years, so attending the Writers' League Conference had been largely about networking for me versus education. But the film festival conference left me feeling raw. On one hand, everyone I listened to made me feel like I'd finally found my tribe after all. I felt at home with filmmakers and screenwriters, more than I'd felt with any other group, from punk rockers to Realtors to strippers. I knew I'd found my niche. On the other hand, for the most part, I didn't exist to any of my amateur filmmaker peers until I was in a position to help them. The *established* writers and producers leading the panels couldn't have been nicer or more accessible. But my fellow attendees were snobs, far from the sweet bunch of literary geeks I'd met at the Writers' League Conference. Most were wannabe screenwriters like me, mostly from LA, where they were already pounding the pavement, networking their brains out looking for their big Hollywood break. I'd lived in LA and knew what it was like—cutthroat and phony. Plus, despite my writing skill, I had a few disadvantages. I may've been just as hungry as the next guy, but I wasn't an energetic, twenty-eight-year-old sci-fi or horror writer (genres that tended to sell best). I was a forty-one-year-old stripper in Austin, Texas, who wrote dark, edgy dramas about sex work and addiction. My stuff was a harder sell, and living outside of LA at the time was still considered a major disadvantage. Basically, I felt all weekend like I was at my high school prom without a date, wearing braces and headgear.

But the pull was unmistakable. By the end of the weekend, I knew without a doubt where I wanted my writing career to take me. And at least one producer took notice, asking me to send her the first twelve pages of my script on Monday morning.

SUZY WANTED ME TO WRITE the script for her best-selling book *Wasted*, about a lesbian love triangle that had ended in murder. I wasn't sure how much control she had over that decision, but apparently not much because it never happened. So, until I could get one of my own scripts off the ground, I returned to other projects at hand. My Free Will Astrology horoscope came right out and said it was time for me "to write an autobiography." I liked the sound of that and quickly progressed on memoir revisions so I could send super-agent Mary Evans my first fifty pages soon.

Meanwhile, business at Exposé had become scarily slow, and the night shift manager had a (blatantly illegal) policy that all night shift dancers had to stay until closing time, which was simply too late for me. So I returned to Perfect 10 in the hopes that their business lunch crowd would be an improvement. Thank God it was. My first day back I made almost six hundred dollars, double what I was pulling in at Exposé. My new schedule would have to be three days a week, one spent at Perfect 10, and two at Exposé. In my younger days that wouldn't have been a problem, but I'd had back problems all my life, and something happened in early October that wreaked havoc in my body, life, and finances.

After fourteen months of hot yoga my back problems had become as undetectable as they'd been since my teens, when they'd started. My daily sciatica was gone. As was the occasional debilitating spasms I experienced off and on for two decades. Then, directly after four-days-in-a-row of work, exerting myself by twisting, arching, bending, and contorting in Lucite heels without warming up or stretching afterward, followed on day five by an intense yoga class, I arrived home with a heavy bag pulling on my shoulder. My phone was in the other hand as I talked to Lalo who wanted me to come over and help with Rita. He'd recently gotten an improved custody deal—while his ex was forced to go to therapy—and he was struggling with time management. He needed someone to stay with Rita while he finished a work task she couldn't accompany him to. His new place was right around the corner from me, but I felt emotionally torn, wanting to help out but not having the time or energy to do so. Suddenly, I felt something snap in my lumbar area. A slow searing wave of pain spread all through my back as I dropped the shoulder bag and choked out, "I'll call you back," to Lalo. My knees buckled and I hit the floor.

I knew in an instant it was bad. I'd been through this scenario more times than I could count, and over the past decade each incident took longer and longer to recover from. But never more than a few days to be back up and around…until this time. I spent five days on my back on the couch, then two more hobbling around in severe pain before I was able to get back to work. A few days afterward, I re-wrenched my back, then weeks later re-wrenched it again. October 2008 was the most painful month of my life, yet somehow, I managed to work a decent amount, albeit in significant pain. I desperately needed the money, especially now that I had no insurance and would clearly have to start seeing a chiropractor.

Much later, I got an MRI and showed it to a neurologist, a dry, serious man who exclaimed in uncharacteristic shock, "What the hell did you do to your back? My God, you have the spine of an old lady!" My lumbar was severely degenerated with one herniated disc, two bulging discs, and two more "on the way." I didn't know how it happened. My only guess was a combination of teenage meth addiction, coke, crack, alcoholism, fifteen years of dehydration, eight years of endurance running, and twelve years of stripping. Plus, perhaps a genetic predisposition (since my dad also had spinal issues).

I did my best to strengthen my core to help support my spine as much as possible. But the ensuing years would be challenging, especially the first two, through mid-2010, when the pain was daily and severe spasms returned without warning, almost once a month. Sitting for even moderate periods brought on back pain, and just walking around the block became impossible due to the hip pain it caused. I couldn't find a comfortable position to sleep in for months. Even reaching too quickly for a towel could result in multiple days on my back. Worst of all, every eight-hour shift at the club resulted in forty-eight hours of sharp pain in my lower back and hips.

I had a physical job, after all. And my body had seriously betrayed me. I soldiered on as best I could, but the fear and anxiety the situation instilled in me was truly demoralizing.

Fruitless & Faultless

November 9, 2008

Current Location: Gates of Hell
Current Mood: *Try me*

The metal padlock on my front door has its brand name etched into the outer face plate. Every day I come home from work, yoga, or Whole Foods (the only places I go anymore), look down to slide in my key, and *every single time* misread the word FAULTLESS as FRUITLESS.

In ALL CAPS no less.

I'm not sure why my mind plays this trick on me, but the humor is wearing thin. I like to think my perception is clearer than that, but I guess perception is subjective. Anyway, my goal lately is to write one blog post a week, which is all my writing/yoga/work schedule allows. Here are the best and worst stripper stories I have for now.

Customer #1

"What are you doing here?" He seemed genuinely perplexed, almost frustrated as if he shouldn't have to be pointing this out to me—the obviousness of my dislocation.

Comments like that tend to piss off most dancers but I thought it showed as much insight into who I am as disdain for what I do. He meant it as a compliment, and besides, it's not always easy for outsiders to appreciate the complex beauty of this work. He was at Exposé that day only to treat his worker to lunch at the restaurant of his choice and while said worker was having a ball, I'd noticed his boss politely shoo away every dancer to approach. He'd even turned his chair to face away from the stage, but I noticed him watching me for a while and so I eventually pulled up a chair.

"I earn enough money working two days a week here to support my five day a week writing schedule."

I got a nod of approval for that, with a follow up question. "Don't these guys drive you crazy?"

"Sometimes," I shrugged. "But I like the atmosphere; I feel at home here. I like my customers and enjoy making their stressful lives brighter. I'm good at it. Obviously, it's not my ideal situation, but I'd rather do this than my last job, selling real estate. There's more integrity in this industry, if you must know...not to mention less work for the same pay."

I got a bigger nod of understanding then. Turns out he was a Realtor, too, and wanted out as much as I did. We shared disgust with the national association—NAR (and for the record, never believe a word they say), then he wished me well with my writing and paid for the ten minutes I sat chatting with him. I wished him well with real estate and kissed his cheek goodbye. I didn't realize how much I'd appreciate his comments until a full week later, when the following incident occurred.

Customer #2

"Is there any chance we can meet outside of here so I can watch you masturbate?"

He's asking me this in the middle of a lap dance, so I answer him quickly, "No, I don't do that sort of thing," and continue dancing. (For the record I masturbate, I just don't invite creepy strangers over to watch me.)

I'd met this well-dressed, gray-haired man-pig three weeks ago. He's returned to see me twice. We don't talk much because he gets two dances as soon as he comes in and then leaves immediately afterward, except for the one time he stayed to inquire about my workout routine and where I go to yoga.

"God but you're so fucking hot. You're so fucking sexy." He says this with a sudden, awkward grab at my breasts, giving me a painful squeeze before I can move out of reach. His hips are bucking up like a baby in a highchair who's overly excited about a spoonful of strained peas heading its way. I twist out of his grasp and push myself off his lap, finishing the dance from a foot away.

"You know, I think we may live near each other," he continues.

I stop moving altogether. "How in the world would you know where I live?"

"Well just stuff you said about where your yoga is and how far of a drive it is from your home..."

Turns out he lives nowhere near me, but still, I'm completely creeped out by his line of questioning. Then it gets worse.

"I just have to know, what kind of car would a sexy Realtor-slash-stripper like you drive?"

The song ends right at that moment. I collect my twenty dollars but since I'm at a near (and rare) total loss for words, I immediately excuse myself to angrily pace the dressing room. I have not been this pissed off at a customer in years.

Composing myself I head back to sit stiffly in a chair across from him, straining to speak calmly and evenly. "Listen, I have to tell you, it's completely inappropriate for you to...well, *frankly, I'm extremely upset that you would ask me about where I live and what I drive.*"

He flips out, as if he were so fucking slick and sly and stealth he's completely shocked I'm on to him. He starts backpedaling like mad, with *oh, I never meant...*and *please don't misunderstand* and other lame excuses that make no sense and I'm not listening to anyway. I turn my head and make him talk to the hand which just makes him ramble louder, at which point I get up and walk off. He disappeared seconds later.

Twenty years ago, I experienced an attempted break-in by a man alternately pounding on my door and twisting its knob with one hand while jerking himself off with the other. By the time the cops arrived, he'd run off, having seen their flashing lights from a block away. They never caught the guy and I've always wondered if he'd followed me home from Sugar's that night, which would've been quite easy since the club was a mere mile from where I lived, and most nights I'd have been too drunk to notice whether I was being followed. Ten years later, in Vegas, a masked man with a gun was apprehended on my patio seconds from breaking in. I was all alone that night, watching TV. A serial rapist had been on the loose in Vegas for two years at that time, and while my would-be intruder wasn't him, I've never felt completely safe in the world since.

This ain't my first rodeo. I've been around the block enough times to make an entire Cirque du Soleil troupe dizzy. You take the good with the bad in any business, stay grateful for the former and do your best to avoid the latter. But there are times you must stop everything to make a few basic rules very fucking clear.

My time, my conversation, my beauty, my performance, and yes, my breasts are available to men who appreciate, respect, and pay for them. *The rest of you should read this next bit carefully.* It is not something you want to be confused about.

Fruitless is trying to take more from me than I am willing to give.

Faultless is my position after I arrange to have your elbows shattered for it.

Don't test me. Don't try to pull shit over on me. You don't get to know where I live or what I drive. You also will never know who I am, or *who I know and WHAT THOSE PEOPLE ARE CAPABLE OF.*

CHAPTER 17

November–December 2008

BEFORE THE END OF THE YEAR, I was doing well enough to finally pay off the IRS. Initially, I'd been told I owed $9,600 for 2006. But thanks to my new accountant, whom I was paying with sex, that figure dropped to four thousand, which I paid off before Christmas. It was one of the only good things to happen that fall.

First, the producer who'd requested my script pages ultimately decided to pass on it. Then I got news about Joe.

The last time I had spoken to Joe, he'd just gotten into a new relationship and promised me he would let me know personally if he got engaged. He did not. On November 19, a blurb came up on my computer screen from some entertainment website, announcing his engagement to Ringo Starr's sister-in-law, Marjorie. I knew it would hurt to hear that news, but I hadn't expected how much. I sank into a major funk and the next day wrote Joe a long email that was somewhere between an unfelt congratulations and bitter chastisement for leaving me in the dust. I ended it with sarcastic birthday wishes, as that day happened to be his sixty-first. He didn't email back. I stayed depressed about his nuptials for months.

Then the worst thing happened. My sweet Tippy's precarious health took a turn and when Dr. Burnside came over to examine her, she was forced to tell me that it was finally "time."

My cat sitter, Jenn, once told me she'd never met a more communicative cat than Tippy. Tippy could state what she wanted better than any cat alive, whether that was more brushing, a different style of brushing (more wrist action at her chin versus a long straight stroke down her back), more tuna juice in her dry food, which TV show she preferred (Animal Planet's *Meerkat Manor* was her favorite), what time I should get off the computer at the end of the day, and exactly how she felt about me working such long hours when there was so much important snuggling and brushing to be done in the other room! She always, and I mean always, knew the exact moment I switched from valid real estate work or writing to fucking around on the computer with busy work or reading blogs at the end of the day, and would either walk across the keypad or sit on it to make me stop. Sometimes, she'd sit and yell at me from the doorway, looking away with disdain when I'd turn to her with some lame excuse, refusing to stop scolding me over her shoulder with chastising meows until I'd acquiesced and followed her into the bedroom.

She slept on my pillow curled around my head most nights. One time she tried to curl up on my face. Another night, during a powerfully vivid nightmare, a beautiful angel appeared in my dream, taking my hand, and whispering to me that everything would be all right. When I opened my eyes, Tippy was staring into them, lightly stroking the back of my hand with her paw. When we napped together, she'd always lay a paw on my hand or face, probably because she knew my work-aholism well enough to encourage me to stay and relax instead of jumping up again as soon as I lay down.

She'd been with me for seven years, spending her first fifteen as my youngest sister's cat. I'd agreed to take her somewhat reluctantly after Sarah went to college. Then, within days, I wondered how I'd ever lived without her. During my loneliest years, she was a constant comfort. I had to wonder if she knew somehow that it was okay for her to die when she did, five days after I met the first man I would become involved with since Lalo.

Guest blogger Tippy-Kitty Speaks...

December 9, 2008

Current Location: Curled up on my heating pad, as always...
Current Mood: loved

My name is Tippy. I am Casey's cat. I'm guest-blogging because Mom's had an "emotional day" whatever that is. I think it has something to do with me but I'm sure she'll be fine. She's tough that way.

So, Mom and I have both been sick for over a week. Mom had a sinus infection, then she got the twenty-four-hour flu and didn't eat for an entire day. My kidneys don't work well so I get dehydrated, sometimes real bad, and then I just don't feel good, like now. I've been eating less every day for a week. I'm down to four and a half pounds; I used to weigh almost nine. Mom's young and healthy and recovered quick. A new friend brought her juice and medicine to put under her tongue. She's fine now, except worried about me. I'm just old, almost twenty-two in cat years which is about 100 in people years. I'm hanging in there.

Mom called those pretty lady vets, Dr. B and Charla, her assistant. They poked and prodded and stuck me with needles. They put liquids under my skin and then I felt better, got hungry, and ate. All the ladies seemed very excited about this. I was just tired and took a long nap.

Dr. B told Mom about a lump in my abdomen, which might be something called cancer. I'm old...these things happen. I've had a good life. Mom spoils me and I get to eat in bed every day. Sometimes I pee in bed, too, but Mom just does a lot of laundry with only a little grumbling. She thinks I'm worth it because I keep her company and we have fun together.

She brushes me a lot and that makes me purr, and though it sounds different than it used to—kinda frail and sputtering—it always makes Mom happy to hear. She still sings to me; Stevie Nicks and Big Head Todd are my favorites these days. And she takes me for walks in the grass whenever I want. Sometimes we see squirrels and sometimes I just sniff the wind. Occasionally people come up and pet me and tell me I'm beautiful (I am), or we watch the boys play Frisbee across the street.

Someday, maybe soon, I'll lose interest in this stuff. Or maybe I'll stop eating again. It's not easy being 100 years old. Even if you're the most spoiled cat in the world, sometimes you get real tired and need to nap forever. I'm counting on Mom to know what to do then. These things happen.

Mom's book, *The Secret Language of Destiny*, says that those born in March 1987 (like me) are here to learn the path of Individuation. That my core lesson is to develop greater self-interest and self-awareness, and to release the need to fill the expectations of others. *I'm a cat!* I'd say I've fulfilled that destiny pretty well.

Mom's path is Empowerment. She's strong, so she'll be okay when I go. She's young and healthy and recovers from things pretty quick.

RIP Sweet Tippy [1987-2008]

December 10, 2008

Current Location: empty apartment; full heart
Current Mood: grieving

After seeing Tippy take a turn for the worse late last night, and then receiving her worst-case scenario lab results early this morning, I realized it was time to let my angel go.

My darling kitty was released from her suffering at 4:30 p.m. today by her tender, caring vet Dr. Cecilia Burnside. My incredible friend Suzy Spencer dug a big-ass hole in her pristine new yard at the top of a hill near the lake. We buried her there, in a sturdy, wooden keepsake box, given to me by my friend and neighbor Ted.

A healing White Light was sent through the ether by my beloved friend Rob. JV, as always, never stopped sending love. Ruckus and Landshark called on the phone. Dad, Red, Brad, Lesbian yoga girl, cat-lady neighbor, and many others have all made this day a little less awful.

Tippy was the smartest, most sophisticated, demure, wise, dainty, funny, strong, breathtakingly beautiful cat I ever knew. I was beyond lucky to have her as my best friend for so long. Thanks to everyone who cared enough to comment, as well as those who cared but kept silent (I know you're out there, too, and I appreciate it).

CHAPTER 18

2009

In December 2008, my friend and photographer Todd Wolfson showed a friend of his some pictures he'd taken of me. The friend, Alejandro, promptly messaged me on MySpace, complimenting the candid shots I'd posted there. I messaged back that if he liked those, he'd probably love the real me.

"Where?" he asked. "…*With respect.*"

I gave him my address.

I already knew of Alejandro, who was a beloved local musician. Known for his time in the Bay Area punk band The Nuns, alt country band Rank and File, Austin's True Believers, and an extensive solo rock career, he was seventeen years older than me but didn't look it. Fit and trim, he had the silkiest brown skin I'd ever felt and a voice so velvety and resonant I could've listened for hours to him recite the alphabet. One reason he was so beloved was that, after living with Hepatitis C since the nineties, one day in 2003, he collapsed on stage and almost died. Soon afterward, many of his musician friends and admirers collaborated on a tribute album to assist with his medical bills. While he wasn't exactly Austin's own Bruce Springsteen, he was a hard rocking, well-known, critically acclaimed local icon, represented by Bruce Springsteen's management. Jonathan Demme was doing a documentary on him.

I'd seen him play years before, at the Cactus Café, and had been mesmerized. It was a different kind of show, with an entire string section, versus his usual rock and roll fare, and was truly magnificent. Another time, I'd crossed paths with him at a little venue on South Congress directly after he finished sound check. I liked his thick black hair, hip fashion sense, and slightly intense presence, but I played it cool when he strode by, not feeling sociable that day or interested in meeting anyone. Still, he locked eyes with me and said hello, drawing out the word while giving me an openly seductive smile. Alejandro was charismatic to the nth degree, and it stopped me in my tracks, but I'd let it go, smiling back at him briefly before turning away. Five years later, there he was in my MySpace inbox, asking if he could come over.

He was married with a five-year-old daughter. I couldn't care less about either. I was married to my writing and had countless needy men draining my energy and affection every other day at the club. Neither of us were primed for a traditional relationship, but the boy was sexy as fuck. He tended to message me in poetic blurbs and song lyrics, and I liked it a lot. He appealed to my artistic side—the side that wasn't constantly stressed about rent, bills, and real-life drama. He was a flesh and blood fantasy, and I needed that in my life right then as much as food, water, and shelter.

I woke up feeling poorly the day he was due to come over, like I'd caught a mild bug, fatigued and the slightest bit nauseated. Still, I managed to take a bath and put on mascara, a cute vintage tank top, and tight sweatpants. Having been alerted that I was under the weather, he showed up with a bag of goodies including juice, incense, over the counter flu meds, and a candle. He was wearing tight dark jeans, pointy shoes, a white shirt, and a black pinstripe jacket. I loved black pinstripe jackets. *He's even cuter than I remember*, I thought.

We talked about his band, touring schedule, and Hep C diagnosis. I gave him a condensed version of my life story, from the punk years through my addictions, time with Joe Walsh, stripping career, and sobriety. I told him about my writing and a new screenplay I had in mind. He told me about his many siblings, kids, and ex-wives. The whole time I felt self-conscious and unable to be myself. My confidence was shaken lately. Lalo had been easier. We'd met at a strip club, while I was on stage no less—the one place I felt supremely confident. By the time Lalo had come over a few days later, our dynamic was set. But Alejandro was self-possessed. At fifty-eight he knew who he was, and his sexual energy was a big part of it. Not only had my sexual energy been waning lately, but I was also fighting a bug of some sort and not feeling one hundred percent in my body. He couldn't have been sweeter or more gentlemanly, but it had been so long since I'd tried to share myself with someone other than strip club customers, I feared I was failing miserably. I had walls up. We could both feel them. But we kissed anyway, because when it came to sexual connection, we were both the type to be all in. To be risk takers.

So, it was a risk. And when we kissed, I felt…nothing. *Sometimes that happens*, I thought. *It's me, not him.*

I wanted it to feel like it had with Charles. But Charles and I had spent seven or eight hours together before we kissed. And, like Lalo, Charles had been vulnerable and insecure to a degree, which made it feel safer to open up to him. Alejandro didn't seem vulnerable to me and that scared me a little. So, I told him I was tired, and he said he understood and would leave. But then we were suddenly touching and kissing again, and that did start to feel like something. The next thing I knew we were having sex. And it was good. Alejandro had all the passion, technique, and sensuality I could want. But when it was over—when he came—I went back to feeling nothing. And I knew it was me, not him. That the walls around me were higher than before Lalo, and I had no idea how to find my way around them.

I was torn between needing someone to touch the real me and blocking anyone who came close. I told him as much when we emailed over the next few weeks. Alejandro was as easy going as I was high strung. He repeatedly made me feel like it was okay, that we had nothing but time to let this thing between us play out.

I had a deep mistrust of men. A fear of losing myself in someone more successful, established, or magnetic than I was, like I had with Joe. And a fear of being taken advantage of, like I had been with Lalo. At a certain point in my life, when I was still a kid, around six or seven, when my father started working long hours, he'd stopped protecting me from my mother's rage and criticisms. Joe, at my lowest, most vulnerable point—one step away from dying alone in Las Vegas—had abandoned me completely. Lalo, for an entire year, had used me financially. Until that moment with Alejandro, I'd had no idea how deep my ambivalence about charismatic men like him really ran.

In the year since breaking up with Lalo, I'd opened myself up to countless needy strip club customers and the occasional, once a month, escort client. I showered them in affection and sexual attention for a price that was the going rate, but which I considered less than fair. Most I met at the club. I'd met Sam and Kate through a neighbor. Adam was a new regular escort client—someone I'd been friends with back in 1985 when we lived next door to each other in college. He'd been pre-med back then and had always been like a big brother to me, when I was getting into all kinds of trouble with meth and the punk scene. Adam was a genuinely good guy, a Richie Cunningham type with a shock of red hair and constant smile, who'd swing by my apartment when I was eighteen to ensure I had enough food or see if I might need company. I'd treasured him back then but hadn't seen him since 1986, until he'd looked me up online in 2008 to invite me for coffee. He was a doctor now, doing lectures for pharmaceutical companies. His wife was an alcoholic, and his marriage was on the rocks. He was staying in it for the sake of their two kids, but he sure could use a safe, discreet sex partner now and then, and would I be interested in something like that for the right price? I'd said hell yes, and since then he paid me five-hundred-dollars per date on his monthly trips to Austin.

More recently, I'd run into an old real estate broker friend named George whose sugar babe had just dumped him. We'd struck up an arrangement to travel together on an upcoming weekend for a few thousand dollars. We'd made the deal at a smoothie counter in the downtown Whole Foods Market. He'd asked if it would be too much to ask if we could have sex twice a day while traveling if he "promised to make it the best five minutes" of my life every time. I'd laughed and told him that would be fine. George was a true Peter Pan type, who, while a fine broker, was one of those guys who never really wanted to grow up. I figured he'd be fun to hang out with, with simple enough sexual needs to manage.

Meanwhile, my club customers were becoming more demanding. With the recession in full swing, we'd had an influx of newbie strippers desperate to earn a living, and an outflux of quality customers, most of whom were middle-class businessmen suddenly struggling to make ends meet. More strippers fighting for fewer dollars was never a good thing. And since the new girls didn't grasp their value or have any negotiating skills whatsoever, Austin clubs were quickly devolving into thinly veiled whorehouses. Whereas I used to get asked for a two-hundred-dollar blowjob in the VIP room on rare occasions—maybe twice a year—lately I got asked on a weekly basis for a *fifty-dollar* blowjob, and when I invariably declined was met with a surprised look and a snide "everyone else is doing it."

One day early that year, I woke up to an aggressively sexual comment on my blog. Instead of ignoring it, like I should have, I shamed the guy for telling me he wanted to "splooge all over my toes." For the next two days he escalated his abusive comments. Turned out he was a customer at Perfect 10 and he was threatening to spread lies and rumors about me there to make my work life hell. My regular commenters rallied to my rescue, berating the guy on my behalf, which didn't slow him down but did warm my heart for their efforts. Eventually, I was forced to block all comments and log IP addresses until the whole thing blew over, but it left me feeling vulnerable and exposed...like every time I opened myself up, someone tried to take it further than I wanted it to go. Further than I should be expected to go.

I was working my way through it all. But until meeting Alejandro, I hadn't quite realized how draining it had been.

❧

Six weeks after our first date, Alejandro asked to see me again. I was worried it would be awkward or feel like...nothing at all, so I decided not to care one way or another. To go with the flow for once in my life and enjoy getting to know a guy.

He arrived in his pointy shoes carrying a guitar. We hugged and kissed in the middle of my living room for a long, long, time. It felt natural and delicious and definitely like...something. Something potentially special. We talked and laughed, and then had sex, and for his entire two-hour visit never left each other's arms. As he was getting dressed to leave, he told me he was going on the road for two weeks and would call while he was gone. "What will you be up to?" he asked nonchalantly.

"I'm going to Mexico, actually."

"That sounds fun. With who?"

"I ran into an old real estate colleague recently, who offered me three thousand dollars to spend the weekend in Isla Mujeres with him."

Alejandro paused, taking that in. Then, with a tilted head, he asked, "Well...if he's paying you to join him, I mean...don't you think he's going to expect sex from you?"

"Yeah," I replied with a smile. "And he's going to get it."

Alejandro looked at me with a new expression on his face. One of curiosity, intrigue, and I daresay admiration.

"Okay then," he laughed. "Well, have a great time and a safe trip, I guess."

ALEJANDRO CALLED FROM THE ROAD like he'd said he would, telling me things like, "I think you're beautiful. Hearing your voice makes me feel so good. I'm fascinated by you. I can't wait to see you." Mostly we texted or sexted each other. I asked him if he saw other women the way he saw me.

"Not in Austin," he said. "I've never cheated on my wife in Austin until meeting you."

He was sweeping me off my feet. As much as I'd let him, anyway. In February, he played a gig at the Cactus Café. When I arrived, I found my name taped to a preferred aisle seat. He played amazingly, perfectly in his element, and I was justifiably blown away. At one point he came into the audience to play three songs, one of them directly in front of me. I knew without him telling me that he'd arranged it that way. We had to be discreet, because although his marriage was not going well, many people knew his wife, so he had to pretend I was just another audience member. Except he played an entire song just for me, and during the show caught my eye repeatedly.

Afterward, I waited for him in the crowd while he signed things for people. He raised a finger at me, letting me know he'd be over in a bit. When he came, we chatted from a respectable distance without touching, though I was dying to put my hands all over him. He still had other people to talk to and asked me to wait in my car for him, saying he'd call when he was done. I sat in my car at the curb thinking about how tired I was and that I had to work tomorrow. About how many times I'd waited on busy musicians who always took longer than they expected. About putting my needs on hold for someone else's career and schedule. For every lover I'd ever had and every man I'd ever loved.

It wasn't Alejandro's fault. He'd gone out of his way to make me feel like the center of his attention, to make me feel incredibly special at the show where he was the star, and I was an audience member. But I'd let Joe's career and lifestyle sweep me up and derail me from my dreams—something I'd never forgiven myself for, nor learned how to keep from happening again. I'd wasted so much time trying to make a relationship work with Lalo when in truth we'd have been far better off as lovers, leading our own lives, separate from each other. I wanted to be with Alejandro in a way that honored us both, but I had a terrible habit of not seeing the right path while trudging down the initial attraction/chemistry road. Only in hindsight did I tend to figure it out and only with much frustration and chagrin. I wanted to get it right this time and thought staying vigilant was the best way to do that. To be vigilant of every time I was giving up my time and energy to someone who prioritized their schedule and career over mine. Not that he would do that...except of course he would because who in his position wouldn't? Alejandro had an established career. He literally couldn't date someone who wasn't at least a little flexible with her schedule.

I waited for him in my car until he was done with the post-gig schmoozing. I also promised myself it would be the last time I did that for him or anyone.

ON VALENTINE'S DAY, Alejandro came over at one in the morning after a gig. I was sleeping but left the door unlocked for him. He touched me, his cool fingers tracing my warm leg, kissing me, though I was too sleepy to properly kiss back. Until he was naked on top of me, fingers inside me and out, until *I* was inside out, kissing him back hard, the way he liked it, and digging into his shoulder with my nails as I came from his touch. When we finally turned on the light, he gave me a forty-year-old edition of Kahlil Gibran's *A Tear and a Smile* and a beautiful moonstone drop necklace.

He asked me one day if I was good at living with someone.

"No, not really."

"Hm, I've always lived with someone," he said thoughtfully.

     Kristin Casey

He was clearly more of a relationship person than I was. I expected what we had to last only as long as it took for him to want something more serious. I treasured our time together and tried not to get too attached. It wasn't hard since he was on the road a lot and lived a ways outside of Austin, so we didn't usually get to see each other more than twice a month, anyway.

He said if anything happened to him I should log on to his email account and delete all our messages.

"If that happens will I have to hear about it on the radio?"

"Don't worry, I may have a few good years left. Or maybe I'll live to be ninety-seven," he said with a wink.

I thought about that for a minute then finally asked, "What do your doctors think?"

Alejandro smiled. "They think I've got a few good years left."

UNBEKNOWNST TO ME, my hormones were out of whack. My once vibrant sex drive, my lifelong constant companion, was sketchy at best and had been for months. And I'd been crying a lot for no apparent reason.

Alejandro came over one day for an hour, before a gig he had at The Continental Club. We made love, then talked. He said he wasn't so sure I needed men in my life. Or maybe just one, the right one… "A together one," he said.

I said, *I don't know anymore*, then teared up a little. Somehow, he could already see how my work and lifestyle were going to interfere with anything we tried to create romantically.

Alejandro's wife was going through some stuff. Feeling weak, unhappy, and depressed. He said he wasn't good with needy women. I felt like I had two settings lately: strong as hell and needy as fuck. I didn't think Alejandro would be thrilled about either. He was a happy-go-lucky guy. I was anything but, and it put a strain on us. We had moments that were beautifully tender and sweet, with potential for intimacy, love, and mutual support. But his schedule was such that, often, the only time he could get away to see me was at three in the morning after a gig or on a writing day I wasn't willing to give up. He was outwardly understanding, though I sensed he thought I was a bit Stalinistic about my writing. *Easy for him*, I thought. An established minor rock star who didn't have to worry anymore about building a career or credibility in his field. He was highly respected, by critics and fans alike. I was just getting started. And while he had seventeen years on me, I wasn't getting any younger.

He sometimes worried that I was getting bored and wondered if I liked him as much as I claimed to. I was never bored, and I liked him quite a bit, but I was under so much pressure to make headway with my writing, pay bills, and keep all my customers and clients happy, that I didn't have much energy left for him or our relationship. My affection reserves were empty. And with my imbalanced hormones, I felt less sexual and womanly than I had in a long time. That part I couldn't bring myself to tell him. That I was beginning to feel detached from my body more and more frequently, and sometimes it happened when I was with him. But it wasn't about him. I was just imbalanced. Carrying too many burdens. And he wasn't in a position to take any of them off my hands.

We decided it would be a good idea to try to spend an entire night together. He promised to figure out a time he could sneak away discreetly. He had a camera crew following him around for most of March. "Don't bring them here," I joked. "There's not enough room."

He came over after a gig at The Continental Club, arriving at four in the morning. We made love for two hours, though I was too tired to talk afterward. I felt withdrawn and my walls were up. Not because of him, just too much work and stress that month. He asked about my escort clients, then decided he didn't want to hear much. After a long silence he said, "I know this is futile, but what are you thinking right now?"

I just laughed. I loved how well he read my moods, even if neither of us fully understood why I had them. Still, I remained distant through the night, and when he left, I closed the door a little too quickly.

He wanted me to leave my baggage behind when we were together. I wanted that, too, but I told him it wasn't that easy. I paid the bills with sex work, which had lately become incredibly draining. It had become so much a part of my life that I sometimes had to fantasize about whoring in order to climax when I was with Alejandro—I mean, what the hell was that about? I guessed I needed to feel valued to get off. To feel fairly compensated for what I was putting out in order to relax into the pleasure of the moment. Cash represented that. It met my needs. Cash was what I needed more than anything at that time in my life, by far.

Looking back, I think in my heart I wanted a savior and was perhaps a little mad that Alejandro wasn't him.

In April, he figured out a way to spend the whole night with me by telling his wife he had to leave on tour one day earlier than he did. I agreed excitedly, completely forgetting that I had plans to see Adam that night, for a five-hundred-dollar fee I couldn't afford to give up. I toyed with the idea, but I simply couldn't cancel the paid date. When I told Alejandro, he was brokenhearted about it.

"I'm sorry. I'm so sorry," I kept repeating.

"Don't say sorry," he said. But then neither of us spoke until one of us finally said goodbye and hung up.

We made up three days later, on a long, productive call. He said he liked me more than he ever meant to, more than he ever wanted to. He said everyone in his life was wondering why he'd been so happy lately and it was because of me. He couldn't tell them because I was a tightly kept secret, but he thought about me all the time. I couldn't wait to see him again and ran out to buy him a red jasper pendant, the first gift I'd bought anyone since Lalo.

I continued to see Alejandro through May and June. We agreed that I wouldn't talk so much about work or my past relationships. It wasn't fair to compare him to my ex-boyfriends like I did sometimes. To judge his behavior on their past misdeeds and hurtful acts. He liked that I was open about it all, but also said that sometimes he wished I was a radio he could simply turn down. I laughed at that, then continued talking about past relationships and current customers and clients, to his frustration.

When we had sex all our problems went away. It got better with every date. We'd spent our entire six-month relationship in private, usually in my apartment and usually in my bed. It was only when real life got in the way that we had tension and disagreements.

I was still revising my memoir and my first script, as well as starting my second script, and devoting a lot of time to all three. I'd managed to save a little money and in June went to Beverly Hills for a facelift that resulted in complications. Frankly, it was flat-out botched. Once again, I had entrusted my body to someone who took advantage of it and damaged me, this time to great expense. All of this stressed me out and made me testy with Alejandro over little things like him showing up early for a date before I was ready. We argued about it, then worked our way through it. A week later, we got together after his gig at La Zona Rosa.

I wasn't feeling like myself. The facelift had fully drained my bank account except for two thousand dollars that went to car repairs as soon as I'd returned from Beverly Hills. I was dead broke with facial nerve damage I couldn't afford to address. So, I was in a dour mood when I went to meet Alejandro at his friend's house, where he'd secured the adjacent garage apartment for our latest tryst. As we lay quietly in bed next to each other, I found myself wondering how I could best extricate myself from the relationship.

My hormones were still off, and my sex drive was practically nonexistent. The phrase "dead inside" came to mind regularly that month. My work, writing, and surgery had all been ridiculously draining. Alejandro deserved more than I had to give him. And I didn't know what to do about it.

As we lay there in silence, all of a sudden, he told me he loved me. And all I could think was how could we possibly be on such different pages?

I didn't see him for months after that. I saved what little sexual energy I had for the now twice-a-month escort appointments that enabled me to stay afloat while working on my writing projects. I plodded through strip club shifts that became more disheartening every week, and through it all prayed my writing would pay off in some way that enabled me to quit sex work while still in my early forties.

❧

FOR ONLY THE SECOND TIME in my adult life, I had almost no desire for sex. I felt empty inside. So of course, that's when Paul, Rob, and Larry all reappeared in my life. Paul's girlfriend had relapsed on heroin, so he was suddenly single again and wanted me to meet him in LA. I decided not to go but it was nice to be asked. Rob invited me to his gym and taught me some MMA holds and sparring, though he didn't make a move on me, and since my sex drive was so low, I wasn't complaining. Months later, I saw him again and we had sex for old times' sake. Larry invited me to Vegas for two days but then had a work emergency after one, leaving me there on my own for the second night, which was a lot less fun.

In September, I called Alejandro. I'd missed him and we had a nice talk. He'd been in Mexico for a month, surfing and writing songs. His marriage continued to deteriorate, and they were heading for divorce. I explained to him why I disappeared so suddenly, about all the apprehension and distrust in me these days and wanting to spare him from it. About our incompatible schedules and the string of misunderstandings between us. About my need to rein in my stress so it didn't affect everyone I encountered. "I don't want you to see me looking so angry and unappealing all the time," I told him.

He said he understood, though I suspected he was taking it more personally than it was. I certainly would have. But how could I explain feeling dead inside and having almost no sex drive? It was embarrassing and depressing. My entire life was becoming embarrassing and depressing. I cried myself to sleep almost every night. Alejandro was never going to stay with a woman like that. If I hadn't ended it when I did, he would've done so himself in a matter of weeks.

Two months later I called, in a good mood and missing him. We met in his room at the Austin Motel, talked about our relationship, my anger, and his understanding of it. Then we made love and talked some more. He joked about being a fifty-eight-year-old rocker, wondering aloud if it might look a little ridiculous.

"Honey, I'm a forty-two-year-old stripper," I laughed. "If anyone looks ridiculous here, it isn't you."

We got together again a few days later. I'd gone to see Bob Schneider at Antone's and danced my ass off for two hours, like I used to when I was younger. Then I raced over to The Continental Club to catch the last of Alejandro's set. As usual, he had a group of crazy happy dancing girls at his feet near the stage, but when I walked up, he caught my eye and smiled, then sang the rest of the set to me. Afterward, he pulled me out the back door and we ran back to his suite at the Austin Motel. My back was killing me from dancing all night and my coochie was sore from grinding on customers all day before. But I didn't care; the sex was just that good, some of the best we'd ever had. It was the last time we were together like that, and it was nice to go out with a bang. An encore of our best material, so to speak.

The following year, Alejandro released a new album. On it was the song "This Bed Is Getting Crowded." He dropped by to give me a copy and tell me the song was about me. "It's about a woman who's constantly talking about the other men in her life while in bed with her lover."

I had to laugh. Yeah, I did that somewhat. It often took place in bed because most of our relationship took place in bed. I was always trying to explain why I was the way I was by telling him stories of my past, it was true. It was just another misunderstanding between us, or perhaps a different way of being. We were such different creatures. Him, so open and loving. Me, so guarded and mistrusting. He once jokingly offered me five hundred dollars "to please just say 'I love you' while we're doing it." I admit, I kind of adored him for that—the most vulnerable moment of clarity he'd ever displayed in regard to our incompatibility. I'd just laughed affectionately before telling him there wasn't enough money in the world to make me say that, to him or anybody. A real relationship between us never would've worked but I was eternally grateful for the fun we'd had trying.

While it was hardly the first time I'd partnered with a man who wasn't right for me, it was the first time I'd seen it early on and done something about it before creating a bunch of drama and chaos for both parties. I'd finally developed dating discernment, derived from my many years of dating consciously and abundantly. I'd learned a lot about chemistry and compatibility in my forty-two years. What I would do with that knowledge and wisdom remained to be seen.

Aching Back, Amazing Front

November 16, 2008

Current Location: Upright!
Current Mood: cheerful

I finally found a new chiropractor who's both cheap and good, which means I'm finally able to work a full shift *and* do a decent job on stage. My hips aren't as swivel-y as usual, my back not nearly as arched, and my floor work less sweeping and sensual, yet it's still far better than any stage work I've done over the past five weeks.

So, today I'm dancing on stage to a mere five customers (most of whom are more interested in watching the UT game on TV than watching me) when a gorgeous brunette dancer I've never met approaches. I assume it's to tip me (which we ladies do for each other once in a while), but no. She wants a quick chat.

"Can I help you?" I say, squatting at the edge of the stage. I notice a group of three other dancers nearby paying close attention, as if they know what she's about to say and are in on it.

"Are those real?" she asks with genuine curiosity, not a trace of mean girl competitiveness.

"You mean my tits?" A stupid question but I'm surprised to be having this conversation with a colleague literally in the middle of my stage set. Whatever, she has a great vibe, so I answer. "Yeah, they're real."

She takes one step back for emphasis and declares, "Those. Are. AMAZING."

I burst out laughing while she continues showering my tits with praise. Holding up all her fingers, "A ten—they're a TEN!" she says and heads back to confer with the others who nod approvingly.

So, I got that going for me.

CHAPTER 19

2009–March 2010

I'D DATED ALEJANDRO FOR most of 2009, but through it all a lot else had been going on with my work and writing. Early in our relationship I'd gone to Mexico with my broker friend George. He'd paid me to spend the weekend with him and his wealthy friends riding scooters around a tropical island, eating fish tacos, drinking limonadas, and having quick, playful sex twice a day. It was an ideal moonlighting opportunity that unfortunately didn't come up regularly. I continued with my twice-a-month, hourly escort dates and stripping two or three days a week at Exposé and Perfect 10. Working with a degenerated lumbar spine was challenging, but I was still earning enough to get by and had even saved five thousand dollars for a facelift.

As the year went on, however, my income trended farther downward. The Great Recession was in full swing. And at Perfect 10, for nearly half my eight-hour shift we were required to do half-price dances—ten dollars apiece instead of the usual twenty, with more "extras" (touching, sucking, digitally penetrating) expected by customers every day. There was no upselling in Austin VIP rooms. We only took customers in there if they promised to buy two or more dances, but dances were still ten or twenty dollars apiece in every room of the club—the same price they'd been two decades earlier, back when there was no touching allowed. Stage tips tended to be two dollars, though sometimes customers still gave one, while expecting to grab or poke my private parts while there.

A friend once told me that before reading my blog he'd assumed all strip club customers were insecure losers, but that based on my genuine regard for them, some must've been confident, successful, and even sexy. And he was right—some were charming, smart, creative, and sexy. I made a killing one night in Vegas off comedian Drew Carey. He'd treated me like a princess for hours and been almost obscenely generous all night. I'd heard through friends at Sugar's that George Clooney had once gone in and taken some of their dancers with him on a mini vacation to Florida. I'd also heard rumors that Steve Carell was known to treat strippers with generosity and respect.

But the good ones weren't just celebrities. They were the men next to you in the pew at church or the bleachers at a Longhorns game. They were lawyers with free advice, doctors who asked about my health, massage therapists who gave complimentary back rubs, and non-massage therapists who did their best. They were veterans who needed to relax, retirees who doted on me, and wage-earning laborers who tipped on every stage and bought me bracelets on Valentine's Day. They were filmmakers and writers, inventors and volunteers, intellectuals and academics who stimulated my mind while I stimulated their libidos. They were fathers and grandfathers, athletes and techies, grease monkeys and rock stars. Some of them were lovely, generous, appreciative humanitarians…and others were absolute fucktards.

❧

On Valentine's Day, I sat with a distinguished, elderly gentleman whom I'd met weeks earlier. He hadn't had time for a dance that day but had since come to the club three times looking for me, the first two on my days off. Having finally found me again, he rushed me into the VIP room where he excitedly presented me with the strip club version of romance: strawberries, canned whipped cream, and cheap champagne—none of which I touched since the strawberries weren't organic, I was averse to eating anything from a can, and for obvious reasons couldn't drink champagne. (I thanked him for the thoughtfulness anyway.)

He was eightyish, small, and frail, yet well-kept, and probably handsome once upon a time. He wore black dress slacks, a gray golf shirt, and black golf sweater. His eyes were pale blue and watery, like the lowest layer of an iceberg. He was upfront about what he wanted from me and was happy to pay extra for it—lots of friction and pressure, stroking, grinding, and hot breath released directly onto the crotch of his pants. He wanted to see me smile as I pleasured him while gazing into his eyes. To feel aroused by me while pretending to himself the feeling was reciprocated. He wanted to feel young again. He wanted to feel like a man.

He complimented my body, voice, clothes, poise, and lap dance skill. And while he wasn't grabby at first, as soon as I was on his lap his mouth dove for my nipple like a starving, demonic infant, teeth bared, tongue jutted out like a tiny, pink, slimy spear.

I recoiled. "Whoa!" I said, as sweetly as I could. "No tongue, okay? That's my number one rule."

"Of course, yes, yes, I understand," he conceded, proving his sincerity with two dry pecks on my cheeks. "You're so lovely, dear, so beautiful and sexy…" His dreamy, watery eyes shone with satisfaction as his wrinkled fingers delicately traced my breasts. Softly, politely, happily. He was getting exactly what he wanted and reciprocated with multiple appreciative sighs. He told me I was exactly what he'd been looking for. I was exactly what he needed.

"My pleasure, honey. Hope to see you again soon." I was about to leave before he stopped me briefly.

"Can I give you one more peck?"

"Of course!" I smiled, leaning in to offer my cheek. As I did he parted his thin, dry lips, just like before, and jutted his pointy, wet tongue out again, too quick this time for me to avoid it connecting with my upper lip. I pushed him against the couch. "Seriously?!"

He looked offended. *He* did. *Him.*

"You agreed," I snapped. *"No tongue."*

His eyes narrowed. As if I'd misbehaved. *Me.*

I demanded an apology, and though he initially refused, I wouldn't leave without it. Finally, he caved and then immediately looked shamed.

I didn't care. In fact, his shame felt so satisfying to me that I cheerfully accepted his apology, changed the subject, and got him laughing about something or other in no time. I didn't know if he'd come back to see me, though I suspected that he might. I was the kind of dancer he'd been looking for. I was exactly what he needed.

Around that time, I met another new customer—a tall, wiry country boy in small eyeglasses with messy short hair, approaching me on second stage. I was in a good mood and gave him a great mini show, for which he tipped me exactly one dollar, slid into the side of my thong. One dollar, which he apparently thought was worth one purposeful swipe of his finger from my hip to crotch where he then hooked it to swipe *inside my thong.* One dollar for a finger full of my off-limits flesh.

"You're a sneaky little man, aren't you?" I shouted as he scampered away, looking down at the floor with either satisfaction or shame…I had no idea which.

Another time, on main stage, I was summoned over by a frizzy-haired man in his thirties with a huge, gold coin medallion around his neck. His table was at the stage's edge—apparent justification to stay seated as he held up—but not *out*—a one-dollar bill, forcing me to crawl on my hands and knees and lean precariously forward to snap it in my thong strap. As I did so, he used his other hand to squeeze my right breast.

I pulled back, covering my chest protectively. "Uh, groping is actually not on the dollar menu."

"Oh," he replied brightly. "Okay, then. Sorry."

I resumed dancing. Two minutes later, he held up another one-dollar bill, still seated. As I did my standard mini dance, he got sidetracked by a waitress but then quickly turned back and handed me the dollar (because I wasn't about to lean over for him this time). Suddenly, a look of regret crossed his greasy, stubbly face.

"Hey, could you dance a little more? I kinda feel like I got shortchanged."

Again, I had to sit back momentarily before replying. "I just danced nearly naked, two feet from your face, in exchange for *one* dollar and *you* feel shortchanged?"

"Well, I didn't mean…uh, er…to offend you." He seemed baffled.

"Honey, for the price of a stick of gum, you want more than the great show I just gave you and that's not supposed to offend me?"

"I'm sorry, I'm from New York, okay? Give me a break…c'mon, high-five me!" He beamed and held up his hand for a high five.

I didn't know what else to do but take it in mine, look into his eyes, and state calmly, "Please be a little more thoughtful to the next dancer, because *seriously, dude,* neither of us give a shit where you're from."

In truth, I sometimes found it difficult to work up much anger over that stuff. Most guys were more clueless than malicious, but the cumulative effect propelled me to post on my blog about it a lot. Medallion guy was one of six major fucktards I had the displeasure of catering to in one week, not to mention that the previous day had been utterly dead. It was one of those days when a dozen girls wandered from VIP to the main floor every twenty minutes or so, making the same rounds to the same guys, looking more and more dazed as each hour passed, sighing in unison and exchanging sympathetic looks and eye rolls, then, finally, laughs in that unfunny way of frustrated camaraderie.

That day, I'd spent a few minutes with one sharp dressed businessman. He was in his mid-forties, with dark hair carefully combed back from his tidy receding hairline and perfectly trimmed to his crisp, white collar and snazzy tie in shades of maroon and burgundy. He was in insurance and needed "a place to kill two hours between appointments today." He sat by the rear stage, nursing one iced tea the entire time, tipping no one, and buying zero lap dances.

Before I had time to guide the conversation toward a lap dance, he launched into a spiel on every kind of health insurance policy I might be interested in (though I hadn't asked, because I wasn't). I changed the topic repeatedly trying to get him in a sexy frame of mind more conducive to buying dances, but it didn't work. He flatly declined before asking with a wink-wink-nudge-nudge if I "do any extracurricular work?" But when it turned out he couldn't afford my escort rates I left him to his watery tea. I was due on stage anyway.

Near the tail end of a kickass set, while dancing to Ian Moore's "Harlem," I was surprised to see Insurance Guy trekking from the back of the room. He had that look of awe I loved, that said either, "I had no idea a woman your age could have such an amazing body!" or "Holy shit, you can really dance!" I was guessing the latter and it turned out I was right because as he slipped a dollar in my thong he stated emphatically, "Wow, you are a true *artiste!*" which I appreciated, but still. This was a man who made his living in sales and yet expected a dozen dancers to provide him two hours of exceptional exotic entertainment, by paying one dancer one dollar plus one compliment.

IN MAY 2009, I QUIT EXPOSÉ after a disagreement with the owner about the quality of strippers he'd been hiring. They were young, but also flabby, sloppy, and trashy. It was bad for business and the handful of high caliber dancers still there, myself included, were sick of it. Three times that month I'd lost out on potential lap dances for refusing to let customers suck or lick my breasts. One smelly

                                        Kristin Casey

old man tried to convince me that other girls were French kissing him in the VIP room, something I never would've believed before but, sadly, of late, did. When another distinguished looking, elderly man greeted me by taking my hand and pressing it so confidently to the bulge in his khaki shorts, I knew he'd gotten away with it multiple times.

"Listen, honey," I informed him. "If I'm gonna make a living stroking cock, I'll simply post on *Craigslist* from the comfort of my own home, thanks very much."

I auditioned at Exposé's sister club, Palazio in South Austin, where I was hired immediately. The first thing I noticed was the lack of smell, and not just Exposé's dead squirrel in the ceiling smell, but the utter lack of smoke, mold, booze, sweat, and fruity body spray that permeates every strip club in the country. It was clean, plush, and sexy in that timeless red velvet meets colored lights way. The other dancers were friendly and professional. Not once on my first eight-hour shift did I witness drama, drunken displays, sloppy behavior, or sleazy dancing. All sixteen dancers except one had an exceptional body with natural perky breasts. The customers were mostly businessmen, versus Exposé's blue collar and hoodie types. I had the most profitable day I'd had all month.

The following month, I attended a screenwriter Pitch Fest in Burbank, California, pitching my first script, *Speed Punk*, to a dozen producers and managers, six of whom liked the story, four of whom asked me to email the script. I was told that constituted a high level of interest, especially for a dark, edgy drama about a teenage drug addict. The next script I planned to write—a crime drama and love story about a drug dealer and high-end escort— was even more commercial. Considering the topics I was most inclined to write about, I was heartened that films like *The Wrestler*, *Boogie Nights*, and *Leaving Las Vegas* had gotten made. I was hoping to find managers and producers to love my work the same way I loved those films.

Back in Austin, I heard from one of the producers who'd requested my script. He didn't think the main character was innocent enough to be sympathetic. She dove into drugs too eagerly, he said, and all I could think was that the dude clearly needed to get out more. Had he never seen *Traffic*, *Trainspotting*, *Drugstore Cowboy*, or *The Basketball Diaries*?

I blew him off and patiently waited to hear from the other three interested parties. In July, once I'd recovered from the facelift I'd also had done while out in LA, I returned to work at Perfect 10 and Palazio, only to find my two best regulars were both MIA due to drops in their income from the recession. Also, though taking a month off had helped ease my daily back pain, once I was back dancing it returned with a vengeance.

In August, I told everyone I knew to stop calling and emailing so I could focus on writing my second script. My relationship with Alejandro had faded to almost nothing, leaving only work, yoga, and writing. Because of my back injury, I'd had to quit doing most forward extensions in yoga, which I didn't mind, other than the fear that it was metaphorically a bad sign as it related to moving forward in life. The writing, however, was going gangbusters. My screenplay characters were talking to me all day and night, telling me who they were and how the story should play out, in ways better than on my original index card outline taped to my dining room's mirrored wall. Two months later, I attended my second Austin Film Festival Conference, networking my brains out and pitching my second script—unfinished—interesting two reputable producers by the end of the weekend.

Work was the real issue, as side effects from the recession continued to plague me. One day, a regular at Palazio—a wealthy, educated man who tipped me well on stage but never bought more than one dance—casually said, "I don't know what you're doing here. You could do a lot better than twiddling your thumbs all afternoon in a sleepy South Austin strip club."

He'd just returned from the Toronto Film Festival where he'd hung out with Ridley Scott and Steven Soderbergh. He'd also just asked me out for the second time since meeting me three weeks earlier (and I'd just turned him down for the second time because I found his offer of compensation offensively low). We were in the VIP room. I was watching him eat shrimp cocktail, hoping when he was done he'd buy a dance or tip me for my time. He did neither, but before leaving did offer some advice: *You should search Craigslist for men to pay to see you outside the club to get through the recession.*

There wasn't much I could say in return. Nothing summed up my situation better than that conversation right there. What an educated, sophisticated, successful man saw as the best option for a talented, self-educated, aging-yet-elegant gal like me was to either date him or date *Craigslist*.

By September, the recession had infested Palazio too. One day I watched a girl I'd never worked with before—supremely average in every way, with the most blank expression ever—grind against a customer on third stage so hard he had to grip its edge to stay upright until she was done *two minutes later*. When it was over, he handed her a crumpled one-dollar bill and sat back down.

Blank Girl proceeded to lay on her side with one leg kicked toward the ceiling, held awkwardly by a weak grip on her ankle, leaving the knee slightly bent in that graceless "newbie dancer" way (meaning too stupid or lazy to lock out her damn knee). Using her free hand, she then weirdly groped around her crotch for a while (presumably to ensure it was still there after banging it against that customer for two minutes for the price of a French fry). Eventually, faux masturbation ceased, she lay there, blank, bent, and awkward, with her puffy, pink-thonged crotch on display till the song blessedly ended. Donning an elastic fishnet dress, she plopped onto the nearest chair to return to staring blankly at the ceiling, oddly, never approaching Crumbled Dollar Guy at all.

I took in the entire display sitting stiffly on a VIP chair, nursing my usual back pain and wondering, *why can't I let this go?*

Until recently, I'd truly enjoyed my work as a stripper. But the higher expression I thought I was bringing to it was slipping through the cracks. One night, a self-described "plump, lazy customer" frantically waved me over from across the room because, as he said, "You're an amazing dancer with the best body in here."

Then, in the middle of my second lap dance he not only tried to rub his hand all over my thong and then finger my clit, but he had the nerve to complain when I told him three times "Sorry, I don't allow that."

I managed to keep his hands off my crotch, but as soon as the song ended he coldly announced we were done. Shortly thereafter, I was summoned to another corner by a married couple to dance for the wife—a sixty-year-old, incredibly beautiful, fit, elegant woman who tried to suck my nipple the instant my bra came off. Later, I was taken to VIP by an old man in a huge cowboy hat, Texas Tech shirt, and high-waisted women's jeans, who, midway into my second song tried to slip both thumbs inside my thong. As I politely nudged them away he instantly stiffened then promptly told me "we're done."

During my final set that day, eight young men in their twenties sat at the edge of main stage, politely tossing and placing two-, three-, and four-dollar tips for me on its edge. One bought a lap dance after my set and didn't try to violate me once. He told me I was beautiful and sexy, then returned to his friends where he continued to tip other dancers on stage. My shift finally over, I changed clothes, tipped out, and went outside where three of his group of twenty-somethings were waiting for a cab.

"Have a great weekend," I said, as they waved and nodded and flashed me knowing smiles—the kind men get when they've seen you naked and liked it, that look of having shared a sexy secret— while also being bashful and tongue-tied.

As I passed them on the way to my car, one called out, "Good job!" His friends laughed and ribbed him for the goofy comment, but I was genuinely touched by the heartfelt compliment. I had the urge to hug him but my back hurt too much to pivot in his direction.

Soon after, I drove to Dallas in search of a more upscale work environment, finding it at Spearmint Rhino—a beautiful, lush, tasteful space, clean as could be, with a huge, spotless, fully stocked ladies' rooms with functioning locks on every stall door (nonexistent in Austin). The music wasn't too loud, my fellow dancers passed out tips and compliments to each other freely, and the customers had better hygiene, grooming, and money than at any club in Austin. Lap dances were twenty-five dollars across the board and half my customers gave me thirty. Unfortunately, the three-hour drive was hell on my back, and travel expenses and higher tip-outs gobbled up most of the extra money I made. Also, by the end of my second week, I'd derived a better idea of how many extras Dallas customers expected, and it turned out to be exactly in line with the bullshit I dealt with back in Austin.

I returned to Austin and checked out the last two decent clubs there—The Yellow Rose and Sugar's, both of which had major problems. The Yellow Rose was clean and comfy; however, their music was so loud I lost my voice halfway through every shift and started experiencing bouts of intermittent tinnitus after work. (Their decibel reader stayed between ninety-eight and one hundred all day, a full fifteen points higher than OSHA advocated as safe to avoid hearing loss.) Desperate to protect my hearing, I quit two weeks later. Sugar's had been my original strip club back in the eighties, where I'd spent five wonderful years. So, I was disheartened to see how run down and filthy it had become. Also, extras at Sugar's were off the charts, with actual penetrative sex taking place in their VIP booths. I quickly quit there too. Instead, I resigned myself to working at Perfect 10, where the building was riddled with mold and smoking was allowed, leaving my head frequently throbbing and my throat and nasal passages raw and stinging. I also worked at Palazio, where the club was either mostly empty or full of customers who expected major extras.

I worked on Thanksgiving, which I did every year when I could. I like working holidays because, though the crowd was sparse, few enough dancers showed up that I tended to do well anyway. With only nine dancers versus our typical thirty to forty, not only did I stay busy, but I had a chance to meet some new customers whose favorite dancers hadn't bothered to show up. And I quickly learned why these guys weren't, and never would be, my customers.

I was once told by a customer that I gave the naughtiest clean dances he'd ever seen. I liked that description and thought it suited me. What he'd meant was that I managed to give him a rock-hard erection without ever actually stroking his dick. Giving a great dance like that practically made me high it felt so good. But by the end of Thanksgiving Day, I'd been informed twice that I was a "really clean" dancer and, by one man, "possibly the cleanest dancer here." Neither of those men meant it as a compliment. They were exactly as thrilled about that little discovery as I was to learn how sleazy all my stripper sisters had become. Since my boundaries hadn't changed in three years, clearly everyone else's had deteriorated quite a bit. Especially after one customer launched me into a string of dances with next to no opening conversation and then, during my second lap dance, proceeded to pull his penis out of his pants to beat off furiously as if it were the most normal thing in the world.

"Uh, I don't actually allow that sort of thing."

"Really? Okay…sorry."

And back in his pants it went, because apparently outrageously inappropriate behavior didn't necessarily exclude good manners. But when he wouldn't stop rubbing it frantically on the *outside* of his pants during my third dance, I quit moving altogether, leaned back and sipped my seven-dollar Voss water until the song ended.

The next inappropriate customer I sat with was a different sort, the kind who liked to think he was emotionally connected to the dancers. That we had rapport and were genuine friends with him. He said he liked to try giving dancers orgasms as a tip...*because who wants to be saddled with all that extra burdensome cash?*

He claimed to be a professor of some sort and said he could speak multiple languages including Japanese. He'd traveled the world and was married to a wonderful woman, though he felt bad for "having become a sex addict in recent years."

Sensing he was trouble, I talked him out of going to the VIP room and gave him two dances on the main floor instead, during which he rubbed his hands all up and down my arms, back, and neck as if I were a frostbite victim. He even tried to rub my ears and chin as I writhed and contorted out of his reach, desperate to keep his grimy hands off my delicate, clean complexion.

❧

MOST STRIPPERS were earning one fourth to half our earnings from 2007, two years earlier. I was in constant pain from dancing with a lumbar full of fucked up discs. The toxic environment of fending off tongues and hands all day was making me hard and bitter. I was pretty sure all the good effects of quitting smoking twelve years earlier were being undone by the secondhand smoke I was forced to breathe in, not to mention what was quite possibly black mold infesting Perfect 10, as evidenced by the black ceiling tiles and constant respiratory issues my coworkers and I dealt with.

In January 2010, Perfect 10 installed lap dance booths in their VIP room, a dozen shadowy, hooded cubicles for which they charged forty dollars for customers to rent for an hour, not one penny of which went to the strippers invited in there with them. It was the moment Perfect 10 management became straight-up pimp daddies. With all that privacy and no security or a single bouncer on site, it was no surprise that two of the four times I went in one of those booths I found used condoms on the floor.

Sugar's and the Yellow Rose had the same style of private booths installed in their VIP sections. They charged customers a tad more, but the result was the same—Austin strip clubs were now officially thinly veiled brothels. Only Palazio tried to keep their VIP room clean, and by clean they basically meant everything was fine except blowjobs and intercourse.

In March, at Perfect 10 during the second song of my main stage set, three customers approached the stage at once to tip me. As I was accepting a tip from one of the men, another of them leaned over and licked my butt cheek. I whirled on him, demanding to know how someone could reach his sixties without learning that licking strangers without their permission was *not okay*? He seemed shocked that I minded at all, and that right there was one of the last incidents to push me out of stripping for good.

The next day, on my way home from Palazio, I stopped to fill my tank, when an Ed Harris look-alike, wearing a green golf shirt in a black compact car, lowered his window to ask if he could take my picture. I assumed he was a professional photographer doing candid shots of people out in the world or something, so after hesitating briefly I shrugged and agreed.

"Great, thanks," he replied, snapping a picture with what looked like an expensive Nikon camera. "Because I'm going to go pull over down the street and jerk off to it."

I stared at him blankly for a moment then returned to cleaning my windshield. I had no idea what to say. I just wanted to get home at that point.

"You're just really pretty," he continued. "I bet guys pull over all the time when they see you."

"I wouldn't know," I answered, removing the gas spout from my tank.

"You wouldn't wanna watch me jerk off, would you?"

That's when I started to laugh, unable to help it. "No, I wouldn't," I finally said, getting in my car.

"You sure are pretty," he called out again before I slammed my door and drove off.

Ten days later, the butt licker from Perfect 10 came back to see me. He tipped me on main stage without incident and then requested a lap dance. Once I got to his table and started the dance, I told him, "Please don't touch my face. Also, no licking or sucking."

"What?!" he wailed.

He literally looked like he might cry, shaking his head back and forth like a frustrated child, saying, "Jeez, I don't even know what to do with myself."

"Why don't you just relax and let me do my thing because I'm pretty sure you're going to love it if you'd just give it a chance."

Which he did. In fact, so much so he bought four dances in a row, dishing nonstop compliments the entire time. When it was over he told me that from now on every time he came to the club he wanted me to dance for him because I was "amazing!"

Two weeks later, I did four lap dances for a round-faced, soft-spoken, thirty-something contractor wearing the roomiest, thinnest sweatpants imaginable with nothing on underneath. For four straight dances, I had to maneuver around his boner and the moist tent pole it created. As soon as I was done and sat down for a breather, he asked me if I'd accepted the Lord Jesus Christ as my personal savior.

"Not lately," I quipped, only to be bombarded with bible quotes and other ramblings about his religious beliefs.

The last customer I sat with that day was a tall, blond, middle-aged Republican from Tyler, Texas, whose job working for a senator brought him to Austin on occasion. He insisted on renting a booth where he immediately tried to finger me. When I said no he asked for a hand job. I said no to that too. Then during my first lap dance,

I had to grab his hand from my crotch and twist his wrist to make him stop trying to jam it inside my thong.

"That's not happening," I told him.

"It's cool," he said. "I get it. You're a type A personality who needs to be in control."

"I may be type A," I replied. "But the reason I'm not letting you finger fuck me is because I don't do cheap, low-end, piecemeal sex work because *I'm not a starving peasant or drug addicted streetwalker.*"

I was literally having to physically protect myself from daily sexual assault in the workplace. Stripping had gone from an erotic visual performance to an interactive, penetrative, sexual experience. Something had to give.

No Crying In Strip Clubs

July 17, 2009

Current Location: dancing as slow as I can
Current Mood: worried

My second stage set is at two thirty, after the lunch crowd has finished their meals and indulged in whatever allotment of dances their thinning wallets dictate. Just off main stage is Ciara, one of the best dancers we have—a real dancer—with a tight, lean body and impossibly flexible hips who can kick straight up into standing splits the same way you and I would blink an eye. Her pole work is effortless. Even just leaning against it she knows how to throw one hip out and both shoulders back, so it is still *dancing*. She's like me that way, knowing that every second, every limb, every joint, every *move* counts.

Now it's my turn, and I'm watching myself in the mirror, moving extra slow today, achingly aware of every step, every turn, every twist, arch, slink, spin, spin, spin. A tiny smile is frozen in place—it is all I can manage as I grit my teeth to keep from crying out in a high-pitched wail about the deep, sharp pain in my lower back. It has barely left me for seven days. The smile and the constant awareness of each next step—from pole to pole to floor vent that blows my hair into a pretty fan around my face—helps keep the tears at bay. If I think about where my right foot will be two seconds from now I won't have to think about the hot poker digging into my spine and I won't start crying. I won't collapse into a weeping, crippled puddle on the stage.

There is nothing less sexy than an aging, injured stripper. Nothing less appealing than a forty-one-year-old with no good options and a dwindling bank account. Nothing less attractive than fear of financial insecurity bordering on desperation. If I don't power through I won't make my quota. And if I don't somehow heal my back, I cannot continue this dancing. If I can't continue dancing, I can't afford to keep writing. If I'm forced to take a straight job for minimal pay, I'll have to give up the one and only part of my life that means anything to me. If I don't have time to write, I will shrivel up and die inside.

I am on stage in this agony because I need the exposure—it's a slow day, and even more dancers arrived to work thirty minutes ago, making it an equal ratio of men to women yet again. There is not one dancer-free customer for me to approach, not one customer even looking at the stage right now. It's just Dave Edmunds and me up here, his badass British guitar licks and my fucked up degenerated discs…two underpaid performers doing their thing in a Round Rock, Texas, strip club on a sad and lazy Thursday.

Sometime later, after my six-song set and a small but decent influx of customers, I'm taking a break in the dressing room, the sharp pain having receded to a dull ache. I'm standing at my locker because sitting makes the pain worse, staring at my phone propped up on the top shelf wishing someone would distract me with a text. Perhaps a Hollywood producer with financing for my script or Ed McMahon calling from the grave with a million bucks for unlimited chiropractic care. Instead, a petite, adorable dancer I've never met, a soft-spoken, young, black girl with a gorgeous smile and Jessica Rabbit figure passes by my row of lockers. I watch her, trying to remember what it's like to walk with such ease, with a heavy dancer bag slung over one shoulder.

She catches my eye and stops. Smiling sweetly, she says, "Oh hey, I've been meaning to tell you for the longest time, I just love watching you on stage, *every time*. Just because you're so, oh, you know… *graceful*!"

I thank her, probably two or three times, enough to make her uncomfortable I think, though she keeps smiling as she shyly scoots out the door. I sink softly against the lockers, trying to avoid any position that will spark the deep, sharp pain in my lower back again. I'm trying so hard not to cry.

CHAPTER 20

Spring, Summer, Fall 2010

I was writing my third script, *True Love and Hot Yoga*, a rom-com about a romantically naive woman trying to navigate a complicated dating scene and hot yoga practice simultaneously. It was going well, however, by now I had a better idea of what I was up against as far as making it in Hollywood, especially as a middle-aged Texan unwilling to move to LA to network her exhausted ass off. Everyone I'd sent my first and second scripts to, while mostly highly complimentary, had declined to option them. Super-agent Mary Evans must not have been impressed with my memoir pages since I'd not heard back after emailing them and following up with her twice. Stripping was no longer paying the bills and had become a drudgery I'd never known it could be. I wondered more and more if I was on the right path or simply wasting my life. I needed a backup plan for my backup plan. Hell, I needed a new plan altogether.

One day in early April, I sat down with a legal pad and wrote out two lists. One of everything I liked to do, from being with men to brushing my cat, from sex to yoga to dancing, writing, swimming, researching, organizing, studying psychology and sexology…all of it, every little thing I could think of. That list had around twenty entries. Next to it, I wrote down every single thing I was good at, including sex, yoga, dancing, writing, swimming, real estate, taking care of kids, and motherfucking brushing my cat. From there, I determined where those two lists overlapped. Next, out of those eight or ten overlapping entries, I looked for the money. Which of those pursuits that I both liked and was good at might lead to work where I'd finally earn some decent money?

There was only one thing on that list: *sex*. Or intimate companionship, to be precise.

By the end of the day, I'd created a profile on a sugar daddy site under the name Cecilia Dahl, praying I'd find one or two kind, lonely, generous gentlemen to help me stay afloat until I could figure out my next move—until I could figure out which vine to grab before the one I'd been clinging to snapped in half.

I didn't get a couple of bites. I was *deluged*. By the end of the week, I had two hundred messages to sort through. As it turned out, I was exactly what all those potential sugar daddies had been seeking: a mature woman they could relate to, who happened to look young and fit, but wasn't flaky, immature, or self-centered, like most twenty-somethings on that site. I let it be known that I was available for lunch and dinner dates with "quality private time afterward" at my place or in their upscale (four or five star) hotel room. When I quoted my rates, made clear my offerings, and stated my boundaries, they thanked me, thrilled to find someone who knew exactly what she had to offer and wanted in return and wasn't afraid to put it out there. "None of the women here know what they want. It's so frustrating!" was a phrase I heard a hundred times from those men.

Most couldn't afford me. That made it easy to quickly delete one hundred and eighty messages. Of the remaining twenty I chose ten to meet in person for coffee dates over the next six weeks. In half that time, I realized I didn't need introductory dates to judge compatibility. As a stripper, I had fourteen years of experience quickly assessing a man's character. I could do it so well all I needed was a short email exchange and one follow-up phone call before setting up a paid date. I booked two per week for one month.

The first thing I bought with the money I earned was a quality vacuum. I'd never been so excited or satisfied as the first time I used it, watching years of ground in dust and dirt get sucked out of my living room carpet. Next came a new wardrobe, entailing multiple visits to every outlet mall around Austin. Until then, I'd only owned enough quality designer clothes to have four upscale outfits to wear. Four dates with the same gent before I'd have to upgrade my yoga pants and flip-flop wardrobe. And because those four outfits spanned the range of warm weather to cold, it would be ideal if those four dates spanned all four seasons—which was less than ideal for someone trying to build repeat (monthly or weekly) business. Thus, much of my first few months' income went to shopping for designer clothes to suit the affluent men taking me to every fine dining restaurant in Austin, Dallas, and Houston.

I officially quit stripping in June. In late July, my sugar baby work came to a standstill but I didn't budge on my rates or boundaries. In August, everything blossomed again. I had regular clients in Dallas, Houston, and Austin. I started working ten to fifteen days a month, building my client base on three separate sugar daddy sites. It went so well, I decided to go full pro. To build my own website as a professional companion—a high-end escort whose focus was less on sex and more on relationships and genuine, authentic, intimate connection with a select group of likeminded gentlemen.

By the end of that year, I'd doubled my stripping income. By the end of the following year (2011), I'd tripled it. In 2012, I quintupled it—working half the hours I'd once worked as a stripper for five times the income. By then, I only saw clients between six and eight days a month. The rest of my time was my own, to write, read, workout, shop, swim in Barton Springs, see friends, and go dancing. I spent a couple of days a month on marketing, handling website issues, doing photoshoots, building and maintaining profiles on Eros.com and Slixa. Still, I had more free time than I'd had since starting my life over sober. I was more fulfilled and happier than I'd been since my twenties when I'd been in love with my very own rock star.

Someday I would write about it. Someday writing would be the medium through which I would help facilitate sexual healing, but for now I still needed to engage in it, for the benefit of my clients and, I suspected, myself. *I still needed to heal.* To heal my lingering fear of intimacy and vague distrust of men. To instill in myself the ability to maintain boundaries and trust that I held enough value that I had a right to those boundaries. To discover that some men, good men, would recognize that fact and happily abide them. To finally learn to how to share myself with someone in an empowered way—knowing exactly what I had to give, what I was willing to share, and what I was not. And know that it would be honored…or that if it wasn't I could walk away and find someone else to respect me and what I needed. I knew how to be vulnerable. I'd learned how to be authentic. I was damn good at setting boundaries (though I still needed work on maintaining them with exceptionally persuasive men). And now those three life skills would help me attain my biggest goals—financial freedom and time to devote to my writing.

My companionship clients honored me in every way. They craved intimacy as much as sex, and the sex they craved wasn't an anonymous one-night stand, but the kind they could have over and over with the same woman, not just to satisfy an animal urge but to provide a genuine sense of connection. Our appointments played out like any typical courting and dating process. They took me to dinner, concerts, movies, and museums. We went parasailing, hiking, ice skating, river rafting, and once on a Grand Canyon helicopter tour. We went to resorts for soaks in hot springs and couples' massages. We went to Vegas to gamble and see Cirque du Soleil. They took me shopping for designer bags, shoes, and clothes. We cooked together and binged Netflix shows. One took me on a tour of the University of Texas business school and liberal arts department. I met a few of their friends, colleagues, and business partners. A couple of them met my friends and my sister.

And, of course, we had sex. Lots and lots of fabulous, mutually satisfying sex.

One of my first clients, William, was a UT professor who wanted nothing more than to help me financially while living vicariously through me and my writing (something he'd always wanted to try but hadn't). Another of my early clients was a lovely young software engineer named Jon, whose wife had been sick with an autoimmune disease and hadn't had sex with him for two years. Jon and I had amazingly fun, passionate sex as often as he could afford it and lots of cuddle time afterward. He was definitely my favorite, and even though I didn't kiss other clients, I kissed him every time I orgasmed. Another client, Eric, was a surgeon in Dallas who was so overworked he had no outside life to speak of except our lustful monthly trysts. I saw a darling oil and gas executive in Houston every month for years, for St. Regis room service, good conversation, and playful quickie sex. I saw many oil and gas guys, finance guys, bankers, developers, entrepreneurs, surgeons, and lawyers—oh so many lawyers. Many of these men I saw regularly for years. They treasured me and delighted in me in ways strip club customers once did but hadn't since the recession. They did more to provide for and protect me (from poverty, stress, exhaustion, and misery) than my own father had been able to manage.

And when our dates were over, I went home to have my life to myself—my bed, bathtub, fridge, Netflix queue, and all the rest. All the privacy, autonomy, and solitude I craved, with a line of generous, loving gentlemen awaiting an opening in my schedule, every time I opened Cecilia's inbox.

Was I still looking for that charge I always got when winning over the affections of an otherwise taken man? Was I just looking for another way to be the prized "other woman"? I suppose that dynamic was a perk of the work, but I didn't fault myself an old habit. I'd forgiven my father his failings and during my years as a companion grew closer than ever with both my parents. I also genuinely cared about my clients, and I believed I just as genuinely deserved their attentions and generous financial consideration.

I was unabashedly, unashamedly thrilled about the money. The money and freedom it would buy me...freedom to pursue my writing, and frankly, some semblance of a life with more fun, friends, relaxation, and personal time than I'd had in longer than I could remember.

Everything looked different suddenly. Work, men, money, sex, autonomy, service, karma, balance...I felt like my life had been reconfigured. Everything was no longer a struggle, no longer pure drudgery. I was primed for a new and better form of expression. I suddenly saw how I had something of value. How I *was* something of value. I didn't know if my writing would ever take off. The cold truth was I was still improving as a writer, and even if I became great someday there was no guarantee of ever becoming a success at it, especially in the film and TV industry. But my companionship was prized highly, and on the open market I was quickly considered one of the very best in the business in the country.

Nothing quantifies like money. And while not every woman needs to have a price tag on her time to feel valued, I did. Unlike my clients, I didn't necessarily need regular companionship, a good listener, or abundant affection for myself—not as much as I needed time to write, create, and build a future—but I had those things to *give*. So, what else would I want in return but money?

Sure, if I'd been in love I'd have craved companionship and sex. And when I finally found a knowledgeable doctor to rebalance my hormones, I got my sex drive back in early 2011. But I could still call up Lalo, Paul, or Larry for the occasional roll in the hay whenever I wanted. Meanwhile, all my best skills of making men feel heard, seen, and appreciated, were in high demand in the world. I'd had no idea how in demand. But now that I did, you better bet I was running with it.

EPILOGUE

O̶ne day in the summer of 2010, two months into my professional companionship journey, I sat at my makeup mirror tweezing my brows, thinking how lucky I was to have finally landed in the next phase of my life. To be thriving financially and emotionally, knowing I was right where I was supposed to be for the first time in a long time. *All I have to do*, I told myself, *is stay young, fit, and healthy. As long as I maintain a youthful, vibrant energy I can justify my high rates and enjoy a life of luxury, finally.*

Just then, a glint of something white and wiry caught my eye, near my right temple.

Please be a T-shirt thread or piece of lint, I prayed. But alas, it was my first gray hair, firmly attached to my head. Isn't that always the way? As soon as something comes to life, it starts dying. But whatever, I thought, plucking it roughly from my scalp. I'll worry about that tomorrow. Or never…who knows.

My Free Will Astrology yearlong horoscope for 2011, my first full year in the business of professional companionship, was as prescient as ever:

> *In 2011, you will have the chance to weave your fortunes together with an abundance of allies who are good for you. They will be your equals, they will share at least some of your most important values, and they will respect you for who you are.*

Don't shy away from the demands that such invigorating collaborations will make on you. It would be less work, after all, to fall back into reliance on more prosaic relationships that don't ask so much of you. Please don't take the easy way out, Libra. Rise to the occasion!

Overall, I kept my energy and vibrancy up for a beautiful and fulfilling twelve-year career, during which I traveled all over North America. (For various reasons, I turned down most offers to leave the country.) While I never allowed reviews—the truly high-end ladies never did—by 2013, I'd become the highest paid Internet escort in the state of Texas.

During that time, my third screenplay made the top five percent of the biggest screenplay contest in the country (the Academy Nicholl Fellowship), yet I never managed to option or sell it, or either of my two others. I did, however, get my first book, *Rock Monster: My Life with Joe Walsh*, published by Rare Bird Books in 2018. I never found out what Joe himself thought of it, since his wife made him sever contact with me in 2011.

I wasn't able to have much of a personal dating life for most of my career as a professional companion. But in 2018, I met someone special whom I dated casually for a year, reminding me that I, too, needed companionship and a personal (versus professional) sex life, which I've had in some shape or form ever since.

In 2016, I got a series of PRP injections in my back that relieved me of most of my daily back pain, so much so that I was able to recategorize it as mere "discomfort" most days. That same year I trained to become certified in a type of sexual healing known as Surrogate Partnership, an evolution of the modality originally invented by Masters and Johnson (detailed in the Showtime series *Masters of Sex*). I then started an intimacy coaching practice and soon afterward became a certified sexuality counselor through the Sexual Health Alliance (SHA).

In 2022, I retired from coaching and professional companion-ship alike, and made writing my main medium finally, throwing myself into two more memoirs to follow-up *Rock Monster*. You're holding one in your hands. The next, about my twelve-year companionship journey, is coming soon.

END

ACKNOWLEDGMENTS

First, a massive thank you to every man in my life from age fourteen onward. From my first lover (Casey Barber) to my first attempted lover (that hot grad school guy I met as a freshman in high school), to my last lover ever (whoever you may be), to every strip club customer (okay, almost every customer) and every coaching, companion, and escort client who enriched my life to a degree nothing else could reach. You all taught me more about the fabulous and fascinating male psyche than most women are lucky enough to see, and more about my own inner workings than I'd ever unravel on my own steam.

Thanks also to my amazing team at Rare Bird Books, Tyson Cornell, Guy Intoci, Alexandra Watts, Mike McNamara, Delia Bennett, and especially my brilliant editor Hailie Johnson whose inspired input and diplomatic candor was vital in making this book what I always hoped it could be.

A deep nod of gratitude to my powerhouse publicist Scott Lorenz at Westwind Communications, for a level of support, creativity, and problem solving I've never before experienced. Also tremendous appreciation to my business manager Mick Lee for filling in every blank and smoothing out every pothole I never saw coming but she did miles in advance, every time.

Thanks to John Ford, Octavio C., and Doug M. for the quiet support and bouts of unexpected generosity. Huge thanks to Nancy Eldridge, Ciara Conway, Dory Bartlett, and Justin Craig for the years of friendship, sound-boarding, and unwavering encouragement. My undying gratitude goes to Louis Black for the cheerleading, championing, and especially ensuring that this woman writer finally had "a room of her own."

Above all, thanks to Miles Everson for the endless love, daily joy, and incalculable support, without which none of this would've been possible. You're the best thing to have happened to me and I can't express enough how grateful and happy I am to have you in my life.